# The Millionaire's Advisor™:

## High-Touch, High-Profit Relationship Management Strategies of Advisors to the Wealthy

Price $195.00

**Institutional Investor NEWS**
INTELLIGENCE FIRST

*Institutional Investor News* is the premier provider of breaking news tailored for senior industry professionals in the global financial markets. Through 20 newsletters and other information-based products, we deliver critical market intelligence to help industry decision makers stay on top of a winning business strategy. Our worldwide team of reporters and editors uncover the facts with exclusive, in-depth information on emerging trends, market analysis, industry leader profiles, competitor intelligence and business leads. Senior executives around the globe rely on Institutional Investor News' authoritative market insight as the most reliable source of proprietary investment and financial news.

www.iinews.com

# The Millionaire's Advisor™:

High-Touch, High-Profit Relationship
Management Strategies
of Advisors to the Wealthy

by Russ Alan Prince and Brett Van Bortel

A publication of
Private Asset Management,
Institutional Investor News

## Preface:

We have worked with all levels of advisors, but our greatest focus and interest is with elite advisors—advisors serving millionaires, and who have become millionaires themselves.

Two things strike us repeatedly about this group of advisors to the millionaire client. First they are all individuals and unique in their own right.

Secondly, each is remarkably similar to one another. Similar not in superficial traits, like clothes or accent. Rather similar in the path or strategy they took to becoming elite advisors. The path that we have seen elite advisors take to their present success is simple, but not easy. Simply put, the commonality amongst the vast majority of these elite advisors was that they, consciously or unconsciously, focused predominantly on cultivating affluent clients that shared the same values, interests and goals as the advisor.

At first, this seemed too simple to be THE answer. However, the more we saw, the clearer it became how important this simple approach was. The benefits of this simple approach are like the pebble that starts the landslide. By focusing on people like themselves, they enjoyed their work, they connected with clients in powerful ways, they avoided toxic clients, they limited the risk for burnout, they had simple but effective service models, they lived the 80/20 rule, they were referred by their best clients to even better clients. In short, they became elite advisors. The goal of this book is to provide a map that shows the way to joining this group of advisors to the millionaire.

# Index

**Dedication:**

*To Jerry,*

*Today and Tomorrow*

**Russ Alan Prince**


*To Victoria,*

*Your name says it all …*

**Brett Van Bortel**

## Acknowledgement:

This book would not be possible without the guidance and mentorship of so many of my colleagues, clients and co-workers. I want to especially thank Scott West for his unflinching ability to create an environment that allows people to realize all of the potential they desire. Dominic Martellaro for his endless energy and pioneering insights & drive. Gary DeMoss for his astute guidance, wisdom of experience and incredible mentorship. My thanks additionally goes out to several others. Jack Zimmermann for his entrepreneurial courage. Mark McClure, Jim Yount, Frank Muller, Eric Hargens and Dave Linton for their contributions. Mark Lie for his ability to turn abstract ideas into clear visuals. To all of you, I believe you're the best in this business at what you do. To Karen Maru File, thanks for helping turn diamond ore into polished gems (and the especially heavy buffing on Russ's contributions). Finally to my department at Van Kampen Consulting, you are the most talented and entrepreneurial group I've ever had the privilege to work with. I owe a special thanks to Kristan Mulley.

— Brett Van Bortel

**Author's Biographies:**

### Russ Alan Prince

Russ Alan Prince, president of the market research and consulting firm Prince & Associates LLC, is a leading expert on the private wealth industry and on advisor-based distribution.

Russ consults for leading financial institutions on strategic and marketing issues. He is called upon to develop marketing plans, for tactical competitive advice, and for guidance on expanding presence through strategic alliances, product development, and executive development.

He provides a variety of coaching and consulting services to financial advisors who target affluent markets. Russ is a seasoned developer of proprietary prospecting and sales and relationship management systems, and he also provides high-end customized practice management programs.

### Brett Van Bortel

Brett Van Bortel, Director of Consulting Services at Van Kampen Consulting, has directed, developed and delivered numerous consulting programs to financial advisors since 1997.

The core goal of all of these programs is to improve the advisor's business. His dominant focus has been in the development of an industry leading affluent marketing program. This program was based on the research of Russ Alan Prince and one of the largest studies ever done on the affluent market. Additionally, it is one of the few that converts marketing insights into actionable steps and measurable results in an advisor's business.

Mr. Van Bortel has been published in numerous industry publications and regularly speaks to, and consults with, financial advisors regarding many aspects of their business.

# Section I:
# The Millionaire Market and The Advisors They Hire

*"Of what can be bought, the rich*
*have the great luxury of being able*
*to buy the best of everything"*

— Thorstein Veblen

# Chapter 1
# The Millionaire Market

> *"The best things in life are free but*
> *you can save that for the birds and bees*
> *Give me money, money, that's what I want"*
>
> — The Beatles

### Chapter 1 Critical Question:
**Have you heard more and more people tell you that you need to "move your book up-market?" Have you read articles recommending that you "concentrate on the affluent?" Are you under pressure to increase the productivity and profitability of your practice?**

If you are an advisor looking to build your practice in today's marketplace, the odds are pretty good that someone has recommended that you target wealthy investors. If you have read any trade literature in the last twelve months, you have read articles urging you to focus on millionaires. No matter what organization you work with, you have undoubtedly been urged to increase your productivity (and profitability).

And, you know they're right. The problem isn't *what* you should do, but rather *how* to get it done. Whether you're talking about sending a man to the moon, or your production through the roof, *what* to do is the easy part, *how* to do it is the hard part. However, the *how* is the dominant focus of this book, based on the best practices of many advisors, whose actions and wisdom this book is based upon.

Millionaires, while a relatively small portion of the total population, command the vast majority of the private wealth throughout the world. More than ever before, they're desirous of working with high-quality investment advisors. The key is for you to be one of the "chosen few" advisors who have centered their practices on the millionaire market.

If you are like the advisors we talk with on a daily basis, you are wondering if the millionaire market is really all that big. Well it is, and we'll show you around it, in this chapter. Even if you accept that the millionaire market is big, you may wonder whether or not there is room for you. There certainly is, and we can prove that to you as well.

### Millions of Millionaires

The first step in developing any business strategy is to "size and scope" the market, and the same is true with your practice. We must begin by gaining a clear picture of the size and scope of your client markets.

There are a couple of ways you can do this:
- Look at your own clients – which ones are the most profitable?
- Look at the top investment advisors – what clients do they target?
- What parameters do top advisors use to gauge clients?
- Look at wealthy people – how many are there?

### A Millionaire Audit of Your Practice

Let's start with a look at your own clients. Do you know which ones are the most profitable? You are probably keeping a close eye on this, but let us suggest a simple process for you in case you haven't checked this out in a while. Take this simple exercise.

## Exercise: Finding Your Most Profitable Clients

*Instructions: List your top 10 clients, then complete the chart, making estimates where necessary.*

| Client Name | Total investable assets ($) | Assets you manage ($) |
| --- | --- | --- |
| 1. | | |
| 2. | | |
| 3. | | |
| 4. | | |
| 5. | | |
| 6. | | |
| 7. | | |
| 8. | | |
| 9. | | |
| 10. | | |

Here are a few things to notice about this exercise. First notice whether the clients who came to mind were the clients who demand a lot of your time or were the clients who make you the most money. A lot of advisors make the mistake of paying too much attention to their demanding clients, and not to their most profitable clients. It's easy to fall into this habit because of the tendency to oil the squeakiest hinge.

> **A lot of advisors make the mistake of paying too much attention to their demanding clients, and not to their most profitable clients.**

You may have noticed that you were quick to know the amount of assets you managed but had to think about what the total investable assets of your clients were. Don't make the all-too-common mistake of thinking you manage all your client's assets. These days, most people – especially wealthier people – have several investment advisors and one or more on-line accounts. How can you possibly know which of your clients has the most potential for you unless you know where all of their investable assets are?

Now to the main point of this exercise. Sit back and ask yourself these questions:

- Which of these clients is my most profitable client?
- Which is potentially the most profitable?
- What is the relationship between a client's wealth and their current or potential profitability to me?

Notice that the wealthier the client, the greater their profitability to you. The wealthier the client, the more they contribute to your productivity. Here is the answer to the first question: <u>The wealthier the client, the more profitable</u>. It's a reality in our business that doing an asset allocation plan for a client with $100K takes as much time as a client with $1M, except it's much more profitable with the $1M client. Do you have any millionaires in your client list (yet?). If you do, you will see this relationship. If you don't, you can still see that the wealthier the client, the better the profitability.

This easy exercise, an audit of your own practice has caused you to see that wealth is correlated with productivity and profitability. How can you boost your practice? Follow the curve. Follow the trend line up. Increase the wealth of your book.

### Benchmarking Your Practice and Its Stage of Development

There is another way we can look at the question of your best market strategy. We can look at what top investment advisors do. You have been around. You know people who are at the top of their game as investment advisors. You have been to conferences and you have seen top people speak.

Who are their clients? Are they millionaires?

They are usually millionaires, once, twice, sometimes many times over.

We have some research on this for you to consider. In our studies we have found that advisors pass through four distinct stages in their career. The Exhibit 1.1 below is based on data from a study of registered reps, but we have found the same stages in studies of all advisors, from independent financial advisors.

In general, advisors start out with low production (under $400,000) and few clients (less than 150). This is Stage I. They grow by adding clients, so Stage II is distinguished by production that is still on the low side, but the number of clients booms to over 150. In Stage III, advisors become more skilled at capturing more assets per client, and so production goes past $400,000 for the first time. Finally, Stage IV success is attained. These advisors are at the peak of their career with top production coming from fewer (a comfortable number) extremely wealthy clients.

## *Exhibit 1.1:*
### *Top Producers*

|  | Production Under $400,000 | Production Over $400,000 |
|---|---|---|
| **Under 150 clients** | **Stage I:** Just starting out, production and client numbers low. | **Stage IV:** Most productive and profitable. Practice trimmed down to just the clients that count. |
| **Over 150 clients** | **Stage II:** Beginning of growth phase. Client numbers growing – approaching take-off point in production | **Stage III:** End of growth phase; production numbers going up. Now spin off the less profitable clients. |

Source: *The World of Registered Representatives* (*www.iihighnetworth.com*, 2002)

Take a minute to think about these findings in relation to your own practice. How would you answer these questions:
- What stage am I at now?
- What stage are the investment advisors I admire at?
- Which stage do I think would be the most profitable for me?

The top investment advisors in the field are generally Stage IV advisors. They are at the top of their game, focusing all their efforts on taking superb care of relatively few extremely wealthy (highly profitable) clients.

Your reflection on the investment advisors you most admire (and your review of our data) has reinforced the insight that you already have about the correlation of client wealth and productivity (and profitability). So again we ask: how can you boost your practice? The answer, follow the best. Base your business model on the best in the industry. Benchmark the leaders, change your practice and the wealthy as well as personal wealth will follow. This is what this book will help you achieve.

## Millionaires—America's Greatest Growth Industry

Just how many millionaires are there? How about 5 million? That is the current estimate for the number of millionaires in America. Some authorities estimate even more. But 5 million is a very reliable number, even with the recent market volatility.

| One in every 60 people is a millionaire |
|---|

This is one in every 60 people. This is a lot to say the least. But it is also tremendous growth. In 1975, there were just 90,000 millionaires. Millionaires have increased 55-fold in 25 years. Millionaires are America's newest growth industry.

The number of millionaires is going to increase. The fundamentals of the US economy still look strong, and there is no global competitor in sight. The economy will continue to nurture millionaires.

So will inheritances. Boomers are about to inherit the trillions of dollars their parents accumulated. This, the greatest inter-generational transfer of wealth in the history of the world, will create even more millionaires as well as put money in motion.

There are literally millions of millionaires, and many more will be created over the next few years.

OK, OK, OK, you say. Yes there are many millionaires. Yes, millionaires are the way to a more productive and profitable practice. But is there room for ME?

The answer is a resounding YES, BUT… YES, there is room for you, and this section will spell out why. The BUT, is BUT ONLY IF YOU OUTSERVICE YOUR COMPETITION.

Yes, there is room for you in the millionaire market, but only if you make your clients incredibly satisfied. The rest of this book will tell you how to make all your clients happy clients. Here, let's prove that there is room for you.

There is room for you in the millionaires market because:
- Millionaires have multiple investment advisors.
- Millionaires are actually underserved.
- Millionaires often switch investment advisors.

## Millionaires Have Multiple Investment Advisors

Because millionaires have multiple investment advisors the opportunity for being an investment advisor to a millionaire is many times bigger than the number of millionaires. In fact, millionaires have an average of <u>three</u> investment advisors. However, as the client's asset base increases to ten million dollars, the number of advisors increases as well.

| Average Investment Advisors Per Client | |
|---|---|
| $1M to $5M | 2.9 investment advisors |
| $5M to $10M | 3.4 investment advisors |
| $10M+ | 5.7 investment advisors |

When you look at these numbers, it becomes apparent that the opportunity to become an advisor to a millionaire is quite large.

It is three to six times the number of millionaires. In other words, there is a range of 15 million to 30 million job openings to be an advisor to a millionaire throughout the United States. This is good news if you are just breaking into the market.

But, you say. They all already have advisors. They aren't looking for me. That brings us to the next point.

### Millionaires Are Actually Underserved

They <u>are</u> looking for you, provided that you are a high-quality, honest investment advisor. The dirty little secret of the investment advisory industry is that wealthy clients are generally unhappy. Most millionaire clients are <u>not</u> very satisfied with the service from their investment advisors. They are generally satisfied only enough to stay with an advisor until someone better comes along. At the first whiff of someone better, they will leave in droves. In fact, most millionaires are actively seeking a new investment advisor that they hope will treat them better (Exhibit 1.2).

Here is some data. Only about a quarter (26.7%) of millionaire clients rate their primary advisor as "excellent." These millionaires say they have and will continue to refer other millionaires to their advisor, and plan to add assets to their portfolio for this excellent investment advisor to manage.

However, most millionaires do not think their primary advisor is excellent. On the contrary, most (69.7%) think he or she is just fair. If someone thinks their investment advisor is only "fair", they will listen up if someone else has a great investment advisor. They might switch to a new advisor at any time. There is no reason to stay with an investment advisor who is only fair, and not excellent. Of course, they will not do a lot of referring of their friends to this advisor, and they don't plan on adding a lot of assets for them to manage.

And 3.6 percent of millionaires rate their primary advisor as "poor" and are out there actively looking for a new advisor. That new investment advisor might as well be you.

## Exhibit 1.2:
### Quality of Investment Advisors

| Rating of Investment Advisor | Percentage | Consequences |
|---|---|---|
| Excellent | 26.7% | • Will refer others<br>• Will add assets |
| Fair | 69.7% | • Receptive to other advisors<br>• Will not refer others<br>• Will not add assets |
| Poor | 3.6% | • Will switch their advisor soon |

*Source: Cultivating the Affluent (www.iihighnetworth.com, 1995)*

To sum up. There are a lot of millionaires. There is a minimum of three times as many investment advisors working with those millionaires. Most investment advisors are not doing a good job satisfying their clients. AND THOSE MILLIONAIRES WILL SWITCH IF THEY ARE OFFERED SOMETHING BETTER.

### Millionaires Switch Advisors

Yes, millionaires will switch investment advisors if they are offered something better. All they want is good service from their investment advisor. If they believe they can get what they want from someone else, they will switch.

In fact, advisor switching goes on all the time out there.

Sure, you say. When markets are rough clients are more likely to switch because investment performance is off.

Well. Some do, but most don't. We did some research during the longest bull market in history, and we looked at clients who switched advisors.

MOST MILLIONAIRE CLIENTS SWITCH BECAUSE THEY ARE NOT GETTING GOOD SERVICE. In fact, 87 percent of clients who drop their advisors said they did so because:

- "Very little ever seemed to go right in our relationship."
- "I felt more and more distance between us."
- "I wasn't sure if he really knew who I was when I called."
- "I never heard from him. It always seemed like I called him."
- "My confidence in him eroded over time."
- "I didn't have a warm personal relationship with him."

They didn't leave because of poor investment performance. In fact, just about all of these clients (87%) said they were happy with the investment performance they had gotten. They left because their relationship fell apart.

Sure, some clients leave because of poor investment performance (13%). But a lot of times there isn't anything you can do about investment performance (Exhibit 1.3). The good news is that you <u>can</u> always do something about client relationships.

### *Exhibit 1.3:*
### *Why Clients Left Their Advisor*

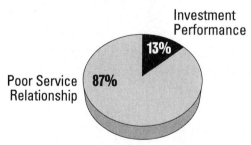

*Source: Cultivating the Affluent (www.iihighnetworth.com, 1995)*

## Chapter 1 Answer:

*The answer to boosting your productivity and profitability is the millionaire market. Millionaires control most of the global private wealth and there are millions of them. Of course they all have investment advisors now. What you need to do is take advantage of the millionaire's predisposition to have multiple investment advisors. Once in the door, you'll gain by out-relationshipping, out-empathizing, and out-servicing the rest of their current advisors.*

*There are millions of millionaires, they all need advisors, and it might as well be you.*

# Chapter 2
# All Millionaires Are Not Alike

*"Rich people are just like everyone else, only wealthy."*

— W.C. Fields

## *Chapter 2 Critical Question:*
### *Think about the concept of asset allocation. How would you explain it to your best client? How would you explain it to your oldest client? How would you explain it to your newest client?*

One thing today's investment advisors are very good at is understanding the technical aspects of their profession. You are undoubtedly good at the technical aspects of your job. You certainly know what asset allocation is.

But here is the point. If you are like the vast majority of investment advisors, you will provide an excellent explanation of asset allocation to your best client. The problem is that you will probably provide EXACTLY the same explanation to your oldest client. And then you will probably provide EXACTLY the same explanation to your newest client.

But are these three clients alike? Do they want the same thing from you? Do they think the same way about investing? Do they have the same levels of experience or expertise in the market? Do they have the same appreciation of technical explanations?

Think about our industry for a minute. For the most part, clients are treated as though they are the same. They get the same explanations of financial concepts. They get the same reports. They are called on the same schedule. They get the same brochures.

Here is the secret (and you know this already). Clients are not the same. They have different needs and wants. They want something different from you, their investment advisor, and from your firm. Clients are people with different personalities. Clients are people with different investor psychologies.

We call this high-net-worth psychology.

Advisors who use high-net-worth psychology in the way they work with their millionaire clients:
- Communicate better.
- Have stronger client relationships.
- Get more client referrals.
- Get more assets to manage.

Do you want a pipeline of client referrals and a big jump in asset capture? Keep reading.

### The Benefits of High-Net-Worth Psychology

When it's not very hard to get into a business we say there are low barriers to entry. The private wealth industry has low barriers to entry. As a result there are many competitors and the industry is highly fragmented. All anyone really needs is a client to get into the business (which is why accountants and insurance professionals are making their moves).

This is a relationship business. Because it is a relationship business, almost any investment advisor can make a living, regardless of the competition. This is as good a time as any to explore how you define "make a living."

For a few investment advisors making a living means getting by. But for nearly all the investment advisors with whom we have studied and worked making a living means a great deal more. It means becoming wealthy themselves. High-net-worth psychology can be very effective in helping you reach the top ranks of the investment advisory industry. It has proven critical in assisting investment advisors in placing more than $100 million under management.

High-net-worth psychology is a systematic way of communicating and working with affluent investors. The use of such systems is one of the critical factors that separate the most successful investment advisors from the rest (see Chapter 3).

Before jumping into the "what's" and "how's" of high-net-worth psychology let's begin by taking a look at where the system came from.

### A Brief Look Back

In 1994, *Institutional Investor* launched a newsletter entitled *Private Asset Management*. The primary audience for the newsletter was, and is, financial institutions targeting the wealthy investor. One of the features of the newsletter was research on the private wealth industry. In particular, the newsletter explored the investment behavior of the wealthy.

Prince & Associates was commissioned to conduct the research on the investment behavior of the wealthy for *Private Asset Management*. In conjunction with *Institutional Investor/Private Asset Management*, we moved way up the knowledge curve concerning the psychology of the wealthy investor.

Based on the research conducted for *Institutional Investor/Private Asset Management*, we produced three research reports that were published in book form. A central component of the research was the psychographic segmentation of the affluent investor – high-net-worth psychology.

Not only have some of the most successful and prestigious private banks, private client groups of investment and commercial banks, brokerage firms, family offices, insurance companies and professional services firms gravitated to high-net-worth psychology, so too have many leading individual investment advisors.

We both work intensively with elite investment advisors around the world and coach advisors who are moving to elite status. Our daily work with investment advisors has provided us with a "living laboratory" where we have been able to develop more and more ways to apply high-net-worth psychology effectively in client-facing situations. That's what it's all about, the ability to improve client-facing effectiveness. That means high-net-worth psychology has to work in the real world, and it does.

We readily acknowledge we owe a great deal of our insights to the elite investment advisors we have the opportunity to work with. More than our understanding, they have shown us how to take the research and transform the findings into strategies and tactics that get bottom-line results. These investment advisors continue to help us refine the numerous applications of high-net-worth psychology.

Why would investment advisors responsible for managing hundreds of millions of dollars be interested in high-net-worth psychology? The answer is that high-net-worth psychology makes them even more effective and efficient. It enables them to better leverage what they already do well. It helps them at the edges and it is the nuances that often make the difference. Elite investment advisors say the primary benefit is that high-net-worth enables them to be more <u>consistently</u> effective. And, for the elite this translates into investment advisory practices with half a billion dollars or more under management.

### *Why High-Net-Worth Psychology Is Important*

You will become more productive and profitable if you are more consistently effective. You already have enough experience working with investors to know they're not all alike. This is especially true of the wealthy. You cannot treat all affluent clients the same. They accumulated their wealth in different ways, think about their wealth differently, and have different ideas about what their wealth represents. You need to consider these differences in the way you interact with them.

It would be nice if we had the time and resources to create a customized strategy for every client or prospect. But there are real-world constraints. It is not cost effective to create customized materials for every single client situation. Even if we could, we sometimes do not know enough about the client to do so. A new client may protect their privacy by being careful about what they tell you. You even can have a client for years and not really know them. What you need is a system for better understanding your prospect's or client's needs and wants <u>as precisely and quickly as possible</u>.

First, you must determine what prospects and clients need and want. When we have asked this question of investment advisors, almost to a person they tell us, "Investment performance." They are absolutely correct. Naturally, clients NEED and WANT solid investment performance. Achieving decent relative investment performance is why they come to you.

But, if you drill down, it's sometimes, but rarely, just about the money – just about investment performance. The best advisors in the business know that to really excel they need to understand a lot more about the relationship and perspectives the client has when it comes to money and investing. Some of the questions that you need to know are:

- WHY do they need and want solid investment performance?
- WHAT does money mean to them?
- WHAT do they look for in an advisor?
- WHERE does their wealth fit in with how they envision life?
- HOW do they prefer to work with their investment advisors?

High-net-worth psychology provides you with a workable, actionable, framework that answers all these questions and more. For starters, high-net-worth psychology organizes wealthy individuals into groups based on WHY they invest – why they are interested in investment performance, why they pick the advisors they do. Knowing why allows you to focus directly on client needs and wants, leading to significantly greater client satisfaction (and we'll see why client satisfaction is so important in Chapter 4).

Based on the research and reinforced by our experience working with the entire gambit of investment advisors, we find that high-net-worth psychology:

- Overall is most effective in marketing and sales.
- Enables you to more effectively convert prospects into clients.
- Increases the retention rate of affluent clients, and the rate at which affluent clients refer others to you.
- Helps you to identify and benefit from asset capture opportunities.
- Provides a methodology that enables you to more easily provide additional financial services to the affluent.
- Is instrumental in enabling you to <u>consistently</u> provide your clients with the exceptional "experience" they want and by which they make many of their investment advisor selection decisions.

## A Small Difference in Performance Makes a Big Difference in Results

Our goal in using high-net-worth psychology is not to have you reinvent your practice. It is our experience that most investment advisors taking the time to read a book like this and continually improve are already working at a very high level. Rather our goal is simply this, *to do the little things more systematically to deliver a consistent as well as higher level client experience.*

The power of a small difference, a small performance advantage over others cannot be overstated, indeed, it's decisive. In fact, it's applicable to all walks of life, whether business, economics or sports. In the Olympics, often just thousands of a second separate the gold medal from nothing at all. Simply put, just a small difference in your performance as an advisor can mean the difference between winning over a prospect, keeping a client or developing a new strategic partnership.

Just to illustrate this concept, the late, legendary Chicago Bears running back Walter Payton was known for his practical jokes and sense of humor. During the off season, Payton was camping in Alaska with his team-mate, fullback Matt Suhey. One morning Suhey awoke to find Payton putting on his running shoes. Suhey asked him what he was doing and he said, "There's a bear outside the tent, and I want to be ready to run if there's a problem."

Startled, Suhey replied, "You can't outrun a bear" (It happens to be a fact that a grizzly bear can outrun a race horse in the first 100 yards, and of course any human.).

Payton tersely replied, "I don't have to outrun the bear, I just have to outrun you."

The lesson of this story is simple. You don't have to be perfect to survive and thrive. You just have to be slightly better than your competition.

Now, how are you going beat your competition in a fragmented, competitive field? How will you leverage client relationships to create an increasingly affluent client base? To date, the most effective system is by using high-net-worth psychology. Investment advisors who have worked with us and who use high-net-worth psychology report results such as the following:

- The ability to reduce the sales cycle by at least 40 percent.
- The ability to create 27 percent additional fee-based revenue annually.
- The ability to produce 3 times the number of millionaire client referrals.

### What Is High Net Worth Psychology?

High-net-worth psychology is a framework, a system, for understanding what millionaires want from their investing, their investment relationships and from you as their investment advisor. At the center of this framework are nine personality types.

Let's briefly explore the characteristics of each of the nine types of millionaire investor personalities (Exhibit 2.1). Let's look at the key needs, values and motivations for each personality. It shows what each type of millionaire investor wants from their investing program. It answers the question <u>why</u> each group wants good investment performance.

## Exhibit 2.1:
### The Nine High-Net-Worth Personalities

*Family Stewards*
- Dominant focus is to take care of their family
- Conservative in personal and professional life
- Not very knowledgeable about investing

*Investment Phobics*
- Are confused and frustrated by the responsibility of wealth
- Dislike investing and avoid technical discussion of it
- Choose advisor's based on level of personal trust they feel

*Independents*
- Seek the personal freedom money makes possible
- Feel investing is a necessary means to an end
- Not interested in the process of investing

*The Anonymous*
- Confidentiality is their dominant concern
- Prize privacy for their financial affairs
- Likely to concentrate assets with an advisor that protects them

*Moguls*
- Control is a primary concern
- Investing is another way of extending personal power
- Decisive in decisions, rarely look back

*VIPs*
- Investing results in ability to purchase status possessions
- Prestige is important
- Like to affiliate with institutions and investment advisors with leading reputations

*Accumulators*
- Focused on making their portfolio bigger
- Investment performance oriented
- Tend to live below their means and spend frugally

*Gamblers*
- Enjoy investing for the excitement of it
- Tend to be very knowledgeable and involved
- Exhibit a high-risk tolerance

**Innovators**
- Focused on leading-edge products and services
- Sophisticated investors that like complex products
- Tend to be technically savvy and highly educated

## Family Stewards

**"Good investing lets me take good care of my family."**
**Investing IQ: ★★★**

The Family Steward invests in order to care of their family. The majority of their investment goals and financial needs will be linked to some larger family issue, like college funding or generational transfer of wealth. Family Stewards often will have privately held businesses, and they like to have their children work in the business. When asked what their goals are for their investments, a typical Family Steward might say, "Good investing lets me take care of my family."

It is highly likely that many of your clients will be Family Stewards as they make up the largest group of affluent investors. You probably already have Family Stewards among your client base. Think of your wealthier clients who have pictures of kids all around their offices, who have their children employed in their businesses, who live modestly yet have a significant asset pool and who are highly motivated to ensure their families are financially secure. How many Family Stewards come to mind?

Family Stewards are average in their knowledge of investing and personal finance. Their investing IQ is three out of five stars, five being the highest. The three stars for Family Stewards shows you they are middle-of-the-roaders when it comes to their financial sophistication. As you will see, there is another group that has only half a star because they are not at all knowledgeable. Conversely, a few high-net-worth personalities have five stars because they are very knowledgeable. According to this measure, Family Stewards are about average.

You must possess expertise to relate to Family Stewards. We'll see that many of the high-net-worth personalities want their investment advisors to be experts. The key to being an expert for a Family Steward is different than being an expert for an Innovator or for an Accumulator. For Family Stewards, expertise is about understanding which services you provide will enable them to best fulfill their primary desire to take care of their family.

You also need to be careful and prudent to mesh with their investment philosophy. Why? Because that is a value shared by the majority of Family Stewards, and they look for financial advisors who share this same value. To accomplish this, you need to show that you are very protective of them and their goals. They need to feel that you understand them and their goals of protecting their family exceptionally well.

An investment advisor working with a Family Steward client might say, "There are a lot of ups and downs in the current market. Let's sit down and look at the situation and make sure your family is protected the way we want it to be."

Family Stewards are highly responsive to a variety of planning services because of their strong motivation to do the best by their families. They can readily understand why planning would put them in a better financial position. Family Stewards are very interested in estate and financial planning, and the majority are very interested in asset allocation services.

Family Stewards are especially motivated when estate and financial planning services are positioned as ways through which they can help their families. For example, an advisor might suggest, "Its good you have decided to do an estate plan. In the plan I just finished, we were able to save on taxes so there was money to set aside for the grandchildren's education." Naturally everyone wants to save on taxes. The key point is that you tie the savings back to the dominant motivation behind their investing – their families. It's not about the products or services you offer, but about the way you position it as a benefit to the client.

Family Stewards are interested in a broad range of investment products that can help them meet their family goals. Among such products are mutual funds, managed accounts, private equity opportunities and funds of funds. The important element for Family Stewards is not the actual investment vehicle; it is the goal of safeguarding their families. The risk profile of a Family Steward tends to be conservative to moderate.

*Your turn:* *How would you explain asset allocation to a Family Steward?*

### Investment Phobics

**"The last thing I want to talk about is investing money."**
**Investment IQ: ?***

Phobics are hard to miss. They don't like investing. They don't know about investing. Investing makes them uncomfortable. Furthermore, they don't want to learn about investing, and they tend to be adamant about remaining financially unsophisticated.

Instead of learning themselves, Phobics would much rather delegate the management of their monies to a trusted investment advisor. So how does a Phobic choose an advisor? You can sum it up by saying that Phobics "probe" an advisor to see if their "gut feeling" tells them they can trust him or her. Only once a sense of trust is established will the assets follow. This is largely because a Phobic is without the knowledge or sophistication to judge a financial advisor analytically, so they do it emotionally.

Phobics are the least knowledgeable about money of any segment. They have a half a star to represent their Investment IQ, which is the lowest of all the high-net-worth personalities. We give them half a star because their financial sophistication generally ends after writing checks and using credit cards. They do not know anything about investments, and they know they don't know. They are looking for an investment advisor to take over complete responsibility.

This trait of passing the responsibility of investing to the advisor makes Phobics a great group to have as clients. For one thing, they are the least sensitive to investment performance of any of the nine high-net-worth personalities. It's a big mistake to try and educate them about financial issues because if you do, their eyes will glaze over, they'll correctly assume you don't understand them, and you'll never see or hear from them again. Instead, you always must work to build personal trust.

To work successfully with Phobics, they need to consider you a reliable and dedicated expert. Here, being an expert means you can take care of, or at least consult on, all their financial matters. They need to be able to count on your presence, your management of all the things they cannot bear to manage and your dedication to their best interests (because they generally don't want to and can't look after them on their own.)

Because Phobics do not want to understand investing, they will focus exclusively on their personal rapport with you, trying to determine whether or not they can trust you.

Phobics are not interested in the various planning services. It is not that they don't need them – most do – but that they are not interested in participating in an extensive financial, estate, investment or tax planning process. The challenge is how to get them to commit to a process they need, but don't have any interest in.

An investment advisor working with a Phobic might advise the following, "Many of my clients don't like to get bogged down in the details of a particular investment. Instead, they've learned they can trust my expertise to find them the best possible investments for their goals. Should they request details, I can provide them verbally or through literature. However, typically they don't."

When a Phobic wants to open an investment account, they are buying you and the comfort and trust they feel with you.

*Your turn: How would you explain asset allocation to a Phobic?*

### Independents

**"To me, successful investing means freedom."**
**Investment IQ: ★★★**

Independents are an uncomplicated group. They seek independence and the freedom to do whatever they want. The way they achieve this is through financial security. They may actually hold a corporate job or run a business, but they aspire to being financially free to pursue a hobby full time, travel, or even start a business around their hobby – such as a tour company for cyclists. Independents are often characterized by having a vague financial goal that once achieved, would allow them to pursue their dream. Once they achieve this goal, they do not always retire and pursue their dream full time. It seems that simply knowing they could cut loose at any time is the liberating feeling Independents crave.

Independents have three stars for their Investment IQ and they are average in terms of their investment knowledge and sophistication.

To work effectively with Independents, you need to be the expert. Here, expert refers explicitly to your ability to provide investment advice that will enable them to do what they want. Independents want you to compensate for their own relative weakness and lack of investment expertise. However, they need constant reassurance that you are focused on the same goal of their investing as they are – financial independence. They will look to make sure that your recommendations and investment style fit with this goal.

In short, they want an expert that is going to get them out of that corporation at age 55. They are not focused on their families (like Family Stewards, however, they won't neglect their family if they have one) and they do not center their decisions exclusively on interpersonal trust (like Phobics). Their hot button is personal financial freedom via astute investing.

Independents typically do not do an adequate job of allocating assets. Consequently, they are interested in asset allocation services because they know they need their assets structured and invested properly. They are aware that asset allocation will help them achieve their goals. However, they aren't necessarily interested in the specific investments (e.g., mutual funds) to which their money is headed. An investment advisor working with an Independent might approach the situation like, "I have put together asset allocation models for many people who have the goal of retiring early, and because I have helped many other people retire early to pursue their dreams, I know what works best for your goal."

Another area of significant interest for the Independent is their interest in retirement distribution planning. Independents know that once they stop working, their money has to keep working as hard and as intelligently as possible. This is especially important to Independents because they are retiring early and will have a longer retirement, and a more active retirement. As such, retirement distribution planning creates another key issue for an investment advisor working with this high-net-worth personality.

Independents have broad investment interests. However, no specific financial product is especially interesting to a majority of Independents, reflecting their relatively average knowledge of investing in general. Some are interested in private equity and others in managed accounts. Therefore, though Independents may express an interest in one of those products, an investment advisor would be wise to distinguish between clients' interests and their needs.

*Your turn:* *How would you explain asset allocation to an Independent?*

## The Anonymous

**"My money is my business and no one else's."**
**Investment IQ: ★★★★**

Did you ever have a wealthy client that took forever to really open up and tell you things you really needed to know? Or did you ever have one ask you "why" you needed their social security number? If so, there's a good chance that wealthy client was probably one of the Anonymous. It will usually take some time before the Anonymous will provide you with much information about themselves. The Anonymous feel that their money is their business and no one else's. This is an obvious hurdle for an investment advisor. However, once you win their trust, the Anonymous client will be loyal – in part because he or she doesn't want to talk to anyone else.

The Anonymous are a challenge to deal with until you truly understand their "logic." They are intensely private people, and do not want to disclose their financial positions to anyone. In order to work with an investment advisor, they need to feel absolutely confident that their privacy will be preserved. They are looking for an investment advisor who understands this and communicates the steps taken by the advisor's practice to ensure the client's confidentiality. For whatever reason, the Anonymous are hyper-sensitive to issues of confidentiality.

The Anonymous have solid personal expertise in investing. They come out at four stars, which places them above average among the nine high-net-worth personalities.

An interesting fact about the Anonymous is that they often come by advisory referrals. In fact, when you receive an advisor referral you may want to consider that the affluent prospect might be one of the Anonymous. Can you guess why you'll never get a client referral from one of the Anonymous? Because they don't talk to each other, or to most anyone else, about financial matters. They simply are uncomfortable or unwilling to discuss this with anybody save the people who absolutely need to know – their other advisors.

In order to work effectively with the Anonymous, you should be extremely discrete and miss no opportunity to emphasize the lengths to which you will go to protect client information. One advisor that works with the Anonymous a great deal tells his clients that he wants them to know that he never discusses any client or client details with anyone outside of his office. He tells them that they may have friends in common throughout town, and they need to know that they can rest assured he will never discuss their account with anyone.

An advisor working with the Anonymous must take great care in handling their client's accounts. For example, every time you send them correspondence over which you have control you should stamp it confidential. You should also send it via a secure delivery service. Finally, always make sure you follow up with a phone call to confirm receipt of the package.

Because they are moderately knowledgeable, the Anonymous want their investment advisors to have considerable expertise. Expertise refers to both investment proficiency and the ability to ensure confidentiality. Many of the Anonymous have not been through the basic planning processes of tax planning and estate planning because they are so tight-lipped about their holdings.

If you can secure the trust of the Anonymous, certain planning services are appropriate, in particular, tax planning and estate planning. A common theme with the Anonymous is anti-government sentiments. They dislike the government's knowledge of their financial dealings via tax returns, and want to pay lower taxes. An investment advisor working with the Anonymous might approach the subject like, "When it comes to your money, the less you have to report, the less the government or anyone else knows."

The Anonymous are attracted to investment products which enable them to preserve their privacy and/or protect their assets from taxation. Annuities fit this mold, as they are attractive from a tax-planning standpoint. Besides, they also avoid probate. For any of these or similar products, you want to be sure to lead with the benefits of the product, that is, that the products will achieve the greater goals of privacy and lower taxes.

*Your turn:*   *How would you explain asset allocation to an Anonymous?*

## Moguls

**"Being rich means power."**
**Investment IQ: ★★**

Moguls are motivated by power. Moguls seek control, influence and, yes, power in their families, business, community and investments. Look for awards, diplomas and credentials on the walls of their offices. Listen to hear if they drop names of powerful and influential people, though not necessarily famous people. Watch their interactions with others. Are they authoritarian or bossy? Are they direct? Very direct? If so, you may be working with a Mogul.

Moguls are not particularly knowledgeable about investing; for this they earn just two stars. In spite of this, Moguls believe they're knowledgeable about investing. Finally, they are not interested in investing per se, but regard it as another forum to flex their power and control.

For you to successfully relate to Moguls, you have to acknowledge their power, and be powerful yourself. A Mogul does not want to work with a shrinking violet. However, Moguls want to be in total control of the relationship. Moguls respond well to flattery and require authority (signoff- verbally or literally) over all investing decisions. Often times, it is beneficial to position yourself as the coach, wherein you make recommendations, but they are the team owner that has ultimate decision-making authority.

To connect with a Mogul, you need to emphasize ways in which Moguls have control over their financial affairs, in which they make the big decisions. You also need to be appropriately deferential. In making a presentation to a Mogul, an investment advisor needs to connect to their basic motivation, for example, "I've developed an asset allocation model that I'd like to present to you to get your approval. I need you to decide between a couple of alternatives."

Moguls find the idea of asset allocation very appealing because it means they can have control over their investments without having to be involved in day-to-day details. Moguls are usually big-picture people. As such, they are interested in asset protection services because they perceive themselves as important, prominent individuals who may be likely targets for lawsuits.

Moguls like products associated with power and with powerful people. They like access to exclusive products because they feel it is an acknowledgement of their power, which explains their affinity for hedge funds, private equity and funds of funds. All three of these products play to their desire for power and to be perceived as powerful.

*Your turn:* *How would you explain asset allocation to a Mogul?*

## *VIPs*

**"There are lots of ways to get respect and investing well is one of them."**
**Investment IQ: ★★★**

VIPs are status oriented. They like prestige and the respect of others. Look around their offices for pictures of themselves with celebrities. These celebrities don't have to be nationally known figures; they may be famous only on a regional or local level. Look also for pictures of their boat, their sports car or their vacation home. Is their office or home furnished luxuriously? VIPs are the profile that looks rich. They prefer designer clothing even in casual dress, and may have several expensive watches.

Many people confuse VIPs with Moguls. To keep them clear and separate, remember for VIPs, investing is about having the ability to buy status possessions. Moguls are about control and power.

VIPs are not especially knowledgeable about investments. However, they might try to impress you with what they think is the right answer. In any case, they will ultimately rely on you as the investment expert.

To work successfully with a VIP, you will need to be particularly attentive and responsive. Applying appropriate deference is also useful. You should especially stress the reputation and prestige of your institution or firm. If you happen to have a famous client that doesn't object having their name dropped, this is the group to do it with (never do this with an Anonymous).

VIPs are not very interested in financial or estate plans as many already have them. Once you establish the general nature of those plans (and how recently they were established) you should advance the discussion to potential product. Down the road, you may find it appropriate to recommend that they review their plans, but do not push the issue too early in the relationship.

One of the VIPs' strongest interests lays in asset protection services because they can see themselves as minor celebrities who may need to insulate themselves from lawsuits. They are also interested in charitable giving because they see donations to various causes as a way to elevate their social standing.

VIPs are especially attracted to investments that have an exclusive aura or cachet. Private equity is known to be difficult to enter, so VIPs like the chance to do so. Another enticing investment category is collectibles because they have the virtue of investment potential as well as ownership of a precious object or status symbol that can be displayed. As an investment advisor, you need to be respectful of this trait, being status conscious when working with them.

*Your turn:* How would you explain asset allocation to a VIP?

### Accumulators

**"You can never be too rich or too thin. Thin doesn't matter, rich matters."**
**Investment IQ: ★★★★**

Accumulators are the "Warren Buffetts" of the world, albeit with lower total assets than Mr. Buffet. They save more than they spend. They tend to live well below their means. They don't exhibit any outward displays of wealth, and in fact have a disdain for those who do. What they enjoy is watching their pile of money grow. The more they have, the better they feel.

Unlike an Independent that may be in an accumulation phase to have the necessary assets to retire, Accumulator's financial goals are rarely linked to some other motive. They just want more. Their goal may be $5 million by age 55. When they hit it, they change their goal to $10 million by age 65, and so on. Accumulators may have families, and while they don't neglect them, their family isn't central to their financial goals the way it is with Family Stewards. In fact, a quote from Warren Buffet himself seems to sum up their attitude. Mr. Buffett said, "I want to give my children enough money so they can do anything, but not so much money that they can do nothing."

Accumulators are the most focused high-net-worth profile on investment performance of the nine. For Accumulators, capital appreciation is an end in itself. They don't want the money to do anything; they just want the money to grow.

For all of their focus on accumulating assets, Accumulators are more knowledgeable than some high-net-worth personalities, but they are not the most savvy investors (obviously diverging from Mr. Buffett in this trait) as denoted by the four stars. Though you may have to educate Accumulators they will be interested in what you have to say and are motivated to learn more.

To work with an Accumulator, you have to continually repeat back to them what their goals and motivations are. They are performance driven, and expect you to be the same way – concentrating on piling up those assets and congratulating each other on successful performance results.

Accumulators are open to various planning services, especially if those services will result in more money. For many of the affluent, and especially for Accumulators, it's not how much you make, but how much you keep. That's why planning services like estate and tax planning are of keen interest. Asset allocation services are also attractive because the point of asset allocation is to maximize long-term results.

Financial planning results in more efficient and effective use of financial assets – an appealing means to an end for Accumulators. An investment advisor pitching to an Accumulator might want to emphasize that they do considerable planning for every client to minimize taxes, ensuring that the client's money will grow as quickly as possible.

Accumulators, more than many other high-net-worth personalities, have broad investment interests. Actually, they are interested in anything that will make them money and interested in whatever will bring them the best return for their risk level. Private equity and even collectibles sound appealing to some Accumulators because those are asset classes in which they are generally not yet investing.

*Your turn:* *How would you explain asset allocation to an Accumulator?*

### Gamblers

**"You have better odds playing the market than at Vegas."**
**Investment IQ: ★★★★★**

Gamblers, as their "name" implies, love the excitement of the market – the drama of investing, the thrill of the big win. For Gamblers, investing is their hobby. For some it is their work, and for a few it is their life. Because of this they are much more performance sensitive than any of the other high-net-worth personalities.

Gamblers are very knowledgeable though they are not always astute. Gamblers believe it is possible to consistently beat the market and they like to recount their big victories. Not surprisingly, they often have a higher than usual risk tolerance. They will call you frequently commanding a lot of your time, but they tend to be active traders as well as long-term investors, applying a percentage of their portfolio to each strategy.

Gamblers love to find people with whom they can talk about investing and need their investment advisors to be as involved as they are. They also like their investment advisors to share in the emotional excitement of investing.

When it comes down to it, Gamblers want a playmate. They want you, as their investment advisor, to be as much of an expert as they are. They also want you to eat, breathe and sleep investing and the market. And, they want you to have an exciting style. They like their investment advisors to be plugged in and energetic.

Most Gamblers say they are not particularly interested in having someone approach them with planning services such as a financial plan unless it is truly state-of-the-art. For instance, consider sophisticated asset allocation modeling. Most asset allocation models deal only with investable assets. For Gamblers, you will need to deal with asset allocation models that incorporate all their assets such as life insurance, real estate and retirement assets.

Gamblers are interested in investment products such as hedge funds and derivatives because there is the possibility of big returns. They like the leverage and risk profile of these investment vehicles. It's their style.

*Your turn:    How would you explain asset allocation to a Gambler?*

### Innovators

**"Derivatives were the best thing to happen to investors."**
**Investment IQ: ★★★★★**

Innovators, like Gamblers, are extremely knowledgeable investors. However, their orientation is different. Innovators like to be at the cutting edge of the money management field. They like new products and services, and sophisticated analytical methods. Innovators often have technical backgrounds, and might be computer programmers, engineers or mathematicians.

Innovators are substantially above average in their investment expertise and they, like Gamblers, have five stars representing their investing knowledge. However, they are tightly focused on the latest thinking in the money management field.

For you to earn the trust, and assets, of an Innovator, you have to prove your own worth in terms of leading-edge product expertise. In other words, if they are on the cutting edge of investments, they want their advisor to be on the razor's edge of the latest ideas. Innovators look to their advisors to keep them sharp. They also expect that you will be as up on modern portfolio theory as they are, and that you look forward as much as they do to opportunities to discuss it. Bear in mind that it is not unusual for Innovators to be running sophisticated analytical software on their own.

Like Gamblers, Innovators are interested only in the most sophisticated planning services. If you are conducting an asset allocation analysis, you should be prepared to review with them the various assumptions built into the model with which you are working.

At the same time, Innovators are eager to take advantage of a number of interesting investment opportunities, including private equity and hedge funds. They are also generally fond of derivatives. These investments fit their passion for leading-edge products. In fact, some Innovators have been known to discuss the mathematics behind swap transactions with their investment advisors.

*Your turn:    How would you explain asset allocation to an Innovator?*

### Chapter 2 Answer:

*One explanation of a concept like asset allocation is not enough, you need at least 9. High-net-worth psychology helps you deliver superb service to millionaire (and other) clients. You can use high-net-worth psychology to bring your practice to a new level, to boost client satisfaction, to get a pipeline of client referrals and aggressively grow assets under management through asset capture. Already you understand the benefits of high-net-worth psychology, how it was developed and what the framework is. The rest of the book is a primer on how you can master the approach.*

| High-Net-Worth Personalities | Primary Motivation | Positioning and Asset Allocation |
|---|---|---|
| Family Stewards | Care of the Family | "I know your top priority is to **take care of your family**. Let me tell you about asset allocation, the best approach we know for managing your investments so you can be **comfortable knowing you have done the best job you can for your family**." |
| Financial Phobics | Avoid financial affairs | "I know **you don't like to get into long, technical discussions** about your investments, so I'll keep it short. Many of the best people in the industry have worried about figuring out what is the very best way to invest, it is asset allocation. If you give me the go-ahead, **I'm going to have a look at what you have got using this approach, and then we can talk again**." |
| Independents | Financial Freedom | "I'd like you to consider asset allocation. **Because your goal is to be financially independent** and flexible, I think asset allocation would be a good approach to explore. Asset allocation allows you to **directly relate your goals to the way your portfolio is invested**." |
| The Anonymous | Confidentiality, privacy | "I have been spending time thinking about your account. There is an approach called asset allocation I would like you to think about. I would like to prepare a **confidential** analysis for your review next time we meet." |
| Moguls | Power, control | "I know you like to **control** your portfolio, and an approach called asset allocation gives you the highest level of **control**. With asset allocation, you *set the overall strategy and make the major decisions*." |
| VIPs | Status, prestige | "Because your portfolio is an important one at this firm, we want to keep you current with the kinds of **investment approaches the leading investors are using**. The approach called asset allocation was proven by **modeling some of the largest pools of money in the country**. we think it's something you should consider given the importance of your portfolio." |
| Accumulators | Asset Accumulation | "As you know, the very best way we know of today to **maximize your long-term investment performance** is asset allocation. Because your **number one objective is investment performance**, I think we should get into this a little more." |
| Gamblers | Thrill of investing | "I know **you have been reading** the materials on asset allocation I sent along. The reason I like it for you is that it's a way **of setting your aggressive risk profile** in the context of asset classes. It will also require rebalancing, so you will have to **stay involved**." |
| Innovators | New investment approaches | "Our **technical people have jsut added some state-of-the art** enhancements to our asset allocation approach I wanted you to know about first. These include . . ." |

# Chapter 3
# What Makes a Millionaire's Advisor™?

*"Most people miss opportunity because it comes dressed in overalls and looks like work"*

— Thomas Edison

### Chapter 3 Critical Question:
### OK, so exactly how do I transform my practice?

You are ready to take the steps to change your practice and your life. You just want to know what to do. Well, the road ahead is paved; we do know what it takes to become a Millionaire's Advisor™. To your benefit, other top producing advisors blazed the trail of this process in a trial and error fashion over many years. Their experience and insights have shed light on a clear, linear process to transform your practice. There is a sequence of steps you need to understand and then implement. The steps, in the order you need to do them, are:

1) Understand and harness the magic of satisfaction.
2) Focus your practice.
3) Develop a target client prototype that works best for you.
4) Identify your client's and prospect's profiles to match with your prototype.
5) Accurately determine client value in evaluating your book.
6) Master high-touch, high-profit relationship management.
7) Systematize client relationship management.

Let's quickly provide an overview of the process. Then we will dig into each element in successive chapters which will allow you to implement these ideas.

# The Magic of Satisfaction

Ask an investment advisor how satisfied their clients are. What you will typically hear is that their clients are very satisfied. If you ask how they know this, they will point to the investment performance they delivered, or note that no one is complaining or say they get along well with their clients.

But really, how do you know your clients are satisfied? We think you can know by looking at your practice as it is. Do your clients stay with you, through good times and bad? If they do, they are satisfied. Do your clients frequently bring you new assets to manage? If they do, they are satisfied. Do your clients bring you new clients? If they do, they are satisfied.

## *The Bottom Line: Relationship Building Builds Business*

One way to really understand this correlation between satisfaction and a successful practice is to consider the worst case – clients leaving their advisors. We have researched this issue. We find that when clients leave investment advisors it is because the relationship has soured, not because of poor investment performance. Look back over your own history with clients. Did the ones who left you do so because of poor performance or not hitting a certain target in terms of returns? Or did they leave because of relationship related problems? In the client's mind it usually is because of some breakdown in the relationship.

The ideal situation is when you combine solid investment performance with solid relationship management to maintain clients and expand your relationship with them as well as win referrals to build your business. In short, by putting a focus on the softer side of the business – relationship management – you will directly impact your bottom line in a powerful way.

## *The Optimal Source of Referrals*

Research confirms that the single greatest source of affluent investors are other affluent investor clients. Theoretically, people talk about any number of prospecting sources for affluent investors. However, the research reveals, in study after study, that client referrals are the single most effective prospecting approach. Nothing else is as productive. Nothing else is as efficient at winning affluent clients.

How does the Millionaire's Advisor™ create these highly satisfied clients? The answer is by figuring out the affluent client's values, goals and needs, and embarking on a systematic campaign to fulfill these values, goals and needs.

The magic to getting referrals takes place before a referral is ever made. In point of fact, a referral won't even be made if the client is not completely convinced that their advisor will take good care of their friend, colleague or family member.

## *The Keys to the Treasure Chest: Creating Highly Satisfied Clients*

The question now shifts to how do you customize your approach to create highly satisfied clients? That's where high-net-worth psychology comes in. This methodology is instrumental in helping investment advisors understand the values, goals and interests of your affluent clients in a clear, simple and effective framework. Each of the nine different profiles has a distinct "financial motivator" that drives all of that profile's investing decisions, as well as what they look for in a financial advisor. The better an investment advisor can understand and integrate what he or she does for a client in the context of this financial motivator, the more highly satisfied the client becomes to the point that they are willing to increase assets under management and the number of referrals they make.

Using the client's financial motivator is a bit like the game of chess. Learning the basic moves of all the pieces is simple, if not downright easy. However, harnessing all of the different tactics you can employ with each profile into a clear and effective strategy is a bit more difficult. Yet, once accomplished, will allow you to be highly effective at winning the game consistently. That is the process the rest of this book will teach you.

## The Need for Focus

Face it, you like some clients more than others. You just get on better with some clients than others. All the investment advisors we talk to agree. Just like we like some people more than others to be friends, advisors naturally like some clients more than others. Advisors seem to have a natural affinity for some types of clients. These are the clients to focus on, and here is why.

### The Case for Focus

Focus happens when you're working with a selective clientele. In this case, we're talking about people whom you genuinely like and naturally relate to. You need to have "chemistry" with your affluent clients. More often than not we find that "chemistry" is present because of core similarities between yourself and clients. To the extent possible, you should seek and develop clients with the same values, goals and interests as yourself. Work with people you have a natural rapport with, people that you share values with.

### Time Management & Profitability Guideline

A major reason for focus is that you simply cannot pay the same amount of time and attention to every client in a growing practice. You have to be selective. Your time is the most valuable commodity you possess. It is literally the only currency you have to spend to build your practice. To optimize your personal and professional life, it is imperative that you use your time as effectively as possible.

The three steps to optimal time management are; Step 1) Determine your hourly rate, Step 2) Ascertain your payout per client, and Step 3) Equitable time per client calculation. The only way it is possible to profitably serve a high number of affluent clients is to have just two or three service models in your practice. You just don't have the time to customize everything to each client. On the other hand, if you force all your clients of many different kinds through just one service model, quite a few will feel unhappy.

### The Benefits of Focus: Sustainability and Scale

You will benefit enormously from the simple principle of building high-touch service models around clients with the same interests, values and goals as yourself. The more you focus on a clientele like yourself, the more efficient and easier your professional life will become. Even better, the more profitable your practice will become. Over the course of your career, this leads to both a sustainable business model you can scale to any size that suits you.

Begin to look at your clients as business lines. Of course there's money to be made by working with <u>any</u> client with money. But the reality is there's only frustration and failure to be made by working with <u>all</u> types of clients. The solution is to focus on two or three types of clients. The profiling system that works best is based on the clients' values, needs and goals. In technical terms, this is *psychographic profiling*. That's a $100 dollar word for people with different values and goals.

## Develop a Target Client Prototype

The beauty of the psychographic approach created in our research is that it simply and effectively categorizes clients and prospects into nine distinct psychographic types or profiles. You can understand the marketplace through this framework and decide who you want to work with.

By using high-net-worth psychology, you can get a very clear idea of the kind(s) of clients you work best with. It helps you quickly understand which client types share your values, interests and goals. These clients should become the core of your practice. They are the ones you want to service to the hilt, so that they refer you to people just like themselves (the same high-net-worth profile). In short, a core of two or three profiles should become the focus of all of your high-touch service efforts.

## Desirability of the Profiles

It should be noted that not all of the profiles are equal in their desirability for your business. Some profiles are particularly relationship focused, rather than returns focused. This means they are even more likely to place a premium on the value of the service you provide and this makes them desirable. On the other hand, some profiles are more demanding than others and require more work from you. All of the profiles should be managed with a high touch service system centered around their financial motivator.

## Identifying Your Own Profile

High-net-worth psychology is applicable to you. You are an advisor, but you are also a human being. You will naturally have a greater intuitive understanding with clients whom share your values and outlook on life and money. If you are like most advisors, you will find that your best clients are those who share this fundamental financial personality. The clients you should build your practice around are these clients as well.

Successful advisors have focused on working with just those wealthy investors with whom they "click." They principally focus on clients with whom they share high-net-worth profiles. Family Steward advisors work best with Family Steward clients, and VIP advisors have a special knack with VIP clients and so on. There is a natural affinity between advisors and clients who share the same fundamental financial motivation.

## *What is Your High-Net-Worth Personality?*

In a later chapter, we provide a Self Diagnostic Quiz to help you determine your own profile. When you complete this self-assessment, you will be in a position to determine your own financial motivator.

You may find that you have one, dominant profile. It could be that you are a solid Accumulator, and you score quite low on the others by comparison. In this case, you have one primary profile. On the other hand, you may see that you have two profiles that stand out, perhaps Family Steward and Mogul. You may even straddle three profiles, and that is OK, too.

## *Implications*

What does all this mean? By determining your own high-net-worth personality you will have a clear idea of which profiles you work most naturally and easily with. And, this is a great head start to zeroing in on the types of clients you will target. As we go on, check this by thinking about your current clients.

Let's say your dominant profile is that of a Family Steward and you also have Mogul and VIP tendencies. Do you find that you would work most easily with Family Stewards, because you yourself are one? Do you also find it easy to work with Moguls or VIPs? Have you found it harder to work with Gamblers or Innovators or Phobics? This confirms your profile. In this case, Family Stewards would be your primary target clients and Moguls and VIPs would by your secondary and tertiary client targets. In developing your business plan, you would focus on the client mix you work most naturally and easily with — Family Stewards, Moguls and VIPs. In this case, you would refer to the chapters that concentrate on these three client types.

Does this mean you should ignore another large profile that you feel you work quite well with? The short answer is no. The self-assessment tool gives you a clear idea of which profiles you will intuitively work very effectively with. However, it does not show you which profiles you could conscientiously cultivate with a little additional effort. Therefore, it is vitally important to carefully look at your results of this assessment.

### Ensuring Compatibility Amongst Your Focus Profiles

To be efficient, you should create as much synergy or overlap as possible in the different profiles you choose to focus on. In other words, not only do you want to work with profiles that share the same interests, values and goals as yourself, but whenever possible you want your focus profiles to have as much in common as possible also. The reason for this is simple. If your focus profiles aren't broadly divergent in their interests, values and goals your life will be easier and your work will be more efficient. For this reason, we provide a methodology to insure a complimentary fit between your focus profiles.

## Identify Your Client's and Prospect's Profiles

Now that you know your profile, the next step is to find out what profile your clients are. You probably have a critical mass of clients like yourself in your book of business, and you may also discover that you have some clients of each different type.

The most common question we get is how do you tell what the financial motivator is for each of your clients? It may look challenging, but actually it is not all that hard to tell one profile from another.

We have developed a method that we recommend to determine the financial profile of a client. This method has been developed with, and field-tested by, top producers. We call it the Profile Diagnostic System (PDS).

### Using the Profile Diagnostic System

Basically, the PDS is a series of open-ended questions to ask your client. Their answers to the questions help you zero in on a client's exact profile by the process of elimination. The PDS is comprised of four open-ended questions, as well as a few follow-up questions. You probably already ask questions like these when working with your clients.

### The Profile Diagnostic System at Work

The PDS works by process of elimination. You use the questions to confirm or reject the possibility of your client being any one of the nine profiles. In Chapter 7 we will use case studies to show you how this is done.

### Confirming Client Profiles: The Trial Balloon

Once you believe you know which profile a client may be, you can use a technique we call the "trial balloon" to see if you are on target. With these follow-up questions, you can confirm your hunch, and proceed accordingly, or disprove it before any damage is done. Creating and floating trial balloon ideas is relatively easy.

You can use all the skills and talents you already have to figure out what financial type your clients are. You already know how to encourage clients to talk to you about what they want from investing. All we do is add several new questions to your usual list.

## Accurately Determine Client Value in Evaluating Your Book

Now that you have determined your own profile and the profiles of key clients, the next step in the process is to evaluate your client book. It is important determine which clients have the greatest business building potential.

### *Determining Client Value*

You may think that the client with the greatest potential is the one with the greatest assets under management (AUM). However, you should look at the idea of client "value" much more broadly. Specifically, you should take into account the potential assets you could bring under management, their pattern of past referrals and future referral potential. By looking at all of these factors, you can develop a very clear picture of a client's value to your business. As you adhere to these four criteria in the evaluation of your clients, you will be able to get a solid gauge of their future value to your business.

Not all clients are created equal. They are different in terms of their high-net-worth profile. They are different in terms of how valuable they are to your practice. You need to evaluate each client you have in terms of their value to your practice.

The reason for this step is that you are about to undertake an approach of high-touch relationship management. You simply can't devote the same, high amount of time to every client. You have to selectively pick the ones to focus on strategically, and these chapters give you a process for doing just that. Now that you have the clients identified, you can move on to the next section that will show you how to develop great client relationships. These relationships will be the basis for your new role as the millionaire's advisor.

## High-Touch, High Profit Relationship Management

With the right motivation and skills, any advisor can make one client highly satisfied. That's not the real issue. The real issue is can you do it with a hundred clients all at the same time? Do it with clients that may very well be the hardest people in our society to please? Do it profitably? And continue to do it year, after year, after year? That's the real issue.

The answer is you can. But only by using High-Net-Worth psychology to build high-touch service tracks for your clients. You must focus on a homogenous core of clients and then get systematic. In other words, you need to create systems where high-touch relationship management happens without necessarily requiring your day-to-day involvement.

## Turning "Relationships" Into Business

We have identified four specific factors that culminate in the client's satisfaction with the relationship – four factors that an advisor can use, like a lever, to raise the ultimate satisfaction of a client. Those four areas comprise what we have called the C.L.A.S. Relationship Management Model – C.L.A.S. being an acronym for the four factors:

- **Client Focus** – Your level of focus on the client's needs, interests and goals.
- **Leadership** – Proactively providing solutions to your client's based on their unique financial motivator.
- **Attention to the Client** – Understanding and providing the level of desired attention, and the motivation for attention.
- **Shared Values** – Demonstrated sharing of core values, common ground and personal goals.

It's no secret that clients judge you according to investment performance and the relationship. But did you know that investors regard the relationship ingredients (C.L.A.S.) nearly four times as important as performance? This means that investment advisors who can deliver solid investment performance *coupled* with high quality relationship management are in an excellent position to develop a highly satisfied clientele, which in turn leads to more assets under management per client and more referrals from existing clients.

When an affluent client classifies themselves as "highly satisfied" more than one out of four affluent clients will increase assets under management each year. These are incremental increases in assets under management year over year, not increases in the value of existing investments. Better still, nearly nine out of ten affluent clients will refer at least one person who becomes a client every six months.

### *Integrating the Nine Profiles & C.L.A.S. for Improved Satisfaction*

C.L.A.S. shows you the four ingredients impacting client satisfaction with the relationship. The nine profiles help you understand what each client seeks by way of the C.L.A.S. model. Said another way, C.L.A.S. is a strategic model that can be applied to all nine profiles to raise their satisfaction level. The nine profiles are the tactical ideas you would use with that profile.

The C.L.A.S. Relationship Management Model is applicable to all nine of the profiles. In the nine profile-specific chapters (chapters 10-18 there are a wealth of additional relationship management ideas.

## Systematize Client Relationship Management

The most effective usage of the C.L.A.S. Model is not to look at it as a grab bag of ideas, but rather to weave the individual ideas into a complete plan, systematically contacting and servicing the client around their profile's unique financial motivator on an on-going basis.

The investment advisors we have seen that do this effectively have been very successful indeed. In fact, our research shows that of those advisors who contacted their client fourteen times or more over a six month period created clients that fell into the "highly satisfied" category 89.7 percent of the time. That means when they employed this systematic process they got more assets under management per client and more referrals almost nine times out of ten. Those are percentages that anyone can make a very comfortable living from.

If fourteen contacts sounds like a lot to you, consider this. We're talking about a brief phone call, an e-mail or some other contact two or three times a month for a period of six months. We're not talking about long phone conversations or turnkey account reviews. We're talking about small, simple contacts made repeatedly and continually to your best clients around what's most important to them. This isn't hard work and no other use of your time leads to such compelling and repeatable results.

The truly beautiful benefit of this process is that once the up-front work of building a high-touch relationship management system is completed, a minimal amount of effort is required by the advisor going forward to maintain the client's high satisfaction rate. It's kind of like driving a car on the highway. The majority of the energy is expended bringing the car up to speed—accelerating. But the car's at 65 MPH, it takes much less additional energy to keep the car at 65 MPH. The bulk of the remaining effort will center around minor customization to the client's individuality .

### The Top Producer's Systematized Use of C.L.A.S.

The way top producers put this to work is very simple, and their process includes three basic steps:

- **Step #1** - generate 15 profile-specific contact ideas for your focus profiles
- **Step #2** - plan the execution date for the profile specific ideas
- **Step #3** - Batch process the profile specific ideas for all clients of that profile on a given day.

We will outline the basic strategy used by top producing advisors. However, we want to not only show you how to build your own plan, but show you an example of a plan for each of the nine profiles. This is exactly what we have done in the last nine chapters of this book. Each of these chapters provides you an actual case study example developed and successfully implemented by an advisor. In addition to this plan, we also provide you ideas for managing and building relationships with each profile.

### Chapter 3 Big Answer:
*You can transform your practice one step at a time using the tools provided here.*

*Essentially the process is to determine your natural strengths and then leverage them as much as possible. By working with clients with whom you have a natural affinity, you will create higher and higher levels of satisfaction. Clients, in turn, will bring you more assets to manage and clients to serve. The key to the process is the client-by-client relationship development plan. The chapters that follow this overview go though the process in detail.*

# Section II:
# Optimizing Your Practice for the Millionaire:
# A Step-by-Step Proven Process

*"Have a cigar,*

*You're gonna go far,*

*We could turn this thing into a monster,*

*If we all pull together as a team.*

*Welcome to the machine"*

— Pink Floyd

# Chapter 4
# The Magic of Satisfaction

*"I can't get no satisfaction, no, no, no, no"*

— The Rolling Stones

### Chapter 4 Critical Question:
### How satisfied are your clients? How can you increase their satisfaction?

When we ask investment advisors how satisfied their clients are, most say that their clients are very satisfied with them and their services. Some point to the investment performance they delivered. Others cite the fact that no one is complaining. A few describe how well they get along with their clients. Our challenge to you is, "How do you know?"

We think you can know by looking at your practice as it is. Do your clients stay with you, through good times and bad? If they do, they are satisfied. Do your clients frequently bring you new assets to manage? If they do, they are satisfied. Do your clients bring you new clients? If they do, they are satisfied.

You see, the way we look at it, satisfaction is not an end it itself. Satisfaction is the lifeblood of a vital practice. It brings about all the other things you want your practice to have; clients who never leave, new assets to manage, new clients to serve. In empirical terms, satisfaction is an "intermediating variable" that results in more assets from current clients and more affluent referrals. With due respect to all the comments investment advisors make supporting the fact that their clients are satisfied, unless they're getting more client assets and referrals on a regular basis, it isn't satisfaction as we (or you) want to see it.

## "Quality Service"

There was a time in our country when people took great pride in the service they provided. Whether a sales clerk at a clothing shop, or the order taker at a fast food restaurant, you could count on good service. Service employees intuitively understood that if you give a client good service, not only are they likely to come back, but they may come back with a friend.

Unfortunately, things have changed. In the present day, "Quality & Service" belong together as deservedly as "Jumbo Shrimp" or "Middle East Peace." Unfortunately, "Quality Service" has become an oxymoron.

While there are many views as to why this has happened, clearly one of the major causes is that those in service jobs today rarely have a stake in the long-term performance of the business they work for. Quite logically, it doesn't matter to them whether or not a customer has a pleasant experience or not, because they will make the same hourly wage regardless. Should the bagel shop they work at go under, they can simply find a new job at the sandwich shop having its "Grand Opening" down the block. So why should they bother to put forth the effort of providing good service? The answer more often than not is they don't.

How does this societal problem affect you as an investment advisor beyond the daily annoyance of having your burger order mixed-up at the drive-thru? It couldn't be more significant. All of us, the affluent included, are constantly subjected to bad service. The result of this has been that the vast majority of us expect mediocrity. We simply hope for the absence of a problem, and aren't surprised if there is a problem.

But every now and again, we encounter a service professional that goes beyond what we ask for. Not only did they give us what we asked for and actually did what they said they'd do by the date they said they'd do it, but they anticipated a concern or a personal preference and acted in our best interests.

What happens when we have this kind of service experience? We go back. In fact we become lifelong customers. In fact, we tell our friends that if they want a good (fill in the blank), "Go see Gary! He'll take care of you."

The critical point here is that getting good service, not just service where nothing went wrong, is becoming increasingly rare these days. As a customer, this is regrettable. However, as an investment advisor in a service industry, this is a remarkable opportunity to be an island of satisfaction to affluent clients in a sea of mediocrity. One top producing investment advisor put it like this, "Every time I get poor service, I don't get angry. I don't get upset. I simply smile and pat my money clip." He knows very well that the backdrop of chronic poor service allows him to become more successful.

## The Bottom Line: Relationship Building Builds Business

For any investment advisor to be successful, they need to master two things. The first of these is to learn to become a knowledgeable, competent and capable investment advisor. In other words, your first priority is to provide a client sound investment advice and access to the best products available based on their situation. Most investment advisors do believe this to be the primary job they have. This is often summarized by both the client and the advisor as "investment performance." Everyone knows – and it's true – that investment performance contributes to client satisfaction.

However, there is a second integral component in a client's overall satisfaction and that is their perception of their relationship with you, their financial advisor. This is often summarized as simply, the "relationship."

Here's the surprising piece, ask yourself what's more important to your overall success as an investment advisor – investment performance or the relationship? While no client wants sub-par investment performance, it's very clear that many of the decisions about who they hire are not based very strongly on investment performance.

When we look at why investment advisors are fired, we find relationship problems, not poor investment performance, are usually the culprit (see **Chapter 1: The Millionaire Market**). What this really tells us is that most affluent investors leave their investment advisors because of relationship related problems. Not performance or lack of hitting a certain target in terms of returns, but everything to do with a breakdown in the relationship.

If you're skeptical about the critical role played by the relationship you might be saying to yourself, "Well sure they said they left because of the relationship, but I bet performance wasn't so great either." As professional skeptics, this answer crossed our minds as well. So, we analyzed the situation. As it turned out, of the affluent investors who said they left because of the relationship, nearly all of them said they were "Very Content" or "Very Satisfied" with investment performance. In other words, good investment performance does not make up for a bad relationship. When you have a bad relationship, the client leaves and their assets follow.

Why would so many affluent clients wish to leave an advisor who is essentially fulfilling the primary objective of the job (delivering solid investment performance)? This is a disturbing question. The answer is that when an affluent client leaves an investment advisor, they aren't going willy-nilly into the yellow pages, or setting up an online account. They are going to another investment advisor. An advisor that they are already working with, an advisor that is coupling solid (or at least acceptable) investment performance with a highly reassuring level of relationship management for one powerful combination.

As noted in **Chapter 1: The Millionaire Market**, the research shows that affluent clients have multiple advisors managing money. More to the point, the more investable assets an investor has, the more inclined they are to have even more investment advisors they (Exhibit 4.1). With less than $10 million of investable assets, the affluent tend to use between three and four investment advisors. However, once the amount of investable assets exceeds $10 million, these centamillionaires employ an average of six investment advisors. Affluent clients are essentially practicing what we have been teaching them all these years – diversification – by not putting all their eggs in one basket, by spreading them amongst multiple investment advisors. It's at least nice to know that these clients are listening to their investment advisors.

### Exhibit 4.1:
**Affluent Investors Use a Number of Different Investment Advisors**

| Amount of Investable Assets | Number of Advisors |
| --- | --- |
| $1 - $5 million | 2.9 |
| $5 - $10 million | 3.4 |
| $10+ million | 5.7 |

*Source: Prince & Associates/Institutional Investors, 2002*

Are we saying that investment performance doesn't matter? Absolutely not. It's essential for any advisor to be delivering performance on a par with his peer group over the long-term. Investment performance is something that every client expects as simply a starting point on their selection of a financial advisor. If you don't have it, or don't deliver it, after a while you're gone.

However, delivering investment performance alone is clearly not enough for most affluent investors. We have seen many instances where the investment performance is spellbinding but the investment advisor was fired. (Ask yourself, do you expect to be able to deliver spellbinding investment performance in perpetuity?)

The ideal situation is when you combine solid investment performance with solid relationship management to maintain clients and expand your relationship with them as well as win referrals to build your business. In short, by putting a focus on the softer side of the business – relationship management – you will directly impact your bottom line in a powerful way.

Another consideration why you should place a lot of emphasis on managing your relationships with your clients is that this component of your success is truly in your hands. If the entire stock market melts, there's a very good chance your clients will feel the heat. You can't control when such events will occur. On the other hand, you are always able to take actions that can enhance the breadth and depth of your relationship with your affluent clients.

## The Optimal Source of Referrals

In the investment advisory business, there is probably no subject as talked about as getting and landing referrals. The topic is beaten to death all too often. However, our research shows that getting referrals is actually quite simple. In the process inherent in high-net-worth psychology, generating and cultivating high quality referrals is in fact quite straightforward. The secret is satisfaction.

Research confirms that the single greatest source of affluent investors are other affluent investor clients. Theoretically, people talk about any number of prospecting sources for affluent investors. However, the research reveals, in study after study, that client referrals are the single most effective prospecting approach. Nothing else is as productive. Nothing else is as efficient at winning affluent clients.

Let's take this one step farther. The Millionaire's Advisor™ is the advisor who is getting the lion's share of affluent client referrals. Their affluent clients are willing, and sometimes eager, to provide these referrals, because they sincerely believe in their investment advisor. That belief is based on the overall consistent high-quality experience their investment advisor provides them. These affluent clients are highly satisfied.

You can compete for these affluent client referrals, but only if you make clients as satisfied as the Millionaire's Advisor™ does. Simply put, the magic to getting referrals is to create highly satisfied clients. Satisfied clients became the advocates (even the sales force) for their favorite advisor as they talk to friends and relatives.

Why are client referrals the preferential means of prospecting for wealthy investors? For the most part, the affluent simply don't go to the yellow pages, or a magazine to find an investment advisor. What they generally do is poll their peer group (friends, colleagues, co-workers, even family) for a glowing recommendation. The operative word here is a "glowing recommendation." They know intuitively that their friend or colleague isn't going to refer someone if they are merely satisfied. Therefore they don't ask, "Who are you using?", but rather "Would you recommend them?" The friend, in turn, isn't interested in sending this person to an advisor that they aren't convinced will take care of the referred. They won't refer a friend to an advisor unless they are highly confident that the advisor won't embarrass them in front of their friend. This level of confidence on the part of a client is established only by an advisor delivering respectable, relative performance and top-notch relationship management.

How does the Millionaire's Advisor™ create these highly satisfied clients? The answer is by figuring out the affluent client's values, goals and needs, and embarking on a systematic campaign to fulfill those goals and needs in a way that fits their values.

The magic to getting referrals takes place before a referral is ever made. In point of fact, a referral won't even be made if the client is not completely convinced that their advisor will take good care of their friend, colleague or family member.

### The Keys to the Treasure Chest: Creating Highly Satisfied Clients

The question now shifts to how do you customize your approach to create highly satisfied clients? That's where high-net-worth psychology comes in. This methodology is instrumental in helping investment advisors understand the values, goals and interests of your affluent clients in a clear, simple and effective framework.

It works like this. Each of the nine different profiles we introduced earlier has a distinct "financial motivator" that drives all of their investing decisions as well as what they look for in their choice of a financial advisor (Exhibit 4.2). The better an investment advisor can understand and integrate what he or she does for a client in the context of this financial motivator, the more highly satisfied the client becomes to the point that they are willing to increase assets under management and the number of referrals they make.

### Exhibit 4.2:
#### The High-Net-Worth Personalities and Their Financial Motivator

| | | |
|---|---|---|
| Family Stewards . . . . | Investing . . . . . | Takes care of my family |
| Phobics . . . . . . . . . . | Investing . . . . . | The last thing I want to talk about |
| Independent . . . . . . . | Investing . . . . | Means freedom |
| Anonymous . . . . . . . . | Investing . . . . . | It's nobody's business but mine |
| Moguls . . . . . . . . . . . | Investing . . . . . | Means power |
| VIPs . . . . . . . . . . . . . | Investing . . . . | Gets me respect, status, possessions |
| Accumulators . . . . . . | Investing . . . . . | Means rich and more money is what matters |
| Gamblers . . . . . . . . . | Investing . . . . | Is an exciting hobby |
| Innovators . . . . . . . . | Investing . . . . . | Is a technical challenge |

Repeatedly we have seen successful investment advisors convert prospects into clients, increase assets under management from a client, and generate referrals from their best clients by doing one simple thing – keeping that client's financial motivator at the center of their relationship with that client.

Using the client's financial motivator is a bit like the game of chess. Learning the basic moves of all the pieces is simple, if not downright easy. However, harnessing all of the different tactics you can employ with each profile into a clear and effective strategy is a bit more difficult. Yet, once accomplished, will allow you to be highly effective at winning the game consistently.

The remainder of this book is centered around providing a simple, step-by-step process to implement a powerful and systematic usage of the high net worth psychology concepts we have discussed.

### Chapter 4 Big Answer:
### Client satisfaction is the key to becoming a Millionaire's Advisor ™.

*You want to build a sustainable practice. This is a practice in which not only do all the most profitable clients never leave, but they bring in their friends and other assets. In this industry, there is a pervasive belief that the reason clients become satisfied is because of investment performance. High investment performance equals satisfied clients. Low investment performance equals dissatisfied clients. In fact, this is not true (which is good news because you do not have much control over the market).*

*What you can control is your relationship with your client. You can use your knowledge of your client's financial motivator to create higher and higher levels of satisfaction. When you increase satisfaction, you end up with what you want which is clients who never leave, new assets to manage, new clients to serve.*

# Chapter 5
# The Need for Focus

*"To do two things at once is to do neither"*

— Roman Sage Syrus

**Chapter 5 Big Question:** Are there some clients with whom you just "click?" Are there some kinds of clients you actually enjoy working more with? Are there some clients for whom going that extra mile is more a pleasure than an obligation?

All the investment advisors we talk to answer "yes" to these questions. Just like we like some people more than others to be our friends, advisors naturally like some clients more than others. Advisors seem to have a natural affinity for some types of clients versus others.

(The reverse is also true, of course. There are probably clients with whom you mix like oil and water – it can be done, but it isn't easy.)

As surprising as it may be, advisors almost never focus their practice on a certain client personality type. We don't know of many instances in which investment advisors have made a deliberate effort to limit their clientele to the people with whom they instinctively relate. Most advisors we know say they can work with anybody.

But is this really true? More importantly, should you work with anybody? Do you really provide the same level of service to clients you really like and those you don't like personally? Let's look at the case for focus.

## The Case for Focus

Focus happens when you're working with a selective clientele. In this case, we're talking about people whom you genuinely like and naturally relate to.

As we discussed in Chapter 4, the most successful investment advisors have learned one critical lesson through the course of their careers to build a clientele like themselves. More to the point, you need to have "chemistry" with your affluent clients. More often than not, we find that that "chemistry" means that there are core "similarities" between yourself and your clients. Therefore, we recommend that you seek out and develop clients with the same values, goals and interests as yourself. Work with people you have a natural rapport with; people that you share values with.

Some investment advisors hone and develop this path by trial and error on an intuitive level. Some accept this path as the wisdom of others, and consciously cultivate it. And some ignore it and seem to set a course for burn out. Regardless, the earlier investment advisors have learned to cultivate clients that they have a natural affinity for the more successful they become.

The necessity for focus becomes even clearer when you analyze how much time you actually have to spend on your clients, relative to financial and business goals.

## Time Management & Profitability Guideline

Your time is the most valuable commodity you possess. It is no exaggeration to say that it is the currency which, when spent wisely through your career, allows you to build financial success. To optimize your personal and professional life, it is imperative that you use your time as effectively as possible.

While that sounds reasonable enough, it is often too vague a goal

(Hey, I want to be efficient!). For this reason, let's start with a more tangible goal common to many advisors, a gross revenue (production) goal of $1,000,000 a year. There are a number of ways to go about understanding how you can achieve this considerable objective. We're going to look at it from a "time" perspective.

The steps to the time perspective are:
- Step 1: Determine your necessary hourly rate.
- Step 2: Ascertain your payout per client.
- Step 3: Calculate time available per client.

Step 1: Determine your hourly rate. To achieve $1 million production, you first need to figure out how much you need to be paid per hour, but before you can do that you need to figure out how many hours you work a year. Let's take a quick look.

There are 365 days per year. Subtract 104 days for all the weekends and that gives you 261 days. Subtract 20 vacation and or personal days and that gives you 241 days. Subtract 9 holidays and that gives you 232 days to run your business and earn your money. (Be aware that 232 days is a somewhat aggressive number.)

How many hours do you work each day? You may work 6 hours or 14 hours per day (and you can certainly plug either number into this model), but for the sake of this example, let's use the standard 8 hour day. Certainly, many advisors work longer hours, but, remember, we are talking about developing a sustainable practice and workload. As such, we have chosen 8 hours per day for this example.

But do you truly have the whole work day to spend on clients? Realistically, the answer is no. Even with a great assistant, you must spend some time in other areas beside client relationship management. You need to devote say 1 hour a day to financial management, 1 hour a day to referral development and 1 hour a day to office management, leaving you with just five (5) hours a day to spend on your clients.

The total number of hours you have in the year to work is 5 times 232, equaling 1160 hours for the entire year.

If you want to earn a million dollars, simple math shows you need to generate $862 per hour (1160 hours x $862 = $1,000,000).

Step 2: Ascertain your payout per client. To achieve this $1,000,000 level, you must look at your payout and average assets under management per client. For example, if you have a 100 basis point payout for your clients, you need 100 clients with average assets of $1 million. Or you need 200 hundred clients with average assets of $500,000, and so forth. Of course, you can go the other way, too (50 clients with average assets of $2 million, etc...).

We realize that an investment advisors production and net will vary greatly from one firm to another. However, by understanding the basic moving pieces, you can determine the number of clients you need given your gross earnings goal.

Step 3: Calculate time available per client. Now you can compute the amount of time you can spend with a client. Please note, we're looking at the issue as if all clients were of equal value to you as well as if they each had the same demands on your time.

Simply divide your total available hours by your total clients. Basically, if you have 100 clients and 1160 available hours, you can afford to spend 11.6 hours per year with (or on) each client. If you're at the 200 client level, you can spend 5.9 hours per year on 200 clients. If you're at the 300 client level, you can spend 3.9 hours per year on them.

Let's say you meet with anyone of these clients in person once a year for one hour. Inclusive of preparation, meeting time and follow up, you are looking at three hours minimum per meeting. If you are working with 100 clients, you now have 8.6 hours to spend on that client for the rest of the year (and only 2.6 hours per client if you have 200 total clients and a mere hour if you have 300 clients).

The question in its clearest form becomes this, "How can you create a highly satisfied client that wants to refer you to their friends, family members and colleagues with just 11.6 (5.9 or 3.9) hours to spend on that individual over the course of a year?"

Eleven measly hours to develop, prepare and execute an "exceed their expectations marketing plan" to the pickiest people on the planet. Easy, right? We all know it's not, but now at least you have a clear picture of the task before you, albeit through our simplified example.

A proven way of effectively managing the relationship is to become as systematic as possible. The idea being to reduce to the extent possible all the time spent in preparation so you can maximize the time with, and value delivered to, your clients.

The only way it is possible to do this is to have just a few service models in your practice. You just don't have the time to customize everything to each client. On the other hand, if you force all your clients through just one service model, quite a few will feel unhappy.

The only way out of this thicket is to give them what they want, when they want, but in a way that is easy on you. The only way this can work is to utilize high-net-worth psychology. Specifically, you need to identify one, two or three focus profiles that you work best with, and then develop a relationship management system for each profile, using it again and again on all the clients who fit that profile. In other words, develop one core service plan, (maybe as many as three) and apply it tens of times to a client group that is homogeneous – a group with the same basic values, interests and goals, a group that has the same profile.

We know you will want to tweak the prototype for each unique client. Nevertheless, the core model you develop will enable you to best utilize that precious resource – time – so that you will be able to meaningfully customize the service model. At the same time, each service model, because it is empirically based, will provide you with considerable leverage.

## The Benefits of Focus: Sustainability and Scale

There are two enormously powerful benefits stemming from the simple principle of building high-touch service models around clients with the same interests, values and goals as yourself. Simply put, it's more efficient and easier, as well as more profitable, to take a focused approach. Over the course of your career, this leads to both a sustainable and highly efficient business model.

### The Importance of Sustainability

Working with clients like yourself will, simply, feel less like work. Clients, in turn, will recognize your natural interest and affinity for them. It will be easier for you to engage with each and every one of them because there is a natural rapport. It's a truism of life and business that people like people like themselves. The old saw "birds of a feather flock together" says it another way. By identifying your own profile and then working with clients who share your profile, it will be less work to connect with your clients on a very personal level.

Now here's the surprising part. You are already unbelievably skilled at working with clients whose profile you share. You will know what your clients want and how they want to be treated because you are just like them. Peter Drucker, the renowned business consultant and visionary put it like this, "figure out what you're good at and work like hell in that area. If you try and be good at what doesn't come naturally to you, you will spend the bulk of your energy working in areas that provide little benefit."

The business benefits of this cannot be overstated. If you persist in working with people that are different from you, people you never really feel you connect with, you will expend an enormous amount of energy for little return. It's the classic mistake of trying to bang a square peg into a round hole. If you persist in this approach, you set a course for burnout. It may be five years, it may be fifteen, but over time, working with clients such as these will wear you down, wear you out and burn you out.

We've all heard of the 80/20 rule (80 percent of your profits come from twenty percent of your clients). The logical inference from this ratio is to "spend" 80 percent of your time on the 20 percent of your client base that give you the most business. Unfortunately, if we work with people whose goals, motivations and personality are vastly different from our own, we unavoidably stand this classic business rule on its head. We end up spending the bulk of our time trying to relate to people whom we have no natural rapport with. Bizarrely, this evolves into a situation where we neglect the clients like ourselves who would be easiest and most profitable to work with, while we misdirect our time and energy attempting to work with clients unlike ourselves. In the end, neither the client, nor your practice, is a winner. These clients can be detrimental to the positive attitude of your staff as well. In fact, we have seen firms that give themselves a Christmas present by voting on the most troublesome client and parting ways with that individual. It's best to eliminate these few clients for the betterment of all the rest of your clients, and your staff.

## *The Power of Scale*

The second powerful benefit of adhering to the concept of working with people like yourself is you take advantage of what Fortune 500 companies call "scale." When the majority of your clients are similar in goals and motivations, you benefit enormously. You can create one service model, and, while needing some client-customization, you can still apply it to all.

You streamline, you simplify and you get systematic. This allows you to focus your mental and physical energy on all of the other issues related to investment advisory management and business development. You will be able to create a highly satisfied clientele in the easiest way possible. We know, of course, that when you achieve a highly satisfied clientele, you hold the keys to getting more assets per client and more referrals.

Contrast this with the idea of finding a client and creating a new service model (re-inventing the wheel). Find another client and create yet another "wheel." And so on and so on. Each time you do this, you expend significant mental energy coming up with the new "wheel", and this has a ripple effect through the rest of your staff. They have to figure out how to handle this new "wheel." There will likely be an entire new set of issues to deal with.

The more of these different types of "wheels" you have, the more difficult it becomes for your practice to run smoothly. It's like a semi-truck driving down the highway. But instead of having the same size and kind of tire at every axle, you've got all sorts of different sizes and shapes. You can bet that's not going to provide a smooth or safe ride for your truck or your business. Clients will surely notice how bumpy the ride is, and you can bet they are going to look for a smoother ride pretty quickly. In other words, they'll start looking for another investment advisor to take over their account.

That's why, if you take on a client that doesn't fit your prototype, there best be several million very good reasons (dollars) justifying the incremental service workload. Let us be clear about our recommendation. Are we saying don't take rich clients if they aren't a focus profile? No, if this falls into your lap, take it. However, we are saying that to optimize your success, you should only ACTIVELY cultivate referrals from the clients with the same high-net-worth profile as yourself.

With this highly satisfied clientele, you will have created a marketing and asset gathering machine. We know from the research and our own experience that highly satisfied clients regularly increase the amount of assets under management with their advisor, the source of which may be income from their business, bonuses, options, inheritance or assets previously overseen by another advisor. Secondly, research coupled with field experience shows these clients will increase the number of referrals they make on a regular basis, bringing new clients to you. Best of all, when you create a homogenous clientele with a profile similar to yours, you will get referrals of similarly profiled clients roughly 90% of the time.

## "Who Do I Focus On?"

If you were to ask this question of a group of investment advisors, someone from the audience would likely shout, "Anyone with money!" While this is true on one hand, it can also be an investment advisor's undoing. The lure of taking any client with money inevitably leads to a practice full of different types of clients with different needs and different expectations. This is exacerbated by the fact that the more money they have, the more attention they feel they deserve. And, they're right.

Where does this net out for you? You'll find yourself running harder and harder to stay in place. By taking any client with money, you don't build one business, but many businesses, each catering to the highly varied needs, interests and goals of your clientele.

As an investment advisor, you know that most conglomerates with diverse and diffuse businesses rarely work. Generally speaking, successful businesses are those that recognize their area of expertise and focus on it. Of course there's money to be made in hundreds of industries, but you won't see Coca-Cola get into computers or cars. In fact, it was Robert Goizeta that truly unlocked the value of Coca- Cola back in the early 80's, by getting out of distractions like shrimp farming, and focusing on their brand and beverages.

The same concept is true for financial advisors. Begin to look at your clients as business lines. Of course there's money to be made by working with any client with money. But the reality is there's only frustration and failure to be made by working with all types of clients. The solution is to focus on two or three types of clients. The profiling system that works best is based on the clients' values, needs and goals. In technical terms, this is psychographic profiling.

### Developing a Target Prototype

The beauty of the nine different profiles uncovered in our research is that it simply and effectively categorizes clients and prospects into nine distinct profiles, allowing an advisor to understand the marketplace and who they want to work with.

## Exhibit: 5.1
### The Bell Curve in Your Book:

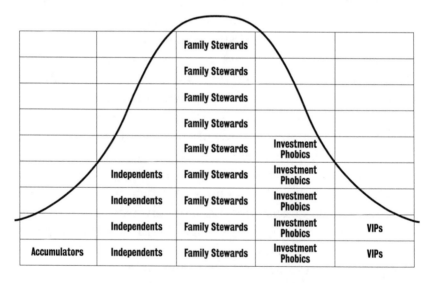

| | | | | |
|---|---|---|---|---|
| | | Family Stewards | | |
| | | Family Stewards | | |
| | | Family Stewards | | |
| | | Family Stewards | | |
| | | Family Stewards | Investment Phobics | |
| | Independents | Family Stewards | Investment Phobics | |
| | Independents | Family Stewards | Investment Phobics | |
| | Independents | Family Stewards | Investment Phobics | VIPs |
| Accumulators | Independents | Family Stewards | Investment Phobics | VIPs |

*One of the most commonly asked questions is, "Should I try to work with all of these profiles, or focus on just a few?" In our view, no advisor can be all things to all clients. The answer is to focus on who you naturally work with best. In fact, you probably are already working predominantly with two or three of the profiles. The trick is to learn which profiles you have a natural rapport with, and focus on these to maximize your success and minimize your workload. Chapter 4 covered this process in step by step detail.*

By using high-net-worth psychology, you can get a very clear idea of the kind(s) of clients you work best with. It helps you quickly understand which client types share your values, interests and goals. These clients should become your service and referral core. They are the ones you want to service to the hilt, so that they refer you to people just like themselves (the same high-net-worth profile). In short, a core of two or three profiles should become the focus of all of your high-touch service efforts. It's certainly acceptable to have clients that aren't one of these profiles, however, you must recognize that they aren't likely to be a source of referrals amongst your profiles of focus. Therefore they will be of less long term value, and not a perfect fit to the high-touch service model(s) you develop for your core.

## Profitability of the Profiles

It should be noted that not all of the profiles are equal in their profitability to your business. Some are relationship focused, rather than returns focused. This means they are more likely to place a premium on the value of the service you provide, rather than be calling you up to complain that their account was not equal to a given performance benchmark. Additionally, some profiles are simply more work than others. We take it as a given that all of the profiles should be managed with a high touch service system centered around their financial motivator. But even with that, some of the profiles will make a high level of inbound contacts because of their profile and this will of course consume more of your time.

For these reasons, we have found it useful to analyze the profiles according to their overall profitability, essentially balancing the time demands they make on the investment advisor above and beyond what goes into the high touch service system, as well as their proclivity toward being Returns or Relationship Focused. The higher the profile's profitability ranking, the better in terms of the long term value to your business.

A question we commonly receive is, "Do individual variances come into play?" The answer is of course "yes." You may find a Family Steward that is more sensitive to performance than the bulk of your Family Stewards, and this client's profitability would adjust accordingly. However, we have found the profiles to be a reliable indicator of this profitability overall.

Exhibit 5.2 identifies the three different measurements you should be considering. They are the profile's tendency to be either relationship focused vs. returns focused. A score of 1-5 indicates the profile is more heavily returns focused. Whereas a score from 6-10 indicates the profile is more heavily relationship focused, the higher the number the more heavily relationship focused the profile. This score is then divided by the client's time consumption. This score will range from 1.1 to1.9, with 1.9 being the greatest consumers of an advisor's time. Using this "Profitability Quotient" will give you a good indicator on the profile's general desirability, by balancing the issue of relationship vs. returns focused and the amount of time consumed by the client.

However, there is one caveat worth mentioning in a given profile's profitability. When you share the client's profile, it will be easier for you to work with them, making their profitability go up. For example, if you yourself are an Accumulator (the profile with the lowest desirability score 0.55), you may still want to strongly consider working with this profile, because they are a group that you will click with quite naturally (this issue is addressed in depth in Chapter 6 and Chapter 9).

*Profitability Equation:*

*(Relationship vs. Returns Score) / Time = Desirability*

## Exhibit 5.2:
*Desirability Analysis of Profiles*
*Based on Time Demands and Returns vs. Relationship Focused*

| Profile | Relationship vs. Returns Focused | Time Consumption | Desirability Quotient |
|---|---|---|---|
| Family Stewards | 9 | 1.2 | 7.50 |
| Phobics | 10 | 1.1 | 9.09 |
| Independent | 7 | 1.4 | 5.00 |
| Anonymous | 8 | 1.1 | 7.27 |
| Moguls | 7 | 1.3 | 5.38 |
| VIPs | 8 | 1.4 | 5.71 |
| Accumulators | 1 | 1.8 | 0.55 |
| Gamblers | 2 | 1.9 | 1.05 |
| Innovators | 3 | 1.7 | 1.76 |

### Profitability Analysis of Profiles
### Based on Time Demands and Returns vs. Relationship Focused

The case for focusing is a compelling one. But just how is it done? We'll lay out a step by step roadmap in the succeeding chapters, but let's first look at some case examples of advisors who have already incorporated the principle of focus into their practices.

# Case Studies:

Seeing how advisors have focus their practice on one profile can give you an insight into how it is done successfully. The following case studies overview tow practices, one focused on Family Stewards, the other Investment Phobics.

# Family Steward Case Study:

One advisory firm in the greater Minneapolis area - JRA Financial Advisors - has a practice that is heavily oriented toward the needs, goals and values of the Family Steward profile. In 1995, Kathy

Moss (President and Partner of the firm) realized that the majority of their affluent clients were simply family oriented individuals. They were affluent by anyone's definition, even wealthy. However, they didn't look like or act like what she expected of "wealthy" people. They didn't drive a Rolls Royce, wear top hats or exhibit big egos. They were people who over time had accumulated wealth by conservatively and steadily building their careers and their businesses. More surprising, their money wasn't their primary concern. Rather their family was their primary concern, and they wanted their money to be applied to taking care of their family. Because this group became JRA's client focus over the last 7 years, Kathy has steadily and continually oriented the practice to the needs of these clients. She didn't consciously say, "I'm dealing with Family Stewards here" (only later when exposed to the research from Prince & Associates did this become clear). Rather, she recognized the common needs, goals and values of these clients and began to orient the practice toward them.

When visited, JRA appears perfectly adapted to the Family Steward client. However, Kathy will be the first to tell you in a straightforward but unassuming manner that they are "always looking to improve and serve their clients needs even better." In short, it's not a static operation, but continually striving for improvement. When you examine JRA, you can identify areas of customization to the Family Steward client along three critical fronts, the office infrastructure, the team's personal style in working with clients and their orientation to the client's values.

### Infrastructure:

The offices of JRA Financial are strikingly different from a typical financial advisor's office and have several attributes which fit hand in glove with the needs and values of the Family Steward Profile. This is evident immediately upon walking into the practice. When a client walks in to meet the receptionist, immediately to the right is a feature rarely seen anywhere else—a children's play room. Not just a room to house children while their parents have their annual financial review. Rather, this is a room complete with a Nintendo setup, games, coloring books, a TV and a host of other toys. Children of clients are free to go in there and play while the parents take care of their personal financial matters, all under the watchful eye of the receptionist whom keeps tabs on the kids through the glassed in room.

This has two benefits to the bottom line of JRA. First, it clearly provides a place for the kids to go during the meeting, allowing the parents to focus on the important issues of overseeing their financial future, making good use of the Planner's time. Additionally, it quietly, but convincingly tells all Family Steward clients that JRA understands their needs and is going to take care of them, even if it requires extraordinary measures. All of this has been achieved, and the client hasn't even gotten past the receptionist.

The practice also has several other amenities that connect with Family Steward clients. It has its own kitchen, library and gym where clients are invited to "make themselves at home" whenever they visit. Occasionally, clients will come to the library to do research or even bring one of their children in that is working on a project for school which is financially related. Kathy sums up the overall goal of their office as being something that "looks established, comfortable and inviting" to the Family Steward clientele.

### Client Interaction:

Clients typically view their satisfaction with an advisor along two fronts—performance and the relationship. To better serve clients, Kathy has instituted a client management structure that reflects this natural tendency of a client to compartmentalize their satisfaction into two areas. As a result, Kathy has assigned two person teams dedicated to every client. Each team is comprised of a Financial Planner and an Account Administrator.

The Financial Planner provides personal planning services, oversees all areas of the planning process and will be the client's lead contact within the organization. The Account Administrator is, however, the **primary** contact for the client. They are responsible for the day-to-day coordination of processes on client accounts and make sure that the plan gets communicated to all necessary members of the JRA team, ranging from the Financial Planner to an Estate Planning Attorney to other support personnel in the office. The Account Administrator will have in-depth knowledge of the client's file and the status of any personal or financial activities. By structuring the "teams" in this manner, both elements of the client's satisfaction with the firm have a point person. The Planner's primary focus is on the planning element. The Account Administrator's primary focus is on the process component. Both emphasize the relationship component, and freely fill in where needed, working "in-tandem" to ensure the client's satisfaction.

Account Administrators will make time for personal conversations with clients during the numerous phone calls they place to insure that things are going smoothly. They make it a point to visit with them when they come in for review meetings with the planner. Kathy notes that oftentimes the Account Administrator will come into the meeting "just to chat" or get an update on an issue that has been part of previous conversations. The clients always respond positively to the fact that the Account Administrator's remember and are interested in the details of their lives. The Planner likewise puts a focus on building relationships with clients. In fact, many of them spend $2/3$ to $3/4$ of a client meeting just catching up on what's been going on in the family. The important information gathered by both the Planner and Account Administrator is then put into the client database by the account administrator so that anyone can access any information they need at any point in the future. Information ranges from births to job changes to specifics on vacations – sometimes including pictures.

The bonds between the firm and clients often become extremely close. For example, one Account Administrator recently had twins of her own. When the news got out to her clients, her office quickly filled up with cards and flowers from them.

JRA holds many client appreciation events to demonstrate to their clients how much the firm values their business. The events occur throughout the year and range in scope and content. Examples of their most successful are:

- Renting out an arcade complete with batting cages, air hockey, video games, basketball court, miniature golf and a DJ for the evening
- A financially oriented "Plan Ahead" seminar with guest speakers on virtually any subject a client might need from a financial professional
- Renting out an entire movie theater for a private showing of the Disney film, *Atlantis*.

It should also be noted that even these events, while clearly designed to entertain and educate their Family Steward Clients, directly impact the bottom line in two important ways. First, they serve to solidify the existing client's loyalty. Secondly, clients are always encouraged to "bring a friend" which inevitably becomes a rich resource of referrals for the firm. This is exemplified by the *Atlantis* movie event. When the invitations were sent to clients, parents and grandparents were so excited by the prospect of a private showing of *Atlantis* shortly after its release that they would RSVP as many as 15 people.

Kathy believes that the follow up can have just as much impact as the event itself. For example, she had the idea of sending toy crystal pendants (featured in *Atlantis*) along with a quote from the film "We are remembered by the gifts we leave our children" to those in attendance. This certainly reinforces that JRA is a family-oriented organization.

### Personal Style:

To work with Family Stewards successfully, it's beneficial to project a value system similar to the clients'. JRA does a very nice job of this right out of the gate. Any client that comes to the office for a meeting to determine if they will hire JRA is shown a brief orientation video on the firm. In this video, the 23 members of the firm are presented as the "JRA Family". Indeed, the firm has a very warm feel to it due in large part to the fact that the team members demonstrate a genuine like for each other. Additionally in the video, a montage of family pictures from JRA are included in the opening sequence to further underline this point and the firm's focus.

All of this has led to JRA developing relationships with their own clients that are nearly as strong and enduring as those between actual family members. Perhaps the most sincere demonstration of this point occurs during one of life's most difficult events. Whenever a client passes away, the firm has a standing policy that a firm representative will go to pay their respects to the client and family. The family always appreciates the show of respect, and more often than not, voices a need during a quiet moment to come see JRA when things settle down. Recently, a long standing client (who had referred multiple family members to JRA) unfortunately passed away. All three planners working with the various family members attended the funeral to show their respect and support to the family. Clearly for JRA, it's not just business with their clients. However, it cannot be missed that this kind of dedication certainly leads to an incredible level of client loyalty and referrals.

## The Results:

JRA does an extraordinary job of building relationships with Family Steward clients and has been extremely successful because of these efforts. It should be noted that any firm can still be enormously successful through a fraction of this level of focus on their clients' core financial motivator. The results for JRA have led to clients for life. Discussion of extending client tenure at JRA is almost a moot point, because clients so rarely leave. Additionally, 95 percent of clients have 100 percent of their assets invested with JRA, which is a very high percentage relative to industry standards. Finally, this level of focus on the client's needs and values leads to approximately 3-5 referrals a week, as well as ensuring that JRA continues to manage the client's assets from generation to generation.

# Investment Phobic Case Study:

One advisor in Florida, by the name of Elizabeth Brickman, is an excellent example of focusing her practice on one profile. Elizabeth has built a very successful business almost entirely with Investment Phobics by understanding this groups desire to establish complete trust with their advisor and then defer decision making to them. To be perfectly clear, she did not wake up one morning and say to herself, "I'm going to build my business predominantly around investment phobics." It didn't happen that way, in fact, it happened almost by accident. Early on in her career, she made a conscious decision to work with people she liked and who liked her. Over the years, clients were so pleased with Elizabeth's warm, sincere and nurturing style that they constantly referred her to their friends, expanding her client base to the point where she no longer accepts new clients unless one leaves. Elizabeth says it best, "Doing business this way just kind of happened. I can't stress how important it is for the financial advisor to be true to who you are, and your clients will find you. These are the people with whom you work best. By being true to who I am my business is exploding, and I'm enjoying work more." In fact, an analysis of her book reveals that 73.7 percent of her top tier (A clients) are Investment Phobics.

How did she do it? By understanding that rather than trying to be all things to anyone, she would be better off being everything to a select kind of client—Investment Phobics. Elizabeth didn't plan to "target" Investment Phobics, it just worked out that way. However, this successful strategy can also be achieved consciously by understanding who you work best with and optimizing your practice for that profile. When you examine Elizabeth's practice, you can identify areas of customization along three critical fronts, her personal style in working with clients, her investment selection and finally her office infrastructure.

## Infrastructure:

Working successfully with Investment Phobics requires a personal style that meshes well with this group's financial motivator. When an Investment Phobic goes to see their financial advisor, they experience a great deal of tension. In their minds, they are going to the epicenter of a world they neither like, nor understand. Accordingly, as they walk into a financial advisor's office, they are like an over inflated balloon on the verge of bursting. The question for the financial advisor is what can you do to relieve this tension? Elizabeth does a great job deflating this tension. She has put a very comforting twist on the standard financial advisor's office. Of course there's a desk with a computer and the other requisite items. However, as you enter the office, you'll see three dog beds each with a nameplate on the front and a Sheltie dog, quietly but alertly resting on it. Then the client meeting area to the right is not over the desk, but rather a pair of elegant, comfortable sofas facing each other over a coffee table with a silver tea service on it. This immediately tells the investment phobic client that this is not going to be an intimidating, obtuse meeting on financial technicalities, but rather a discussion between two human beings.

## Client Interaction:

Though Elizabeth is the client's financial advisor, at the core of her interaction with all of her clients is a genuine friendship. It's the opposite of what you traditionally see, business first and maybe friends. This is reflected in her interaction with clients. If she has a one-hour conversation with a client, it is very typical for her to spend 55 minutes on the phone about non financial subjects and five on financial subjects. How can a business operate successfully this way? Elizabeth explains, "First of all I genuinely care for all of these people. But by not talking about investments, you are feeding the relationship, making it stronger. When you have strong relationships, clients stick with you, add assets and make referrals. I'm very happy talking about non-financial topics." In fact this strategy has been so successful that Elizabeth doesn't do any advertising and grows her practice through referrals. In short, doing what is best for this particular profile also happens to be best for the business.

## Personal Style:

Working successfully with Investment Phobics requires a personal style that meshes well with this group. For example, though Elizabeth does intensive sessions of portfolio work with great technical detail, she does it for lengthy periods away from clients. However, she doesn't involve the client in the details of portfolio development, unless they ask. "I've had too many clients whose eyes glaze over when I get into extensive detail. It's not what they want. They want me to do the work."

This personal style works well with her clients who essentially want the same things. Elizabeth summarizes this thought with, "I receive a lot of fulfillment from this type of client because it arouses my protective instincts. I'm drawn to people that place their trust in me."

## The Results:

The results for both her clients and herself have been very satisfying. Her clients, who by their own admission know little about investing, have done well because they have focused on the long term and followed Elizabeth's advice. Elizabeth believes that "Investment Phobics can do better financially than many other more technically knowledgeable people because they stick to their plan."

This approach has also worked well for Elizabeth's bottom line. Today the vast majority of her clients are Investment Phobics, so her service practice is optimized for this particular group. Her success is best measured by the long tenure of her many clients.

Many of whom have been with her for over ten years. In fact, she has only lost 4 clients in the last 10 years. Additionally, even with a six figure account minimum, her practice has continued to grow steadily through the years, causing her to cap it at a maximum of 200 clients. In any light, it's clear Elizabeth's strategy of optimizing her practice for Investment Phobics has benefited both herself and her clients.

### Chapter 5 Big Answer:

*With only so many hours in the day you need to treat every hour as a strategic asset on the way to your first goal of $1 million in production. The most efficient and effective way to do this is to focus on your natural clients – the client personality or personalities you have the greatest affinity for.*

*This chapter urges you to think the unthinkable. Spend your time and efforts on the clients most like yourself, not on the clients with the most money. Get off the impossible merry-go-round of customizing your approach to every client. Stop making the equally dangerous error of treating all your clients alike.*

*Do what the best do. Focus your practice on your natural client base, those profiles that share your values. You will feel better, perform more efficiently and have happier clients. You will create a cycle of success instead of stress. Want to know exactly how to do this? Read on.*

# Chapter 6
# Identifying Your Own Profile

*"Know Thyself"*

— Socrates

## Chapter 6 Critical Question:
**Have you ever wondered why you "click" with some clients? Conversely, have you encountered clients you just couldn't connect with no matter how hard you worked? Have you thought about your core motivations to invest?**

This book is all about knowing clients, but also knowing yourself. A truism of most advisors is that the clients they work most easily and effectively with (and profitably) are a mirror image of themselves. Typically, those clients will share some significant form of connection with their advisor. This is no accident. It is the way of the world that people like to work with people like themselves.

As an investment advisor, knowing your own high-net-worth financial motivation(s) has many benefits. You will undoubtedly become a wiser investor yourself. More importantly, you will become a better advisor to investors.

Successful advisors, have predominantly focused on working with just those wealthy investors with whom they "click." The most successful advisors work principally with clients with whom they share high-net-worth profiles. Family Steward advisors work best with Family Steward clients, and VIP advisors have a special knack with VIP clients and so on. There is a natural affinity between advisors and clients who share the same fundamental financial motivation.

Even if you are not wealthy at this moment, high-net-worth psychology is applicable to you. Certainly, you plan to be wealthy.

That is one of the reasons you are in this business. In fact, we have found that the nine profiles work regardless of an investor's current wealth level. However, the percentages of each group shift as you go down-market or up (down-market you will see more Family Stewards and Investment Phobics, up-market you will see more Anonymous, Moguls and VIPs). You are an advisor, but you are also a human being. You will naturally have a greater intuitive understanding with clients whom share your values and outlook on life and money.

In this chapter, we will take you through a process of coming to learn about your own investment outlook. If you are like most advisors, you will find that your best clients are those whom share this fundamental financial personality. The clients you should build your practice around are these clients as well.

## What is Your High-Net-Worth Personality?

To determine your own profile, take the following Self Diagnostic Quiz. Simply prioritize the statements below from most important to least important. Be sure to write down the first thought that pops into your mind. Don't stop to think about your answer or spend time second guessing yourself.

# Exhibit 6.1
## Self Assessment Tool

*In the following self-diagnostic survey, we present some investment options. In each group of four, rank the options in terms of how important they are to you personally, with 4 being the most important and 1 being the least.*

1. Please rank each of the following 1 thru 4 with FOUR being most important to you and ONE the least.
   _____ Funding college education for children and grandchildren (A)
   _____ Achieving my asset accumulation goal (G)
   _____ Having enough money to have the vacation home I want (F)
   _____ Getting enough money to retire early (C)

2. Please rank each of the following 1 thru 4 with FOUR being most important to you and ONE the least.
   _____ Having a fun time investing (H)
   _____ Learning about the most sophisticated investment methods (I)
   _____ Having enough money to have the power I want (E)
   _____ Being able to maintain my privacy (D)

3. Please rank each of the following 1 thru 4 with FOUR being most important to you and ONE the least.
   _____ Finding someone I trust to do my investments so I don't have to be involved (B)
   _____ Insuring the security of my family through my investments (A)
   _____ Minimizing the risk of identity theft through proper disposal of financial info (D)
   _____ Having sufficient assets invested to be independent (C)

4. Please rank each of the following 1 thru 4 with FOUR being most important to you and ONE the least.
   _____ Being able to protect the confidentiality of my investments (D)
   _____ Having the assets to buy the things I want (F)
   _____ Being able to focus on the exciting aspects of investing (H)
   _____ Having the luxury of not educating myself on technical, financial minutiae (B)

5. Please rank each of the following 1 thru 4 with FOUR being most important to you and ONE the least.
   _____ Having sufficient investments to feel powerful (E)
   _____ Using the most modern investment approaches (I)
   _____ Using my investments to take care of my family (A)
   _____ Concentrating on increasing the amount of my assets (G)

6. Please rank each of the following 1 thru 4 with FOUR being most important to you and ONE the least.
_____ Having the asset base to live wherever I want to (C)
_____ Having enough assets so others respect me (F)
_____ Hiring a top money manager to oversee my account and forgetting all about it (B)
_____ Maintaining complete privacy over my investment affairs (G)

7. Please rank each of the following 1 thru 4 with FOUR being most important to you and ONE the least.
_____ Finding new ways to keep investing as thrilling part of my life (H)
_____ Applying the most technical investment approaches (I)
_____ Having the investment base to get people to do what I want (E)
_____ Using investment products to transfer assets to family members (A)

8. Please rank each of the following 1 thru 4 with FOUR being most important to you and ONE the least.
_____ Being able to avoid getting involved in the details of investing (B)
_____ Focusing on increasing my assets (G)
_____ Having the assets to enjoy the finer things in life (F)
_____ Insuring my privacy with the investment managers I choose (D)

9. Please rank each of the following 1 thru 4 with FOUR being most important to you and ONE the least.
_____ Having advanced planning and products in my investment portfolio (I)
_____ Being able to use my investments to influence the way things are done (E)
_____ Having the confidence I can live independently (C)
_____ Staying very involved on a day to day basis (H)

Add up all of your rankings for A's, B's, C's, etc in the box below. Based on your answers to these questions, you will have a strong idea of your likely profile(s).

| | Total | High-Net-Worth Personalities |
|---|---|---|
| A | | Family Stewards |
| B | | Phobics |
| C | | Independent |
| D | | Anonymous |
| E | | Moguls |
| F | | VIPs |
| G | | Accumulators |
| H | | Gamblers |
| I | | Innovators |

Now look this over. You may find that you have one dominant profile. It could be that you are a solid Accumulator, and you score quite low on the others by comparison. In this case, you have one primary profile. On the other hand, you may see that you have two profiles that stand out, perhaps Family Steward and Mogul. In which case, you may be a parent from the old school, and want respect and deference from your children, even as you take good care of them. You may even straddle three profiles, and that is OK, too.

Bear in mind, that you likely have a primary, secondary and sometimes a tertiary profile. For example, you may have had a score of 16 on A, 14 on E and 12 on F. This would indicate that your dominant profile is that of a Family Steward, followed by a tie between Mogul and VIP.

## Implications

What does all this mean? By determining your own high-net-worth profile you now have a clear idea of which profiles you'll work best with. And, this is a great head start to zeroing in on the types of clients you will focus on. As we go on, check this by thinking about your current clients.

Let's say your dominant profile is that of a Family Steward and you also have Mogul and VIP tendencies. Do you find that you would work most easily with Family Stewards, because you yourself are one? Do you also find it easy to work with Moguls or VIPs? Have you found it harder to work with Gamblers or Innovators or Phobics? This confirms your profile. In this case, Family Stewards would be your primary target clients and Moguls and VIPs would by your secondary and tertiary client targets. In developing your business plan, you would focus on the client mix you work most naturally and easily with — Family Stewards, Moguls and VIPs. In this case, you would refer to the profile specific chapters at the end of this book (chapters 10-18) that focus exclusively on these three client types.

Does this mean you should ignore another large profile that you feel you work quite well with? The short answer is no. The self-assessment tool gives you a clear idea of which profiles you will intuitively work very effectively with. However, it does not show you which profiles you could conscientiously cultivate with a little additional effort.

This is especially true with the Investment Phobic profile. The chances are quite slim that you, as a trained financial advisor, are going to come out as an Investment Phobic. However, does this mean no financial advisors should work with this group? Remember, Investment Phobics are not only the second largest profile in the affluent market, they are also the most profitable because they place the least demands on your time. These two characteristics make them a very attractive market. As such, Investment Phobics are a target market every financial advisor should at least consider. While you may not share their distaste for financial subjects, as long as you feel you can be empathetic to their orientation to financial services, you have a good chance of being successful with this group. Therefore, it is vitally important to carefully look at your results of this assessment.

If the self-assessment points you to one of the smallest profiles (by percentage of the affluent, see **Chapter 2: All Millionaires**

**Are Not Alike**) you should consider consciously cultivating an affinity for one of the three largest profiles. For example, if you take the assessment and it says you personally are an Accumulator, Gambler or Innovator, you may want to consider consciously adapting your style to one of the largest three profiles. Additionally, these three profiles tend to be more returns sensitive than the other six larger profiles, and they also make fairly significant demands on your time, diminishing their overall profitability. This makes them a bit less attractive than the other six profiles. However, if you yourself are an Innovator, and read all the major publications to stay current on the latest ideas, you will undoubtedly love working with other Innovators and be very successful in the process.

By focusing on one or more of the larger profiles, you can take advantage of their larger numbers with just a little extra effort on your part. Following our example, look at the three largest profiles (i.e., Family Stewards, Phobics and Independents) and see which had the highest score. If your highest score amongst the big three turned out to be Independents, you should strongly consider including Independents in your list of target client profiles. These are the profiles for which you will later build high-touch service plans (see Chapters 10 through 18).

## Ensuring Compatibility Amongst Your Focus Profiles

To be efficient, you should to create as much "overlap" as possible in the different profiles you choose to focus on. In other words, not only do you want to work with profiles that share the same interests, values and goals as yourself, but whenever possible you want your focus profiles to have as much in common as possible also. The reason for this is simple. If your focus profiles aren't broadly divergent in their interests, values and goals, your life will be easier and your work will be more efficient

For this reason, the final step we want to take is to examine your clients on the compatibility matrix to ensure, at a minimum, neutrality between your focus profiles, and preferably a complimentary fit.

How do you do it? Simple, just identify your primary target profile in the left column of Exhibit 6.2 and look to see where your secondary and tertiary profiles fall. Do they fall directly under the Complimentary column, the Neutral column or the Conflicting column?

If they fall under the *Complimentary* column that means there is a synergistic fit between the profiles. In other words, it is beneficial to work with those two profiles in terms of the client's interests, values and goals. There is a strong fit.

If they fall under the *Neutral* column, that means there isn't necessarily a fit, or strong benefit, to choosing that mix. A neutral weighting also means there is no conflict between those two profiles. In short, there's no harm, but no benefit either.

However, if the profile falls under the *Conflicting* column, that tells you that the interests, values and goals of your focus profiles are dramatically different, even conflicting. To work with conflicting profiles is simply counterproductive and draining for any investment advisor.

For example, trying to work with Phobics and Innovators would require the advisor to adopt a radically different mindset from client to client. In one moment an advisor would be totally avoiding technical discussion with Phobics, but in the next the advisor would be asked to dig into the details of the Brinson study with an Innovator. This degree of "wearing different hats" will wear any advisor out and prevent the advisor from maximizing the time they have with their focus profiles.

If you find that your focus profiles are conflicting, you should strongly consider replacing a conflicting profile with a neutral or better still complimentary profile.

## *Exhibit 6.2:*
### *Profile Compatibility Matrix*

| Profile Compatibility Matrix | | | |
|---|---|---|---|
| **Profile** | **Complimentary** | **Neutral** | **Conflicting** |
| Family Stewards | Investment Phobics Independents | Moguls VIPs | Anonymous Accumulators Gamblers Innovators |
| Investment Phobics | Family Stewards Independents | Anonymous Moguls VIPs | Accumulators Gamblers Innovators |
| Independents | Family Stewards | Moguls VIPs Accumulators | Investment Phobics Anonymous Gamblers Innovators |
| Anonymous | | Moguls VIPs Accumulators | Family Stewards Investment Phobics Independents Gamblers Innovators |

## Profile Compatibility Matrix Con't.

| Profile | Complimentary | Neutral | Conflicting |
|---|---|---|---|
| Moguls | VIPs | Family Stewards<br>Independents<br>Gamblers | Investment Phobics<br>Anonymous<br>Accumulators<br>Innovators |
| VIPs | Moguls | Family Stewards<br>Independents | Investment Phobics<br>Anonymous<br>Accumulators<br>Gamblers<br>Innovators |
| Accumulators | Independents | Anonymous<br>Innovators | Family Stewards<br>Investment Phobics<br>Moguls<br>VIPs<br>Gamblers |
| Gamblers | Innovators | Moguls<br>VIPs | Family Stewards<br>Investment Phobics<br>Independents<br>Anonymous<br>Accumulators |
| Innovators | Gamblers | Anonymous | Family Stewards<br>Investment Phobics<br>Independents<br>Moguls<br>VIPs<br>Accumulators |

After having reviewed the compatibility of your above focus profiles, you are now in the best position to determine the one, two or three high-net-worth profiles you should focus on.

### Chapter 6 Big Answer:

*Like your clients, you have a financial motivator that guides your investment decisions. You, too, can be classified as one of the nine financial profiles.*

*But you can't really know and serve your clients until you know yourself. As an investment advisor, knowing your own personal high-net-worth financial motivation has many benefits. You will undoubtedly become a wiser investor yourself. More importantly, you will become a better advisor to investors.*

*Through this chapter, you have figured out your own investment profile. You have also determined your focus client profiles. These client profiles will become the foundation of your client cultivation going forward.*

*The next step is to profile your clients. Since it is not possible to simply hand your clients the self diagnostic quiz (clients hate being "classified"), we have developed a methodology that easily enables you to determine your clients' profiles.*

# Chapter 7
# Identifying Your Client's and Prospect's Profiles

*"The rich aren't like you and me, they're different"*

— F. Scott Fitzgerald

## Chapter 7 Big Question:
## How can I figure out what high net-worth profile my clients are? How can I tell what type a prospect is?

Now that you know your profile, the next skill you should adopt is how to find out what profile your clients is. You especially want to know which of your current clients fit the focus profiles you selected in the last chapter. You probably have a critical mass of clients like yourself in your book of business (like, after all, does attract like). You may also discover that you have some clients of each different type.

Ok, you ask, "How can I tell what profile my prospect is?" or "What is the profile of each of my clients?" Many investment advisors have actually asked us to create some sort of checklist to help them figure out which client is a Family Steward, which one is a Phobic and so on. Unfortunately, it's not quite that simple. But as you'll see, it's not all that hard to tell one profile from another.

We have developed a method that we recommend to determine the profile of a client. This method has been developed with, and field tested by, top producers. We call it the Profile Diagnostic System (PDS). Basically, the PDS is a series of open-ended questions to ask your client. Their answers to the questions help you zero in on a client's exact profile through process of elimination, by listening for the tell tale signs of each profile.

The PDS is comprised of four open-ended questions, as well as a few follow-up questions. You probably already ask questions like these when working with your clients. However, what is different is the nine profiles give you something completely new to listen for. What makes this system work is not so much the questions, but rather learning to listen to your client's answer for the unmistakable traits of one of the nine high-net-worth personalities.

You don't have to ask all the questions in the PDS, just as many as you need. It may take only one to get an idea of a client's profile, or it may take all four and a follow-up. It will vary by client. Now, let's go through the questions, and then show you what to listen for from each.

The four PDS question are:

1. **"What Would You Like Your Investments to Achieve?"**

   Follow-up: "Is it to take care of your family or to be more independent yourself?"

2. **"When You Think About Your Money, What Concerns, Needs or Feelings Come to Mind?"**

   Follow-up: "Are you more interested in accumulating it or in what it can do for you? And what can money do for you?"

3. **"How Involved Do You Like to Be in the Investing Process?"**

   Follow-up: "Is investing something you like to do, or have to do?"

4. **"How Important to You Is the Confidentiality of Your Financial Affairs?"**

   Follow-up: "Is There Anyone Else Who Needs to Be in the Loop on Our Investment Planning Decisions?"

## Using the Profile Diagnostic System

Let's go through the PDS and explain the logic. We'll also see which of the nine high-net-worth personalities each question helps uncover.

### Question #1. "What Would You Like Your Investments to Achieve?"

This question quickly exposes two types – Family Stewards and Independents.

Family Stewards are affluent investors whose primary life motivation is to protect their family in every way possible, including financially. Family Stewards are often owners of businesses, and tend to keep a lot of assets in the business so the enterprise can provide employment and a future for family members. Family Stewards are very forward looking, and are as concerned about education of grandchildren as helping children out with down payments on their houses. So if you ask this question of a Family Steward, you will hear all about what they would like their money to do for their family, ranging from funding the college education of a child or grandchild to taking care of an elderly parent to estate planning that ensures a harmonious division of assets for their children.

Independents will answer this question at the other extreme. Independents seek just that – personal independence. Independents dream about chucking it all and sailing off into the sunset. Their portfolio buys them personal autonomy, or freedom, the thing they value above all else. If you ask this question of an Independent, you won't hear about their family very much, if at all. You will hear about the dream house on the golf course, or sailing around the world, or about being able to retire at 55. Listen carefully, though, for the theme of freedom and independence – not about material possessions.

## Question #2. "When You Think About Your Money, What Concerns, Needs or Feelings Come to Mind?"

This question will help you identify Accumulators, Moguls and VIPs.

The key word "accumulate" will smoke out Accumulators. Accumulators are more financially savvy than most of the other groups. They are singularly focused on just one goal – accumulating more assets. Accumulators are not particularly concerned with what can be done with their money, they are driven to accumulate it. Hence, their answer will be something like, "I just want my money to grow as quickly and safely as possible." Or they may have a specific, long-term goal in mind, like $5 million by age 60.

Moguls and VIPs are interested in money because of what it can do for them. Moguls value money for the power it gives them. Power is all important to Moguls. They like to control people and environments around them. More money enables Moguls to have things more their own way. They tell stories of affiliations and friendships with power figures, like influential politicians, that are not necessarily famous. Also Moguls see themselves as power figures, even mini-celebrities, holding considerable authority in their family, business and community. Listen for these common themes from Moguls.

VIPs are status oriented. They like to be recognized and acknowledged. They like prestigious surroundings and trophy possessions. They tell stories about encounters with celebrities, and often have pictures with them on their walls. They are interested in what money can do for them, but their examples will focus on material possessions; a wonderful new house, fabulous trips, or a new boat. VIPs invest for what it can buy, and the lifestyle it can confer.

## Question #3. "How Involved Do You Like to Be in the Investing Process?"

This question is extremely effective in identifying Phobics, Gamblers and Innovators.

Phobics dislike investing, they are scared of it and are highly intimidated. When you ask them a question like this, you will hear a lot about how much they do not like investing, how they are burdened by it, and that it's one more thing they have to do or worry about. Either that or they will attempt to change the subject completely.

Ask this question of a Gambler or an Innovator, and you will hear enthusiasm and commitment. They like, even love, investing. Gamblers and Innovators are by far the most knowledgeable and expert of all, and this knowledge will come across in their answers. Listen closely to tell the difference between Gamblers and Innovators. Gamblers live and breathe investing. It is their hobby and sometimes their life. Gamblers love the thrill of market volatility.

Innovators are not taken by the thrill of investing but by the intellectual challenge of it. They are technically sophisticated and like to be at the frontier, or cutting edge of the investing world.

## Question #4. "How Important to You Is the Confidentiality of Your Financial Affairs?"

Nobody is going to say confidentiality is not important. Of course it's important to everyone, but only the anonymous are rabid about this issue.

This question is designed to identify one particular group, the Anonymous.

They are fearful and worried about personal security and confidentiality. They need constant assurance that you are protecting the integrity of their information as well as their investments. They are moderate in their understanding of investments. Ask this question of the other types, and you won't get much of a response. Sure, they want their dealings to be confidential, but they are not singularly focused on this issue. In contrast, the Anonymous are. They will explain how central this concern is to them, and how essential it is in any advisory relationship.

## The Profile Diagnostic System at Work

The PDS works by process of elimination. In short, you simply want to confirm or reject the possibility of your client being any one of the nine profiles. Here's an example of how that might typically work.

## Exhibit 7.1
### Applying the PDS

*Question #1: "What Would You Like Your Investments to Achieve?"*

*Answer: "Well, I just want my money to grow. I want to get it as big as possible. I'm not expecting 30% a year or nothing. But I want to take advantage of compounding and am focused on the long haul. In other words, reasonable returns over many years."*

| | |
|---|---|
| Family Stewards | VIPs |
| ~~Phobics~~ | Accumulators |
| Independents | ~~Gamblers~~ |
| ~~Anonymous~~ | ~~Innovators~~ |
| Moguls | |

### Explanation:
The client wants growth. This eliminates Phobics, the Anonymous, Gamblers and Innovators. Phobics can be eliminated because the client understands and is comfortable with investing based on the nature of their answer. Anonymous can be eliminated because issues of confidentiality never surfaced. Gamblers can be eliminated because the client never expressed any of the excitement typically shown by this group around returns or specific stocks. Innovators can be eliminated because the client focused on the result (solid

long term returns) rather than the process (the technical information of how these results could be achieved) that would be characteristic of an Innovator.

But "why" does the client want their money to grow? For their family, personal freedom, power, a yacht or just to accumulate? A follow-up question is needed to clarify the motivation, and the profile.

*Follow-up Question: "Are you more interested in accumulating it or in what it can do for you?*

*Answer: "I'm fairly frugal, don't spend a lot. I take care of my family, but I want to manage that so it doesn't hurt my long term growth goals. I just like watching it grow and grow."*

| | |
|---|---|
| ~~Family Stewards~~ | ~~VIPs~~ |
| ~~Phobics~~ | Accumulators |
| ~~Independents~~ | ~~Gamblers~~ |
| ~~Anonymous~~ | ~~Innovators~~ |
| ~~Moguls~~ | |

### Explanation:
The client said he is frugal, eliminating "VIPs". You'll recall "VIPs" are the high-net-worth personality that "looks rich." The client made no mention that family, power or freedom were his main goals, eliminating all but "Accumulator." The client said he enjoys watching the money grow, a trait characteristic of an "Accumulator." This confirms he is an "Accumulator."

## Confirming Client Profiles: The Trial Balloon

Once you believe you know which profile a client may be, consider floating a trial balloon to see if you are on target. This way, you can confirm your hunch, and proceed accordingly. Or, disprove it early, avoiding a misdiagnosis. Creating and floating trial balloon ideas are relatively easy. Simply follow the process in this flow-chart (Exhibit 7.2).

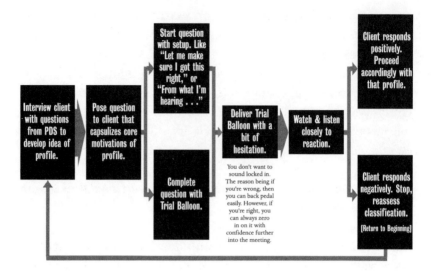

## Exhibit 7.2
### The Trial Balloon

As you can see, the first step in this process is to have an idea what profile the client is. Then you want to confirm this idea. You may think that a specific client is a Family Steward, but it is important that you get it right. That is why it is important to validate your idea by asking "trial balloon" questions.

For example, if you thought someone was an Accumulator, you might try a trial balloon such as: "After having had a chance to get to know you, it seems to me that you are very astute about money. It sounds to me like making the most money possible is more important to you than, say, early retirement or buying a boat or condo. Do I have that right?"

As shown in the flow chart, clients will either confirm your idea about their profile, or they will disagree, and give you more information. Here are some trail balloon questions to use with clients who may be each of the types.

## *Sample Trial Balloon Ideas:*

*Family Stewards*: ". . . It seems your family's well-being is your primary concern. We're going to create a portfolio that's focused on your family, that's going to really take care of them long term. Is that your goal?"

*Phobics*: ". . . I get the feeling you're not that comfortable with investing. Is that true? That's okay because I am, and I am going to do my best to make sure that your goals are met, so that you don't have to worry."

*Independents*: ". . . It's really important to you to have the investment resources in the bank to make sure you can do what you want. From talking to you I sense that what you want is the freedom to do whatever you want. Maybe retire at 55, and pursue some hobby or interest. Is that right?"

*The Anonymous*: ". . . You operate similarly to the way I work with my clients. My key concern is that confidential information stays confidential. When we work together, you can rest assured that confidentiality is one of my highest priorities."

*Moguls*: ". . . I feel that you want to be in ultimate control of everything we do together. My job is to make sure that you have the best advice and information in order to make the big decisions. Do I have that right?"

*VIPs*: ". . . It's important that you know we work with some of the biggest names in the investment management industry. People at the same level as you are. People who know and understand the appropriate investments for someone in your position."

*Accumulators*: ". . . It seems to me that you are very astute about money. You know how to save it, and how to make it grow. I enjoy working with clients like you and I'm going to do my best to make sure we create an investment strategy to make the most money possible. Are we on the right track? Is that what you want from an advisor?"

*Gamblers*: ". . . Investing is exciting for you, just like it is for me. I love everything about investing. Whether it's finding a great stock, watching CEO's on CNBC or doing research on financials. Together, we can make sure we keep up with all of the events going on. I sense that your ideal advisor is one who is as excited about the process of investing as you are."

*Innovators*: ". . . You have a great deal of knowledge about investing, and it's very important to you to use state of the art investment approaches. That's precisely what my firm, and myself in particular, specialize in."

### Chapter 7 Big Answer:
**You can use all the skills and talents you already have to figure out what financial type your clients are. You already know how to encourage clients to talk to you about what they want from investing. All we have done is add several new questions to your usual list.**

**In the chapter before this one, we figured out what your type is. In this chapter, we want to open up a process for you to discover (and confirm) what type each of your clients is. Practice with the clients you feel most comfortable with and then assess your newer clients with this process. Shortly, you will be so comfortable with the process that it will be second nature.**

**But, as important as figuring out what type each client is, the next step is even more important. You need to use this information to restructure and refocus your practice. That is the challenge taken up in the next chapters.**

# Chapter 8
# Evaluating Your Client Book

*"You got to know when to hold 'em; know when to fold 'em."*

– Kenny Rodgers

## Chapter 8 Critical Question:
**How can I work with fewer but wealthier clients? How can I use these client profiles to refocus my practice? How can I be more effective and efficient – so I am more productive?**

So far, you have determined your own profile. You have determined the profiles of clients you have the greatest natural rapport with. You have also determined the profiles of your top clients.

Now, let's convert all of that information into action, and determine which clients have the greatest business building potential.

At first blush, a simple analysis of assets under management seems to be all that's necessary. That is, you may think that the client with the greatest potential is the one with the largest AUM. However, you should look at the idea of "client value" much more broadly. Specifically, you should take into account the potential assets you could bring under management, their pattern of past referrals and future referral potential. By looking at all of these factors, you can develop a very clear picture of a client's value to your business.

Before discussing a system to use in evaluating your clientele with these four criteria, it is helpful to have a working definition of each of them.

### Present Assets Under Management:
This is simply the total Assets Under Management (AUM) of the client with you, their advisor.

### Potential Assets Under Management:
This is the combination of two items.

One way to determine this is based on the assets you are aware of which are not on deposit with you. This can be money on deposit with a competing investment advisor, money sitting in a certificate of deposit at a bank or any other number of vessels that the assets reside in. The common link is that the assets are currently owned by the client and not with you.

Secondly, assets that you are aware of which will be coming to the client at some point in the future. These assets can take the form of a future inheritance, a trust, a bonus, options which will vest in the future, profits from a business, proceeds from the sale of a business, claims from a lawsuit or other such sources. The common link here being that there is a high probability that these future assets will be owned by the client but are not yet owned or illiquid.

### Referrals:
This is simply the number of referrals the client has made which themselves have become clients of yours. While you could do a simple total here, we find it helpful to focus on the most recent referrals. We recommend looking at the total number of referrals that became clients in the last 24 months. By ranking the client according to this, we find (unlike the legal hedge placed on numerous prospectuses) that a client's past performance is indeed indicative of future results. In other words, if they have made referrals that became clients in the past, they are likely to continue.

### Potential Referrals:
This is the most difficult criterion of the four to value. Essentially, the question we want to answer is, "Is this client a center of influence amongst affluent circles?" Said another way, does their personal and/or professional life put them in frequent contact with people you would like to have as clients? A surgeon is an obvious example of someone who would be in frequent contact with other surgeons or doctors and have occasion to make a

referral for you. Contrast this kind of affluent investor with a client who was a lottery winner. They may very well be a large client themselves, but are unlikely to rub elbows with other affluent investors, and, therefore, be a poor source of potential referrals.

Complicating matters slightly is the client's high-net-worth personality. A client may very well dwell in the right circles, but be of a reserved personality that isn't prone to pass your name on to anyone. If the client is quiet and reserved, our experience shows they are less likely to recommend a friend or colleague when the occasion arises. (Note: The Anonymous profile is an example of this. They are very private people. Not only are they less socially active than other profiles, but they typically would not discuss their personal information with anyone. Indeed, they prefer to keep matters such as their choice of financial advisor to themselves and well insulated from the social circles they do engage in.)

In summary, while ranking your clients according to this criterion, ask yourself to what degree do they dwell in personal or professional circles where affluent people reside, and is their personality one that's prone to influence others?

By adhering to these four criteria in the evaluation of your clientele, you will be able to get a relatively solid gauge of their future value to your business. Granted, it is not an entirely quantitative system and does involve some art as well as science. However, it is the best system we have seen to provide the investment advisors instruction into their best clients.

A variation on this approach is to rate the clients on scales that reflect each criteria. Use the following worksheet (Exhibit 8.1) to evaluate your clientele. It provides a simple numerical system to evaluate your clientele along these four criteria. You may note that the numerical scale changes from criteria to criteria. This is done to more heavily weight actual client behavior versus future potential. When you're done, those clients with the highest total score are likely to be the clients with the greatest long-term value to your business.

## Exhibit 8.1:
### Client Valuation System

| Client Valuation System | | | | |
|---|---|---|---|---|
| Instructions: Rate clients on scale provided. Circle the number with the corresponding quintile that the client falls into for that criterion. 1 is worst, 5 is best. Note: the numerical scale changes between 1-5 and 1-3. This is done to more heavily weight actual client behavior versus future potential. In areas with the scale set at 1-3, round the clients downward by quintile. For example, you should circle "3" for a client that is in the fourth quintile for "Referral Potential". Clients with highest total score are the most valuable and where you want to focus the bulk of your time. | | | | |
| **Client Name:** | **Present AUM** | **Future AUM** | **Clients Referred past 24 mos.** | **Referral Potential** | **C.T.V.** (Client Total Value) Total circled #s here |

| Client Name: | Present AUM | Future AUM | Clients Referred past 24 mos. | Referral Potential | C.T.V. |
|---|---|---|---|---|---|
| 1. | 1 2 3 4 5 | 1 2 3 | 1 2 3 4 5 | 1 2 3 | |
| 2. | 1 2 3 4 5 | 1 2 3 | 1 2 3 4 5 | 1 2 3 | |
| 3. | 1 2 3 4 5 | 1 2 3 | 1 2 3 4 5 | 1 2 3 | |
| 4. | 1 2 3 4 5 | 1 2 3 | 1 2 3 4 5 | 1 2 3 | |
| 5. | 1 2 3 4 5 | 1 2 3 | 1 2 3 4 5 | 1 2 3 | |
| 6. | 1 2 3 4 5 | 1 2 3 | 1 2 3 4 5 | 1 2 3 | |
| 7. | 1 2 3 4 5 | 1 2 3 | 1 2 3 4 5 | 1 2 3 | |
| 8. | 1 2 3 4 5 | 1 2 3 | 1 2 3 4 5 | 1 2 3 | |
| 9. | 1 2 3 4 5 | 1 2 3 | 1 2 3 4 5 | 1 2 3 | |
| 10. | 1 2 3 4 5 | 1 2 3 | 1 2 3 4 5 | 1 2 3 | |
| 11. | 1 2 3 4 5 | 1 2 3 | 1 2 3 4 5 | 1 2 3 | |
| 12. | 1 2 3 4 5 | 1 2 3 | 1 2 3 4 5 | 1 2 3 | |
| 13. | 1 2 3 4 5 | 1 2 3 | 1 2 3 4 5 | 1 2 3 | |
| 14. | 1 2 3 4 5 | 1 2 3 | 1 2 3 4 5 | 1 2 3 | |
| 15. | 1 2 3 4 5 | 1 2 3 | 1 2 3 4 5 | 1 2 3 | |

## Chapter 8 Big Question:

Use client profiles to refocus your practice to work with fewer but wealthier clients. Improve your effectiveness and efficiency in order to boost production and profits.

Not all clients are created equal. They are different in terms of their high-net-worth psychology. They are different in terms of how valuable they are to your practice. This chapter has given you a method you can quickly implement to evaluate each client you have in terms of their value to your practice.

The reason for this step is that you are about to undertake an approach of high-touch relationship management. You simply can't devote the same, high amount of time to every client. You have to selectively pick certain ones to focus on strategically, and these chapters give you a process for doing just that. Now that you have the clients identified, you can move on to the next section that will show you how to develop great client relationships. These relationships will be the basis for your new role as the millionaire's advisor.

# Chapter 9
# High-Touch, High Profit Relationship Management

*"You got to serve somebody"*

– Bob Dylan

## Chapter 9 Critical Question:
*I understand High-Net-Worth Psychology and Financial Motivators. But exactly HOW can I implement these ideas? How can I take several ideas and turn it into a plan? How can I make things even easier by using that plan for several clients with the same profile?*

With the right motivation and skills, any advisor can make a client highly satisfied. That's not the real issue. The real issue is can you do it with a hundred clients all at the same time? Do it with clients that may very well be the hardest people in our society to please? Do it profitably? And continue to do it year, after year, after year? That's the real issue.

When simply identifying the real issue is this difficult, you know making it happen won't be easy either. Achieving this lofty goal can seem daunting. How can you balance the apparently contradictory needs of a high level of customization with the claims hundreds of clients will place on your time?

The answer is by using High-Net-Worth psychology to build high-touch service tracks for your clients. There is ultimately only one way to achieve this "Holy Grail" of client relationship management. You must focus on a homogenous core of clients and then get systematic. In other words, you need to create systems where high-touch relationship management happens without necessarily requiring your day-to-day involvement. How do you achieve that? Just follow the system.

The system is a two-fold process. First, we'll take a closer look at exactly what makes a client satisfied. Secondly, we'll look at how to weave this specific information into a high-touch service plan that can be used again, and again, and again. In other words, we won't just give you the musical notes that affluent clients like to hear, but we'll show you the songs as well.

## Turning "Relationships" Into Business

Previously, we showed how client satisfaction could be split between a client's satisfaction with investment performance and their satisfaction with the relationship. We established that the quality of your relationship with your clients is as important, if not more important, in the long-term retention and cultivation of them. However, we didn't go far enough.

To create highly satisfied clients, we need to understand what it means to have a client that's satisfied with the relationship. Sadly, there has not been very much information on a scientific level of what makes a client happy with a relationship. Because most of the available information is anecdotal, it's unreliable. It is not the sort of information you want as the foundation of a viable business plan. Part of the problem is that "The Relationship" is a soft, subjective, gooey concept, especially within a business context. In spite of this gooey-ness, everybody in this industry talks about how important "Relationships" are. However, nobody has really defined in specific terms what makes a client "satisfied with the relationship." No one has scientifically identified the elements of satisfaction with the relationship – until now.

That's where Prince & Associates is different. Our studies bring this term down out of the clouds and identify four specific factors that culminate in the client's satisfaction with the relationship – four factors that an advisor can use, pull like a lever, to raise up the ultimate satisfaction of a client. Those four areas comprise what we have called the C.L.A.S. Relationship Management Model – C.L.A.S. being an acronym for the four factors.

# The C.L.A.S. Relationship Management Model

It turns out that when clients judge their investment advisor, the main areas they weigh regarding satisfaction with the relationship fall into four categories. They are:

- **Client Focus** – Your level of focus on the client's needs, interests and goals.
- **Leadership** – Proactively providing solutions to your client's based on their unique financial motivator.
- **Attention to the Client** — Understanding and providing the level of desired attention, and the motivation for attention.
- **Shared Values** – Demonstrated sharing of core values, common ground and personal goals.

To keep things easy, these four ingredients of client satisfaction are referred to simply as C.L.A.S.

We stated earlier that clients judge you according to investment performance and the relationship. However, what is surprising is that investors regard the relationship ingredients (C.L.A.S.) as nearly four times as important as performance. That's not to say investment performance doesn't matter. Rather it means that investment advisors who can deliver solid investment performance *coupled* with high quality relationship management are in an excellent position to develop a highly satisfied clientele, which in turn leads to more assets under management per client and more referrals from existing clients.

The results of the research on this point are as startling as they are clear. During our study of affluent clients over a two year period, of all clients who fired their investment advisor, nearly 96 percent were "very happy" with their portfolio's performance. So why did they fire their advisor? They were dissatisfied with "The Relationship".

This statistic is a disturbingly negative consequence of providing bad or even average service, but what happens when you provide high quality service?

When an affluent client classifies themselves as "highly satisfied," 25 percent of them will increase assets under management each year. These are incremental increases in assets under management year over year, not increases in the value of existing investments.

## Exhibit 9.1
### Benefits of High Client Satisfaction

1 in 4 satisfied clients increases assests under management each year.

9 out of 10 satisfied clients will refer at least one person who becomes a client every six months.

Better still, nearly nine out of ten affluent clients will refer at least one person who becomes a client every six months. This is the engine that drives every successful advisors practice in working with the affluent. Ultimately, this is very good news because while you can't control the markets and performance, you can quite easily learn to control a client's satisfaction with the relationship.

## Integrating the Nine Profiles & C.L.A.S. for Improved Satisfaction

Now that you have a basic overview of the specific components of C.L.A.S., the question becomes how do you positively impact "The Relationship?" The answer is by combining high-net-worth psychology (the nine profiles and their financial motivator) with an understanding of the C.L.A.S. model. Let us explain.

C.L.A.S. shows you the four ingredients impacting client satisfaction with the relationship. The nine profiles help you understand what each client seeks by way of the C.L.A.S. model. Said another way, C.L.A.S. is a strategic model that can be applied to all nine profiles to raise up their satisfaction level. The nine profiles are the tactical ideas you would use with that profile. For example, "Leadership" (the second element of C.L.A.S.) applies to all nine profiles as a strategic need, but it means something far different to a Family Steward versus an Independent. To a Family Steward, providing "Leadership" means proactively providing solutions on how to fund college for their kids or grandkids, how to build up and distribute a nest egg to the kids so they use it to as a down payment on a house, rather than the purchase of a car. Contrast that with "Leadership" for an Independent. For an Independent, "Leadership" means proactively providing them ideas on how to retire by 50 and or ensure that their money lasts through their retirement. These are the same strategic goals but they mean something tactically different to each of the nine profiles.

# Exhibit 9.2
## Goals, Strategies and Tactics

| | Strategy | Tactic |
|---|---|---|
| *General Example* | *General Example* | *General Example* |
| Win the Presidency of U.S. | Win the Iowa Caucus to take early lead in polls, increasing political contributions and warchest | Drive a "Tractor" across a couple major counties during planting season to generate publicity for the campaign |
| *HNW Psychology Example* | *HNW Psychology Example* | *HNW Psychology Example* |
| Create Highly Satisfied Family Steward Clients. *Financial Motivator:* Taking Care of the Family | Leverage "Leadership" element of the C.L.A.S. Relationship Management Model | Run hypos on cost for college based on the year the client's children turn 18, provide them an investment plan showing how much is needed today for college later, as well as the best investment vehicle (529 or UTMA) |

This may still sound abstract, so let's drill down on each element of the C.L.A.S. model by comparing and contrasting the actual practices of top advisors that focus on a particular profile. This way you will not only get a better understanding of each element of C.L.A.S., but see the actual practices of advisors using this model.

## Client Focus

***Your level of demonstrated focus on the needs, interests and goals of your clients.***

The example we want to provide you is of two advisors, one focused predominantly on the Anonymous profile, the other focused on predominantly the Mogul profile.

Remember that the Anonymous are the profile that is hyper-sensitive to issues of confidentiality. For them, confidentiality is absolutely key. We have consulted with an advisor from Connecticut who demonstrates his level of client focus on this issue by constantly reinforcing to his clients the lengthy steps he takes to insure their confidentiality.

First, he tells them it is likely that they have friends in common, and he wants the client to know up front that he NEVER discusses one client with another, or with anyone else that doesn't work in his office or firm. He mentions that he doesn't even discuss clients with his wife. If the client ever runs into a friend at a cocktail party and discovers that they have the same financial advisor, he can rest assured that the advisor has never discussed any details of his account with that individual.

Next, he tells the prospective client that he takes a great deal of care to protect the confidentiality of their information in his office. He tells them that they may not have noticed but they won't see any client files lying about in his office. He tells them that he keeps all files in his office in a safe, not a file cabinet, but a safe. Only after the client walks in, and the door is shut, will he pull out a key, open the safe and remove the client's file for discussion. When the meeting is over, that file will be back in the safe before the client leaves the office. He tells them that at night when he leaves, he locks the door on his office and that he is the only one with a key. He then locks the door to the building and the building has an alarm system.

Additionally, he tells the clients he will never Fed Ex something to them. He sends all written correspondence via US Mail. Why? Because it is a felony to open US Mail and it's only a zip strip to open a Fed Ex letter. He tells them he never uses e-mail to discuss specifics in a client's account, only for general market updates. In addition, he tells them that all trash leaves his office only after passing through a cross-cutting shredder. He finishes by telling them that the biggest security risk to their information is themselves. He explains that when the client throws out their monthly statements and their trash is placed on the curb, it is no longer their property. Therefore, it becomes vulnerable to anyone that wants to come by, pick it up and go through it. As a solution, he recommends the same cross-cutting shredder he uses in his office for them to use at home for their account statements and any other sensitive information.

All of this is an excellent demonstration of this advisor's level of client focus to the Anonymous profile around their key concern—confidentiality. Is it a bit extreme? Maybe. Is it profitable for this advisor in terms of client retention, increased assets under management and professional referrals? Absolutely.

Contrast that advisor's display of what it means to provide Client focus to an Anonymous with what another advisor does to demonstrate Client Focus to his Mogul clientele. The majority of his Moguls are high level executives at various corporations, and a few society people. Recall that the Mogul profile includes people who like to have control and power. This advisor demonstrates Client Focus to his Mogul clients by drawing the following picture in the first meeting with the client. He starts by sharing with them his philosophy as a financial advisor, specifically stating that he is the coach and they are the team owner. In other words, he makes recommendations, but they make the final decisions, they have the power. He shows them a sample agenda of one of his client meetings. At the top of this document it says, "Executive Summary: Financial Plan for Mr. X." He tells them that he wants to make every effort to be respectful of their time and to make the best use of it possible. Toward that end, he will prepare a draft agenda prior to any meeting for the client's approval and sign-off. He asks that the client review it, write in any edits or additions they have, sign it and fax it back to him. This again gives the client total control of the agenda. Do many clients ever actually make a change? No, but that is beside the point. This investment advisor's main goal is simply to continually reinforce to the client that they are the one with the control and power, and by handing over control of the meetings to his clients, he gives them just that. In closing, he tells them that all interaction will be through him, never a subordinate.

Once the relationship has begun he engages in a few additional practices to demonstrate his level of Client Focus to his Mogul clients. For example, when he meets with the client at their office, he always shows up 15 minutes early for meetings. This subtly says to the client that they are the important one. Conversely, if a client meeting is to take place at his office, upon seeing the client, the receptionist says, "Hello, Mr. Jones, Gary's (the advisor) been expecting you. Let me take you back to his office." This way, the client never even sits down in the waiting area. They are ushered directly back to the advisor's office. All of these efforts are designed to very subtly and non-verbally communicate to the client that they have the control, that they are very important and that they will be treated as such. This is exactly the message Moguls want to hear, and a great demonstration of how you can use Client Focus to your advantage in working with them.

Through this example you can see that the same goal is being met here – a demonstration by the advisor to the client of their level of Client Focus – but the specific form it takes results in two very different approaches.

## Leadership

### Proactively providing solutions to your clients based on their values, interests and goals.

The example we want to provide you is of two advisors, one focused on the Innovator profile, the other focused on the Independent profile.

Remember that the Innovators are the profile that likes to be on the cutting edge of investment planning and products. An advisor looking to provide leadership to this group needs to demonstrate that they are on the "razor's edge" of investment planning and products, meaning they need to demonstrate to the client that their level of expertise and access to resources surpasses the clients. If it doesn't, how can they possibly provide leadership to Innovators?

One advisor in northern California successfully provides "Leadership" to innovators in the following way. He subscribes to a fairly large number of industry publications and newsletters. Because he is an Innovator profile himself, he enjoys reading and occasionally employing some of the ideas in these publications. While he reads these articles, he highlights important thoughts or ideas. He then gives these highlighted documents to his assistant who makes copies and re-highlights all of his highlights. (This advisor feels that a photocopied article with yellow highlights shows personal attention much better than photocopying an article with underlines in pen). The assistant then hand writes a note at the top of each article personally addressed to the client that typically reads something like this, "Jay, I thought you might find this article interesting. I know you like to stay current on new ideas. I highlighted a few key passages if you don't have time to read it all. Call me if you'd like to discuss anything." In addition, he will occasionally hold conference calls with his clients to discuss ideas and strategies presented in the articles. Being Innovators, these clients enjoy an active discussion of these articles with other, informed opinions.

By so doing, this advisor positions himself as the expert and resource for information on new ideas relevant to investment management. He, in effect, becomes the Innovator's mentor and is thus able to provide "Leadership" to his Innovator clients on complex issues.

Contrast that form of "Leadership" with Innovators, with what another advisor from Houston does to demonstrate "Leadership" with his Independent clients. Among Independents, money means freedom. To provide "Leadership" to his Independent clients, this advisor tells them about the extensive experience he has helping people achieve financial independence, pursue their dreams and, most importantly, make sure their money lasts through their retirement. He briefly explains his process, including determining their financial goal, understanding the costs of the hobby or interest they want to pursue and the client's timeframe to create a plan. Then each year to keep on track with the client's goal, he provides what he calls a "progress report," which overviews the progress that's been made to the financial goal and the goal of retirement. As the client approaches their financial goal, the advisor shifts the focus to retirement distribution planning.

To further reinforce his position as an expert on achieving financial Independence, he provides his clients with a copy of an article he had published in the local paper. The article talks about the five biggest myths to achieving financial independence, thoughts on how much is enough and a few brief examples of clients he helped to pursue their dreams. In addition, he keeps a three ring binder with a brief bio and testimonial from people he's helped to reach financial independence in the past. One especially nice touch in these bios is that several of the clients mention that they still use the advisor to make sure their money lasts through their retirement. All of these efforts very effectively provide the "Leadership" Independents seek to achieve financial independence.

## Attention to the Client

### Understanding and providing the level of desired attention, and the motivation for attention.

All clients don't have the same need to hear from their financial advisor and this is especially true for the nine different profiles. Some love investing and will call you constantly to the point of annoyance. Others can't stand the subject of investing and get a tight feeling in their stomach when you call. It's critical to understand how often a client wants to communicate with you and why they want to communicate to achieve a highly satisfied client. Attention to the Client can be summed up with two questions. How often do you contact the client, and they you? And what are you talking about?

Two great examples to demonstrate what this element of C.L.A.S. is all about are the Phobic and the Gambler. The reason these two profiles are such great examples is that they are polar opposites of each other in regard to this element of C.L.A.S.

Gamblers will call you all the time and want to talk about the latest earnings report for a bellweather stock. Phobics, on the other hand, will practically never call you. The only time they tend to call is when they see Peter Jennings mention a particularly bad day on Wall St. and they become anxious. When you call them, you certainly don't want to jump right into the technical aspects of investing but lead in to the point of your call by asking about some other personal interest they have, such as their grandchildren.

The biggest challenge for an advisor to a group of Gamblers is not providing them with enough attention, but keeping them from individually consuming all of your time with numerous, lengthy inbound calls. One advisor that works with a large amount of Gamblers solves this problem and provides "Attention to the Client" by implementing the following two ideas. At the end of every trading day, he has an optional conference call for all of his clients. It allows the advisor to share his thoughts on the markets, individual stocks or important events in one fell swoop with all of his clients. He calls it his "Market Wrap-Up," like the news shows. By so doing, he can address the events of the day once with many clients instead of repeatedly with one client at a time. He also institutes a "three-minute" rule for individual, inbound calls from his Gambler clients. When they call in with an idea, he turns over an egg timer on his desk. He only allows the conversation to go on for a maximum of three minutes. His clients don't mind because he's positioned this as a way to make sure he can be available for his clients anytime they need to call. Plus, the typical Gambler doesn't mind getting right to the point of their investing question or trade. Hence, the three-minute rule acts as a catalyst to speed the conversation along.

By so doing, this advisor is able to adequately provide an effective form of "Attention to the Client" for all of his Gambler clients. However, another advisor that works heavily with Phobics provides "Attention to the Client" in a method that is the exact opposite of what you'd do for a Gambler.

The challenge with providing "Attention to the Client" with Phobics is contacting them in a way that engages them in the process and isn't off putting. First of all, this advisor rarely gets inbound calls from her Phobic clients, unless there is a sudden change in the client's situation or there is a particularly large drop in the DJIA reported on the major network news shows. But inbound calls are the exception rather than the rule with Phobics. Accordingly, this advisor's strategy of providing "Attention to the Client" is centered around the contacts she initiates. With all of her Phobic clients she explains that typically her clients don't like investing and want her to handle it for them. She says that she understands this and doesn't mind at all. She then explains that most clients like to meet once a year face to face to talk about any changes in their lives and see if she thinks this requires any changes to their financial situation. Additionally she says she likes to call at least once every four months to "check-in." For most Phobics, this is plenty of attention.

When she meets with her Phobic clients or talks to them on the phone, she doesn't cut to the chase of the necessary changes to the client's account. Quite the opposite, she simply asks a lot of questions about what's going on in the client's life to get them talking, and then listens. Her goal is to strengthen the trust the client has with her by being a good listener, and showing she cares. Often times, she will spend 45 minutes on the phone with her clients and never even talk about a particular investment. She says it takes a fair bit of time, but it only occurs once or twice a year and is very effective, so it's worth it.

Now that you can see how different the approach for a Gambler is from a Phobic, the important questions to be asking yourself for all nine of the profiles is how often does the client want to talk and how can you best manage this and to remember to lead with the client's dominant interest when you do talk.

## Shared Values

### *Demonstrated sharing of core values, common ground and personal goals.*

The final element of the C.L.A.S. Model is "Shared Values." It is a fact of life that people like to do business with people like themselves. What appears to be going on is that people intuitively feel they can more readily trust someone if they share a similar life situation, or value or goal. They believe that the investment advisor may more fully understand their viewpoint because the advisor's is so close to their own. This concept is summarized by the old saying, "Birds of a feather flock together."

Two great profiles to compare and contrast to gain a better understanding of this element of the C.L.A.S. Model are the VIP and the Accumulator. The shared values you would want to demonstrate with Accumulators are frugality, saving more than you spend, no showy displays of wealth and living below your means. Contrast that with VIPs who view investing as a way to get more status possessions. To demonstrate shared values with them, you want to show that you enjoy the finer things in life— nice car, nice office, good artwork, etc. Displays of wealth with VIPs are not only OK, they are expected.

An advisor in Beverly Hills, California works with a large number of VIPs as the core of his business, and is, in fact, a classic example of the VIP profile himself. He wears Armani suits and a gold Rolex watch. His office has original paintings by a local artist throughout the reception area, halls and offices (in fact some of the advisors clients have even bought paintings from this artist after seeing them in the advisor's office). He owns a convertible Jaguar XKR and takes clients out to lunch in it. When asked if this adversely affects his client's opinion of his fees, he says that most of his clients are like him. In other words, they believe it takes money to make money, and wouldn't want an advisor that couldn't afford these possessions. In other words, his clients share his values.

Now, imagine this same advisor decided he wanted to work with the Accumulator Profile, in addition, to VIPs. The Accumulator would recoil when they saw the Rolex, the artwork or the Jaguar. That's because these are all signs that the advisor doesn't share his values of frugality and living below his means. These displays of wealth are absolutely the wrong thing to do with Accumulators. However, just as strongly, they are absolutely the right thing to do with VIPs.

Part of the reason we feel so strongly that advisors should conscientiously cultivate a clientele like themselves is the power that "Shared Values" has in who they like and who likes them. What we have seen the most successful advisors do is avoid trying to swim upstream by fighting this dynamic and instead turn it to their advantage by swimming downstream with it.

## Applying the C.L.A.S. Model in Full: Family Stewards

Family Stewards are the largest group among the nine profiles, and the desire to take care of their family is the core motivation behind all of their investing decisions. Investment advisors working with this group need to understand this driving principle to maximize the service that they provide this client group. That said, let's look at how the C.L.A.S. Relationship Management Model can be used (Exhibit 9.3).

## Exhibit 9.3
### Family Stewards and C.L.A.S.

|  | Client Focus | Leadership | Attending Behaviors | Shared Values |
|---|---|---|---|---|
| Family Stewards | Thoroughly addressing client needs | Proactively solve client needs & goals | Attention to the Client (# of Contacts & Reason) | Similar belief system and life focus |
|  | - Get to know all of the children's ages, interests and any special needs<br>- Involve key family members<br>- Remember important family occasions and developments | - Learn the time left for each child before college, determine the projected cost of college then and the money needed to fund it today<br>- Emphasize experience in working with family issues, i.e. estate planning and generational transfer of wealth Attention to the Client | - Expect infrequent client originated contacts. Tend to call only if they perceive a problem<br>- Schedule regular face-to-face meetings that follow a regular, predictable pattern | - Share the importance of your own family in your life<br>- Show how your value of thrift benefits the family<br>- Share your own community affiliations and involvement |

Client Focus refers to time management with your clients, the thoroughness with which you address client needs and how effectively you foster client involvement. Because their family is central to a Family Steward, you would want to orient yourself to the Family's needs. For example, when scheduling a meeting with a client, you want to avoid a time that conflicts with a family activity, like a daughter's soccer game, or their quality time at home together. Simply ask the client: "Is there a time we could meet that doesn't intrude on your family time?" By so doing you indicate to your client that you understand their priorities and are willing to accommodate them to the best of your ability, thereby increasing your client's satisfaction.

Client Focus also refers to how thoroughly you address the client's needs. With Family Stewards, you want to thoroughly address their central motivation for investing – their family. Get to know all of the client's children, their ages, interests and possibly special needs. Maybe the client's mother is likely to need a live-in nurse and he's concerned about how to provide for this and college for three kids at the same time. Maybe his daughter is being groomed to run his business (it's very common for the children of a Family Steward to join the family business), and is going to get their MBA, after obtaining their undergraduate degree.

The point is each client is unique, and you need to take the time to get to know their family so that you can thoroughly address all of their needs and stay on top of developments.

Leadership involves proactively addressing their needs and providing solutions as they relate to their family. As affluent individuals, they all have busy lives, and would like nothing better than to know they have a competent expert, keeping a watchful eye on any new developments or concerns that might affect their family's well-being. For example, with a Family Steward you can take the lead on planning for college funding with no more information than the children's birth dates. Take it upon yourself to determine the year each child graduates from high school, how many years to invest money for college remain, and what college they may be considering. Learn what tuition is projected to cost at the time each child will be graduating high school and develop a plan to fund it. Or if you have already established college funding programs, revisit the subject every so often to make sure there haven't been any major changes you will need to make adjustments for. Perhaps the client's daughter has decided to become a doctor, and instead of four years of college education, eight years now needs to be funded. You can then schedule checkpoint reviews with the client when the children are freshman and then juniors in high school to discuss any important developments, like a child's desire to attend a much more expensive private school. Imagine how impressed a Family Steward would be if you proactively developed a plan such as this for their children's education. This is leadership.

Attending Behaviors refers to the fact that you are diligent about responding to any phone calls and questions they have, as well as proactively contact them when necessary. You can positively impact this area of client satisfaction with a Family Steward, by scheduling regular face-to-face meetings with them at a time that doesn't conflict with any family time. Also, Family Stewards like stability in their life, so it's a good idea to have meetings that follow a regular predictable pattern. For example, it might be a good idea to have a client meeting at the end of every school year, as it is a good time to discuss any changes in the children's college preferences or interests. Plus, it helps to jog the client's memory that it's time to meet with their advisor to discuss the children's futures.

Shared Values is the final element of CLAS. We all like to do business with people who are like us, who share similar values. Accordingly, it is helpful to your business relationship to communicate to your client that you share a similar belief system with them and place importance on many of the same values. With Family Stewards, you would want to let them know how important spending time with your own family is to you.

Additionally, Family Stewards typically favor stability over high returns. As such, you might communicate that, like them, you believe in a slow, steady and stable investment strategy. The main point being the more similar values you share with your clients, the more comfortable they will be with you, and the more satisfied they will be with the relationship.

The C.L.A.S. Relationship Management Model is applicable to all nine of the profiles. As such, below is a matrix outlining this same basic applications of the model to all the profiles. Of course, these are just the baby steps in using the model, the actual application of which can be much deeper. There are a number of additional relationship management ideas in the profile specific chapters (chapters 10-18) that follow this one. Be sure to use these in addition to the matrix below in developing your own plans.

# Exhibit 9.4
## CLAS Relationship Management Model Applied to Each Profile

|  | Client Orientation | Leadership |
|---|---|---|
| **Family Steward** | • Involve key family members<br><br>• Remember family occasions | • Emphasize experience in working with family issues<br><br>• When talking about performance, stress reassurance |
| **Investment Phobic** | • Avoid technical discussions<br><br>• Learn a lot about their outside interests | • Encourage client trust by talking about perfectionism<br><br>• Frequently inform them of high quality performance, but do not spend a lot of time on it |
| **Independents** | • Be task driven, and focused on the client goal<br><br>• Avoid technical discussions irrelevant to the client's goal | • Always talk about investment performance in the context of the client's goal — financial freedom<br><br>• Talk about successful experiences in working with similar clients |
| **Anonymous** | • Great attention to client privacy needs<br><br>• Talk about firm commitment to client confidentiality | • Explore client preferences for maintaining privacy<br><br>• Tell client about the firm's security procedures |
| **Moguls** | • Reinforce perception of client control at all opportunities<br><br>• Create decision-points for client (opportunities to make decisions among several options) | • Make them feel as though they are the #1 client<br><br>• Make them feel as though they are working with the #1 firm in terms of investment performance and service |

| | Attending Behaviors | Shared Values |
|---|---|---|
| **Family Steward** | • Schedule regular face-to-face meetings<br><br>• Arrange meetings so that they follow a regular, predictable pattern | • Share the importance of your own family in your life<br><br>• Show how your value of thrift benefits the family |
| **Investment Phobic** | • Fewer meetings<br><br>• Meetings focus on lifestyle (not financial) issues | • Show interest in their lives<br><br>• Talk about your belief that investing is necessary, but that not everyone has to be an expert |
| **Independents** | • Frequent updates on progress toward goal of financial independence<br><br>• Periodic review of the financial objective | • Tell stories about other clients who have lived out their dreams<br><br>• Demonstrate how appealing you think the idea of financial freedom is |
| **Anonymous** | • Fewer meetings than with most clients<br><br>• Short agenda because of time constraints | • Agree that privacy is increasingly important<br><br>• Demonstrate steps you take to insure your own confidentiality |
| **Moguls** | • Meetings organized around decisions they are asked to make<br><br>• Reinforce previous client decisions | • Show that you think their accomplishments are significant<br><br>• Set up choices for the client, don't question their decisions |

| | Client Orientation | Leadership |
|---|---|---|
| **VIPs** | • Provide "first class" treatment (board room, best restaurants) <br> • Give the sense of many people involved on their behalf | • Make them feel as though they are in the same class as celebrity clients <br> • Stress sterling image of the firm |
| **Accumulators** | • Communicate a sense of urgency around financial performance <br> • Involve their other professional advisors (lawyers, CPA, etc. . . ) | • Report frequently on relative performance compared to selected benchmarks <br> • In every interaction, reinforce investment expertise |
| **Gamblers** | • Communicate excitement and enthusiasm for investing <br> • Highest possible interaction with portfolio manager | • Emphasize expertise in taking advantage of market movements and volatility <br> • Communicate trading vs. buy-and-hold orientation |
| **Innovators** | • Want access to top technical expertise <br> • Position yourself as an educational resource | • Bring leading edge investment opportunities <br> • Talk the technical jargon |

| | Attending Behaviors | Shared Values |
|---|---|---|
| **VIPs** | • Schedule frequent meetings to address their ego needs<br><br>• Ensure that the meeting content is not exceedingly challenging | • Drop names of celebrity clients of the firm when appropriate<br><br>• Talk about highly visible people in the community |
| **Accumulators** | • Conduct frequent meetings<br><br>• Focus all meetings on portfolio results | • Reinforce the value of accumulating wealth<br><br>• Show belief that "private wealth is what made this country great" |
| **Gamblers** | • Initiate many phone contacts between meetings<br><br>• Quickly respond to client calls | • Mirror their emotional intensity<br><br>• Show you share an appreciation for quickness, risk-taking, and action |
| **Innovators** | • Have frequent interactions (not just meetings)<br><br>• Focus on industry news, and new products | • Share the belief that innovative, cutting edge investing is the way to go<br><br>• Reflect their technical turn of mind |

As we have shown, the C.L.A.S. Model is a uniquely effective model for you to systematically break down how you can improve your relationships with your affluent clients. Improved relationships can only lead to increased assets under management and referrals.

Integrating High-Net-Worth Psychology with the C.L.A.S. model provides you with a clear path to follow with each of the nine profiles, allowing you to positively impact your client's overall satisfaction level, increase assets under management per client and generate referrals and personal introductions. By consistently implementing these proven methods, you will be able to build a practice that is highly productive, efficient and profitable.

### Turning C.L.A.S. into a Systematic Plan to Raise Client Satisfaction

Now that you have a clear understanding of the C.L.A.S. Model, it's time to look at how other advisors have put it to work. You could simply look at your clients and say to yourself, "Well, I've got a Family Steward here, and their family's really important to them and I should keep that at the top of my mind when dealing with them." In fact, many advisors have taken that path, and indeed had increased success.

However, by far the most effective usage of the C.L.A.S. Model is not to look at it as a grab bag of ideas, but rather to weave the individual ideas into a complete plan, systematically contacting and servicing the client around their profile's unique financial motivator on an on-going basis.

The investment advisors we have seen do this have been very successful indeed. In fact, our research shows that of those advisors who contacted their client fourteen times or more over a six month period created clients that fell into the "highly satisfied" category 89.7 percent of the time (Exhibit 9.5). That means when they employed this systematic process they got more assets under management per client and more referrals almost nine times out of ten. These are percentages that anyone can make a living from.

## Exhibit 9.5
### Contact Strategy

| Contacts/Month | Total Contacts | Customized to Client's Profile | Time Period | Percentage of Clients Converted to "Highly Satisfied" Category |
|---|---|---|---|---|
| 2-5 | 15 | Family Steward | 6 Months | 89.7% |

If fourteen contacts sounds like a lot to you, consider this. We're talking about a brief phone call, an e-mail or some other contact two or three times a month for a period of six months. We're not talking about long phone conversations or turnkey account reviews. We're talking about small, simple contacts made repeatedly and continually to your best clients around what's most important to them. This isn't hard work and no other use of your time leads to such compelling and repeatable results.

The truly beautiful benefit of this process is that once the up-front work of building a high-touch relationship management system is completed, a minimal amount of effort is required by the advisor going forward to maintain the client's high satisfaction rate. It's kind of like building a house. If you build it right the first time, it requires minimal maintenance and a great deal of use. The bulk of the remaining effort will center around minor customization to the client's individuality and identifying a prospect as a given profile and plugging them into your high-touch relationship management system.

## The Top Producer's Systematized Use of C.L.A.S.

The way top producers put this to work is very simple, and falls into three basic steps.

- Step #1: Generate 15 profile-specific contact ideas for your Focus Profiles.
- Step #2: Plan the execution date for the profile specific ideas.
- Step #3: Batch process the profile specific ideas for all clients of that profile on given day.

Let us explain each of these steps.

## Step #1: Generate 15 Profile-Specific Contact Ideas for Your Focus Profiles

In this step, you want to take the two or three profiles that you identified as your "Focus Profiles" in Chapters 7 and 8 and begin the process of creating a service track that is customized to the financial motivator of that profile. For example, if Family Stewards are one of your "Focus Profiles", now you want to develop a series of contact ideas based on the fact that their family has overarching importance in their decision making process as it relates to finances.

This series of ideas should total at least 15 in number. There are two ways that you can develop these contact ideas. Use the C.L.A.S. model to help you trigger ideas. Or you can use the following questions. Take a moment to jot down two or three ideas for each of the following questions, keeping in mind one of your clients that fits the profile as you answer the questions.

1. How can you demonstrate your level of client focus and orientation (to Focus Client Type)?

2. How can you demonstrate leadership by proactively providing solutions (to Focus Client Type's) needs, concerns & goals?

3. How can you most effectively plan your contacts (to Focus Client Type), both the quantity and reason for contacting them?

4. How can you demonstrate that you share the same values and beliefs as your (Focus Client Type)?

As you may have noticed, the answers to each of these questions fall neatly into one of the four elements of the C.L.A.S. model.

The first question was to prompt you for ideas on Client Focus, and then so on down the line with Leadership, Attention to the Client and Shared Values. Go ahead and code each of your ideas by putting a (C) for Client Orientation, or an (L) for Leadership and so on at the end of each idea. This will come in useful when you begin to drop them into your calendar in step two.

In addition to brainstorming your own ideas, you can use some of the ideas we have seen other advisors successfully employ with their clients. In the remaining chapters, you will find a sample client business plan for each of the nine profiles. Find the chapter of the profile that corresponds with your chosen "focus profile", and take a look at this plan. Not only will it give you a clear example to follow, but you will likely find ideas that you can incorporate into your own plan.

In addition to the sample client business plan, we have provided a number of relationship building ideas. It should be noted that you should feel perfectly comfortable using one of the sample client business plans verbatim if you wish, rather than take the additional time and effort to generate your own ideas. However, if you take this route, do remember to take into account the individuality of your client on things such as birthdays in the process.

### Step #2: Plan the Dates to Implement Your Profile Specific Ideas

The next step is to begin to plan the implementation date for all of your ideas. The most effective and simple strategy for planning your calendar involves choosing a date and assigning a specific C.L.A.S. action for a specific profile on that date. For example, on February 1$^{st}$, you send a list of "The 100 Best Colleges" to your Family Steward clients. This action would demonstrate the advisor's Client Focus to the Family Steward client, fitting right into the C.L.A.S. model.

Your next step is to plan all fifteen of your contacts over the next six months for your top three profiles. We've found it easiest to complete an entire plan one profile at a time, then go back and start from the top with the second Focus Profile, and so on down the line.

As you plan your contacts out, try to alternate between C.L.A. & S. contacts for the profile. It's not necessary to have them follow a strict linear flow in this order repeatedly, but rather to evenly alternate between all four elements. However, by alternating between the various elements of C.L.A.S., you create two important benefits. It ensures that you hit each element at least a couple of times over the course of the six months, and avoid too much emphasis on one element at the expense of some others. Over the six months, you should be able to hit each element of C.L.A.S. three to four times.

When inputting your contacts into your calendar, we have also found it helpful to employ a coding system that allows the members of the office to observe at a glance the nature of a given contact. The best we have seen is to abbreviate the profile, then a backslash and the letter code for the element of CLAS being leveraged. For example, a contact with a Family Steward around Leadership would be abbreviated simply as FS/L.

### Step #3: Batch Process the Profile Specific Ideas for All Clients of that Profile on a Given Day

Finally, batch process all of your Family Steward clients at once with a given action. The example we used above was to send a list of "The 100 Best Colleges" to a Family Steward client on February 1st. But don't do it for one Family Steward client, implement this action for all of your Family Steward clients. This way, you take care of that element of the C.L.A.S. Model in one swoop, batch processing the entire profile with a single action. Not only is this clearly the most efficient way to utilize the C.L.A.S. Model, it also creates a clear, on-going "job description" for your assistant to execute day after day (Exhibit 9.6).

## Exhibit 9.6
### Family Steward Client Satisfaction Calendar

— July —

| Sun | Mon | Tue | Wed | Thu | Fri | Sat |
| --- | --- | --- | --- | --- | --- | --- |
|  | 1 (C) | 2 | 3 | 4 | 5 | 6 |
| 7 | 8 | 9 | 10 | 11 | 12 | 13 |
| 14 | 15 | 16 | 17 | 18 | 19 (L) | 20 |
| 21 | 22 | 23 | 24 | 25 | 26 (C) | 27 |
| 28 | 29 | 30 | 31 |  |  |  |

— August —

| Sun | Mon | Tue | Wed | Thu | Fri | Sat |
| --- | --- | --- | --- | --- | --- | --- |
|  |  |  |  | 1 | 2 | 3 |
| 4 | 5 (A) | 6 | 7 | 8 | 9 | 10 |
| 11 | 12 | 13 | 14 | 15 | 16 (S) | 17 |
| 18 | 19 | 20 | 21 | 22 | 23 | 24 |
| 25 | 26 | 27 | 28 | 29 | 30 | 31 |

— September —

| Sun | Mon | Tue | Wed | Thu | Fri | Sat |
| --- | --- | --- | --- | --- | --- | --- |
| 1 | 2 (C) | 3 | 4 | 5 | 6 | 7 |
| 8 | 9 | 10 | 11 | 12 | 13 (S) | 14 |
| 15 | 16 | 17 | 18 | 19 | 20 | 21 |
| 22 | 23 | 24 | 25 | 26 | 27 | 28 |
| 29 (S) |  |  |  |  |  |  |

— October —

| Sun | Mon | Tue | Wed | Thu | Fri | Sat |
| --- | --- | --- | --- | --- | --- | --- |
|  |  | 1 | 2 | 3 | 4 | 5 |
| 6 | 7 | 8 | 9 | 10 | 11 (L) | 12 |
| 13 (A) | 14 | 15 | 16 | 17 | 18 | 19 |
| 20 (S) | 21 | 22 | 23 | 24 | 25 | 26 |
| 27 | 28 | 29 | 30 | 31 |  |  |

— November —

| Sun | Mon | Tue | Wed | Thu | Fri | Sat |
| --- | --- | --- | --- | --- | --- | --- |
|  |  |  |  |  | 1 (L) | 2 |
| 3 | 4 | 5 | 6 | 7 | 8 | 9 |
| 10 | 11 | 12 | 13 | 14 | 15 | 16 |
| 17 | 18 | 19 | 20 | 21 | 22 | 23 |
| 24 | 25 | 26 (C) | 27 | 28 | 29 | 30 |

— December —

| Sun | Mon | Tue | Wed | Thu | Fri | Sat |
| --- | --- | --- | --- | --- | --- | --- |
| 1 | 2 | 3 | 4 | 5 | 6 | 7 |
| 8 | 9 | 10 | 11 (S) | 12 | 13 | 14 |
| 15 | 16 (A) | 17 | 18 | 19 | 20 | 21 |
| 22 | 23 | 24 | 25 | 26 | 27 | 28 |
| 29 | 30 | 31 |  |  |  |  |

Most investment advisors find that this little bit of planning up front makes things run much smoother down the road both in their office and with their clients. It helps all members of their team know what needs to be done well in advance of its required completion date. Secondly, by generating a high-touch relationship management system, the advisors we have worked with have allowed themselves to significantly reduce the number of inbound contacts from clients. This is very significant because it means they have successfully shifted their business from a reactive client management mode to a proactive mode. Proactive practices are not only easier to run but increase client satisfaction more efficiently. The reason for this seems simply to be that a client more highly values having their advisor anticipate an issue than having to phone it in to their advisor and wait for a response.

### Summary

What we have outlined above is the basic strategy used repeatedly by top producing advisors. However, we want to not only show you how to build your own plan, but show you an example of a plan for each of the nine profiles. This is exactly what we have done in the following chapters. Each of these chapters provides you an actual case study example developed and successfully implemented by an advisor. In addition to this plan, we also provide you ideas for managing and building relationships with each profile.

## *Chapter 9 Big Answer:*

*Your first goal is to understand the High-Net-Worth Psychology and Financial Motivator concepts. The next challenge is to understand how to implement these ideas. Chapter 9 has walked you through a step-by-step approach for implementing the client satisfaction aspects of the I-CLAS model. The next nine chapters show you how to work with each of the nine client types.*

# Chapter 10:
# Family Stewards

*"It's a Family Affair"*

— Sly Stone

## Chapter 10 Critical Question:
## How can I leverage my Family Steward Clients and build a large, successful practice?

This is a sample relationship model and business plan for a Family Steward client, and is a general example for a Family Steward. It is important that you not only understand the Family Steward profile, but also each client's individuality. Think of the Family Steward profile as your starting point, and then customize your plan to each individual with those directional insights. You must combine the "Financial Motivator" of the profile with each client's unique character. This is the essential step necessary for success.

By customizing the business plan described in this chapter to each of your target clients, you will be well on your way to success. In this chapter, we will walk you through the general steps, and illustrate each step with a client story.

## PRACTICE BUSINESS PLAN

### I. Mission/Vision
*Create a highly successful investment advisory practice by targeting Family Steward clients.*

The high-net-worth psychology approach forces you to focus on the client segments most in tune with your own personality. In earlier chapters, you figured out your own financial motivator and those of your best clients. If you are reading this chapter, it is because targeting Family Stewards is a suitable strategy for your own style and those of many of your top clients.

## II. Strategy

*Increase Family Steward satisfaction by focusing on their financial motivator of helping their family. Develop and implement a CLAS individual client business plan for top clients.*

Your strategy is to create highly satisfied Family Steward clients, with the ultimate goal of increasing assets under management and generating more referrals. Research proves this cause and effect relationship. Highly satisfied clients bring in more assets and make more referrals. By developing a practice business plan along these lines, you will begin to think explicitly about the actions that will increase your client's satisfaction with you and your services.

You can waste a lot of resources in trying to create satisfied clients. Not all activities are equally efficient in creating client satisfaction. In fact, what makes some clients satisfied irritates other clients.

We have developed a model we call the CLAS model to help guide you in doing only what you need to in building client satisfaction. If you personally are a Family Steward and have a critical mass of Family Steward clients, our recommendation is that you should structure your practice around delivering against the relationship needs of Family Steward clients. (This is also our recommendation if you decide, for other reasons, to target Family Steward clients).

Start by continuing to do an excellent job of providing investment advisory services. You should recognize that investment advisory services are critically important. They put you in position to win on the relationship front. The four components of satisfaction with the relationship – the "CLAS" – actually deliver more value to clients as measured by how much they increase the probability that clients will refer other people to you and that they will add assets to be managed.

For Family Steward clients, the CLAS refers to the way in which you interact with them in order to increase their satisfaction with you and your services. In the CLAS model, the "C" refers to client orientation (the amount of focus on the Family Steward client), the "L" refers to advisory leadership (proactively providing solutions to Family Steward clients), the "A" refers to attending behaviors (contacting Family Stewards) and the "S" refers to shared values (how an advisor shows their trustworthiness to Family Stewards). Research proves that the "CLAS" portions of the model are 4 times more important than investment performance in producing client satisfaction.

The implication is that if you focus on satisfaction, clients will stick with you even if the market creates poor investment performance. Again, the research bears this out.

## Exhibit 10.1
### The CLAS Model

| | | |
|---|---|---|
| **C** | **Client Orientation** | Your level of client focus |
| **L** | **Leadership** | Proactively identifying important issues and providing solutions |
| **A** | **Attending Behaviors** | The number of and motivation for client contacts |
| **S** | **Shared Values** | Trustworthiness and sharing of a similar value system |

### III. Target Clients
*You do not have the time or resources to practice high-impact relationship management with all of your clients. For this reason, you need to focus on your best clients and/or those clients with significant asset or referral potential.*

You can easily do this if you list your Family Steward clients. Then select just your top Family Steward clients, the ones with the most potential for asset capture or client referral. You can use the worksheet below for this purpose. Fill in the client's score on the Client Valuation System (chapter 8, exhibit 8.1), or simply use your estimate of potential assets available for capture and rank them according to what you think their current satisfaction level is — high, medium or low. Finally, for each client, decide on what your goal for increasing the satisfaction is, and fill that in.

## Exhibit 10.2
### Client Targeting Worksheet

| Client Name | Client Valuation System Score | Assets Under Management/ Potential AUM | Current Satisfaction | Satisfaction Goal |
|---|---|---|---|---|
| Jay Hartz | | $200 | Medium-high | Improve to highly satisfied |
| | | | | |
| | | | | |
| | | | | |
| | | | | |
| | | | | |
| | | | | |
| | | | | |
| | | | | |

Once you have completed your chart, look it over. Especially, look for patterns. Are there a lot of assets you do not have under management, or do you not know? Do you think your Family Steward clients are as satisfied as they could possibly be, or might there be room for improvement? Have you selected the right clients for targeting? If not, revise your list. Once you have the right clients targeted, proceed to the next section to develop a relationship plan for each and every one of these key Family Steward clients.

### IV. Individual Client relationship Planning
*Create and implement for each Family Steward client an individual relationship plan designed to raise satisfaction to targeted levels.*

Creating an individual client plan can best be explained through an example. Let's take a sample client, Jay Hartz, who is a Family Steward and who has high potential as a client. He owns a closely held company, he has many professional contacts and many community contacts through his involvement with his children. This accounts for his high priority as a client to target, as he potentially has assets available to capture and is well networked. Client networks create the potential for new client referrals.

You have known Jay for some time. After you learned about investing personalities from this book, you began to think of Jay as a Family Steward. You sat down with Jay to confirm his profile. You used the questions in the guide, and Jay talked mostly about wanting to create a good life for his wife and children. He mentioned being very active with his children, coaching a soccer team and being an Assistant Cubmaster in his son's Troop. It was actually easy to confirm that Jay is a Family Steward, and you verified your classification of Jay with several trial balloon questions. You decide to classify Jay as a Family Steward for the purpose of creating a plan.

In addition to knowing that Jay is a Family Steward, you know him as an individual. You bring both streams of knowledge to bear on your development of this individualized plan.

To change client satisfaction, you must make quite a few client contacts over the course of six months. You set a goal of 15 contacts with Jay. Then you map out what a six month plan of contacts might look like. As you develop your plan, you mark each action item with a (C), (L), (A) or (S) to designate which component of CLAS you are impacting with a specific action item. Some action items will impact more than one component of the CLAS Model. The goal is to impact each area 3 to 4 times over the six month plan. You use this plan to guide your actions over the coming time period. Of course, you expect deviation from the exact plan – it is intended as a general guide. You should document your actual contacts by date, event and code them C,L,A or S.

## Exhibit 10.3
### Individual Client Relationship Development Plan

**Client name:** Jay Hartz

**Background:** Jay owns a successful construction company. He and his wife have 3 children, 4, 7 and 9. You have helped him with mutual fund investments, but not with any planning.

**Financial Motivator:** Family Steward

**Investing I.Q.:** Average

**Target Contacts:** 15 contacts

| Date | Goal | Action |
|------|------|--------|
| July 1 | Identify a special family occasion and send a small gift item. (C) | You know the client goes up to the family cottage in Michigan every year for a long 4th of July weekend. Knowing this, you put together a small fun pack for the client's kids, including a disposable camera for each child. You also include a simple handwritten note that says, "Hope you have a great weekend! Thought your kids might have fun with these, and maybe you'll get some memorable shots." (If you do, send me one for my wall." (If you have a lot of Family Steward clients, consider creating a wall with photos of all of his clients and their families in your office.) |

| Date | Goal | Action |
|------|------|--------|
| July 19 | Provide leadership to the client by being proactive on important family issues. (L) | Put together an analysis of college funding for the client's children. Since you know their ages, you know the number of years left before they would be attending college and you can get college tuition estimates from recognized experts for those years. Send the analysis to your client with a note saying, "Jay, I came across some information I thought you should be made aware of. Enclose is an analysis of what college tuition is projected to be, both in-state and out-of-state, when each of your children graduate. I recommend to my clients that the sooner we put together a plan, the more time we have to let compounding begin to work for us. I'll call in a few days to see if you'd like me to put together a plan to fund each of the kids' educations." |

| Date | Goal | Action |
|------|------|--------|
| July 26 | Follow-up with the client on the college funding analysis you prepared. (C), (L), (A) | Call Jay and discuss the future costs of education. In addition, re-emphasize that the sooner a plan is developed, the more time there will be for compounding to work and less out-of-pocket contributions will need to be made. Your goal is to get his approval to put together a financial plan for each of his children's educations and meet with him to implement the plan later. |

| Date | Goal | Action |
|---|---|---|
| August 5 | Arrange face-to-face meetings in a regular, predictable pattern. (A) | Schedule a meeting in your office, followed by lunch with Jay to approve and sign your plan to fund his childrens' educations. Tell him that you'd like to set up an annual "Back to School" review of each of these accounts to keep him informed and ensure he is satisfied with the progress. Mention that you think it is a perfect time to review them, because with the kids going back to school, it will be at the top of everyone's mind. Ask him if he thinks this is a good idea. If he agrees, schedule the date in your calendar for next year and send out a reminder to Mr. Hartz a few weeks beforehand. |

| Date | Goal | Action |
|---|---|---|
| August 16 | Demonstrate your own values of thrift and savings. (S) | Take several steps to communicate your value of thrift to clients like Jay. Even small things like having an assistant clip coupons for a basket in your waiting area with a sign that says, "A penny saved is a penny earned. A penny invested is a nickel." Other ideas include starting a "dollar a day" investment account in your office to demonstrate the power of saving and investing even a small amount over time. You can display the daily total on a marker board in your waiting area. When clients come around once or twice a year, they will be able to see how much even one dollar a day can grow. |

| Date | Goal | Action |
|---|---|---|
| September 2 | Foster client involvement and satisfaction (C), (L) | Statements are sent out at the end of the month. Give Jay a call to "see if he had any questions about his statement." You point some sections you think are important. Simply asking clients if they have any questions will help clarify anything they were unsure about as well as make them more comfortable to freely ask questions they may have in the future. Helping them "feel free to ask any question" will go a long way towards maintaining a highly satisfied client for two reasons. First, the client will feel you are accessible and approachable. Second, it keeps any discontent they have from festering into a problem that could threaten the account. |

| Date | Goal | Action |
|---|---|---|
| September 13 | Communicate the importance of your family and spending quality time with them. (S), (A) | When you go on vacation, send out an advance notice to your clients to let them know you will not be in the week of September 16th thru the 23rd. Include in your note that you are going on a fishing trip to Canada with your family. Provide them with the name of someone they can call in the office in the event of an emergency. This not only reinforces that your family is your priority, too, but also demonstrates once more the superior level of concern and service you provide your clients. |

| Date | Goal | Action |
|---|---|---|
| September 30 | Demonstrate your own long-term, conservative approach to investing. (S) | Carefully select reading materials for your waiting area. Get reprints or copies of articles you especially like that you believe closely match your own long-term outlook on investing. Then, stamp them with your company name, phone and message saying, "Complimentary Copy." By doing this, you convert your waiting area from a hodge-podge of magazines into another opportunity to convey your own philosophy and values to your client. |

| Date | Goal | Action |
|------|------|--------|
| October 11 | Involve your clients key family members in the investing process to learn of any unique needs (L), (C) | Take Jay and his wife out for lunch with the goal of making sure that she also has an understanding of the investment plan that has been established. This will provide an opportunity to get to know Jay's wife and answer any questions she may have. Spend time getting to know them both and identify any unique needs they may have. For example, you learn that Jay is concerned about the costs of houses for her children and wants to set up a separate fund to provide a down payment on a house for each child. You also find out that she is also concerned that they haven't updated their will since having their kids. |

| Date | Goal | Action |
|------|------|--------|
| October 14 | Respond to their needs quickly and efficiently, and foster client involvement. (A), (C) | Take advantage of your meeting with both spouses. Demonstrate your responsiveness to their needs by sending a brief memo outlining your recommendation and plan based on the special needs they communicated to you—building a nest egg for each child. Additionally, you can refer a lawyer that can help them update their will. You close by saying you will call in a week to see what they would like to do. |

| Date | Goal | Action |
|------|------|--------|
| October 21 | Keep your word by doing exactly what you have said to help establish trust. (S), (A) | Follow-up with a phone call to Jay to see if they want you to implement your plan to build a nest egg for each child. Additionally, ask if they would like the lawyer you know to contact them about updating their will, as well as when would be a good time to call. |

| Date | Goal | Action |
|------|------|--------|
| November 1 | Keep your clients posted on new developments or information concerning their investing strategy (L), (A), (C) | You already know the Hartz's children are their central concern due to the college funding and nest egg accounts you have established for them. As such, you have made it a priority to keep an eye out for developments on this subject. You ran across an article that outlines how much college is going to cost and how few people are prepared for it. Its projections are covered by your current plan. You send it to your client with a brief note that says, "Jay- Thought you'd find this interesting. It projects future costs of college. We're in good shape. I'll continue to keep an eye out for new developments." |

| Date | Goal | Action |
|------|------|--------|
| November 26 | Remember major family occasions. (C), (A) | In your lunch with the Hartz's back in October, you learned that the Hartz's anniversary is December 1st. You send a quick note congratulating them on their 20th. In this highly personal remembrance, it's not appropriate to bring up any other business concerns. However, by simply remembering and sending them a card, you demonstrate to them that you regard them as a very important client. |

| Date | Goal | Action |
|------|------|--------|
| December 11 | Demonstrate the importance of your own family in your life. (S) | Send out a holiday card to your clients that includes a photo of you and your family. Posed shots are fine, but a photo of you and your family involved in an activity together is even better. Include a brief caption under the photo. For example, if your photo is of your family during a community summer festival where you all volunteered to grill hotdogs and hamburgers, include a caption saying, "Working the Grills at the Winfield Good Old Days, August, 1999." |

| Date | Goal | Action |
|------|------|--------|
| December 16 | Send the client your annual holiday gift. (A) | Send the Jay and his family a holiday gift, which can be enjoyed by the whole family, like a fruit basket. Be sure to consistently send a gift at the same time each year and preferably the same item. This financial advisor always sends out two fresh Hawaiian pineapples every year. It's just a bit unique and clients regard it as a small treat that they can count on once a year. This may sound trivial, but it goes a long way towards helping reinforce to the client that you are reliable and can be counted upon. As their financial advisor, this is a net positive impression. |

## V. Collect Relationship Development Ideas

*Constantly collect new ideas for relationship-building activities with Family Steward clients.*

Here is a list of quick, highly effective ideas that you can use to stay connected to a Family Steward's "family tree." Utilizing one or more of these tools on a regular basis will reinforce how well you understand the Steward's values and serve as a consistent reminder of your high standards of service.

Some advisors pre-code activities such as these with a "C", "L", "A" or "S" to help in their client planning.

## Exhibit 10.4
### Relationship Development Ideas

➢ Keep an eye out for articles or books, which parents can use to teach children financial responsibility and pass them along to Family Stewards.

➢ Gift a magazine subscription to your Family Stewards. It costs very little and is a monthly reminder to them of your level of service. Be sure to choose a magazine that dovetails with the family's interest. For example, if they like to go bicycling together, send them a subscription to a biking magazine.

➤ Create or suggest exercises that parents can use to promote financial understanding with their children, such as opening a bank account, establishing a budget, setting a goal such as (buying their first car) and developing a savings plan to achieve it.

➤ In your initial client meeting, ask your client to draw their family tree. This shows you their view of the family and may contain surprising information about a parent or uncle who may turn into a qualified prospect. Also ask them to include the full names and birth dates of all family members. This information can be used later to send out birthday cards to all.

➤ Send out birthday cards to the husband & wife, but also to the children. Ask yourself what is more impactful to a Family Steward. Sending a birthday card to a 50 year old man, so that they can say, "Good, he didn't forget again this year." Or, sending birthday cards to the account holder's children, so that the kids become excited and tell the account holder about it. The latter is much more powerful.

➤ Run hypos on the cost for college based on the ages of the children and the amount of assets it would take to fund college today at a given percentage. The more you can proactively address their problems, the stronger the relationship will become.

➤ Use your office as an active relationship building tool. Communicate that you share the same values of "family", "community" and "conservative investing." Put pictures of your own family and community involvement throughout your office. Some advisors even include photos of themselves and the little league teams they coach and sponsor as a clear, non-verbal way to tell Family Stewards that they have been around awhile and that they have roots in the community.

➢ Offer to record and preserve the client's Life Story for generations to come. Obviously this is not something you would do. However, there are firms that specialize in interviewing clients, editing and producing audio family heirlooms capturing a parent's or grandparent's wisdom forever on a CD. Best of all they are fairly affordable ($295 and up) if this service is offered as a value added item for a service such as estate planning. One such company can be found at www.legacyrecordings.net. An alternative way to achieve a similar effect, is to give your clients a book on genealogy or family tree software that will allow them to record their life story on their own, and pass it on to future generations. A book called, To Our Children's Children does a great job of this and is a gift any Family Steward would appreciate.

➢ Collect and send magazine or newspaper articles about non-financial topics that may be of interest to Stewards. Topics could include:
  • Helping your Child get into College
  • America's Top 100 Universities
  • Your City's Listing of the Top 10 Family Restaurants
  • A Review of Children's Films
  • 25 Ways to Keep your Child from Being Bored During Summer Vacation
  • Family-Friendly Vacation Spots and Hotel Chains
  • 10 Books to Read Aloud to Your Children
  • Tips on how to Relate to Teenagers
  • Favorite Local Family Attractions

➢ Keep an eye out for tickets to family-oriented events, such as circuses, ice skating shows, children's theatre, movies, etc. Periodically offer tickets to your family steward clients.

➢ If one of your Steward clients has a child who is involved with high school sports, stay on top of what's going on and strike up a conversation about it with the Steward. You can also clip out newspaper articles and box scores that mention the

Steward's children and send them out with a congratulatory note. The same principle can be used with other children's interests and activities, such as inclusion on the honor roll, college entrance exams, college selection, etc.

➢ Set up your own seasonal events, such as pumpkin carving contests, Easter egg hunts, sledding, sleigh rides, nature hikes, father/daughter or mother/son events, etc . . .Use the Sample Prospecting Idea shown here as a template to organize the event.

➢ Familiarize yourself with the interests of the Steward's children (baseball, swimming, ballet, horseback riding, etc.). Look for related gift opportunities such as a personalized Louisville Slugger bat, tickets to a touring ballet company, a horseback riding lesson and send them to the Steward to pass along to their kids.

Search out Family Steward oriented websites for additional relationship management ideas to brainstorm with your staff. Here are a few examples:

www.aaced.com
The American College Entrance Directory site features important information for choosing a college or university to attend. It provides profiles for more than 3,500 schools, and includes information from academic requirements and scholarships to virtual tours.

www.ed.gov/pubs/parents/Reading
This site is sponsored by the U.S. Department of Education-Office of Educational Research and Improvement. It gives parents tips on helping their children learn to read.

www.savingforcollege.com
This site is dedicated entirely to college savings plans. It includes links such as, articles, new developments and a message board. It boasts having the most comprehensive, current and objective information available regarding qualified state tuition programs.

www.moviemom.com
Moviemom.com is a site that helps parents choose movies for their children to watch. It features movies for all ages on video and in the theaters.

www.kidvidz.com
This site helps families use media for fun and education. It is a family media resource site and suggests special interest videos for children.

www.babycenter.com
Babycenter.com provides expert advice about pregnancies and having a baby. It even provides customized weekly newsletters based on the due date of the baby's birth.

www.justuskidz.com/parents.html
This is a general site on parenting and family. It is a starting point to parenting resources and includes topics ranging from potty training to homeschooling to adoption.

www.childsafety.org
This site provides parents with child car safety information and is published by the Child Passenger Safety Advocacy. It features information ranging from monthly checklists to car manufacturer information.

www.childsecure.com
This site is a general health and safety site that provides parents with discussion groups, and various links such as recall alerts, medical glossaries and vaccine calculators.

www.rightonthemoney.org
This site provides straightforward advice for people who want to make better financial decisions for themselves and their families. It offers several topics to look at, including caring for parents, wedding bills as well as kids and investing.

www.familymoney.com
This is the website for Family Money magazine. This finance magazine says that it focuses on what is really important—making a better life for your family.

www.parentingteens.com
Parentingteens.com provides parents of teens with resources, insight and support. It features weekly parenting tips and site upgrades, as well as a parent forum for parents to chat and exchange ideas.

www.parentsoup.com
This site is targeted to parents of teenagers. Features include receiving e-mail newsletters, chat rooms and expert advice.

www.integrityonline2.com/specialfamily
This is the site for Special Family magazine. It is for families who live with any type of physical or mental disability, including visual and hearing impairments.

www.irsc.com
The Internet Resources for Special Needs Children (IRSC) website is dedicated to communicating information relating to the needs of children with disabilities. It provides valuable information for parents and other people who interact with children who have disabilities.

http://users.sgi.net/~rollocst/amuse.html
This site features a national and international directory of amusement, theme and water parks, as well as family entertainment centers. The directory provides locations of each, as well as direct links to websites.

www.grandtravel.com
This site provides ideas for special vacations for grandparents and their grandchildren. Vacations range from domestic to international, and the site provides contact information to make reservations.

## VI. Implement Prospecting Program

*Create and implement an ongoing new client prospecting and development program guided by these same principles.*

Family Stewards are great clients to target as they tend to be well networked, and willing to refer friends to friends. Your task, as an advisor who welcomes referrals, is to create opportunities for your current clients to introduce you to prospective, new, ones. There are several ways for you to do this. You could work with clients one-on-one to get referrals, asking to meet people they know for lunch or coffee. Advisors we know who are most successful tend to have events (or a series of events) where these introductions can occur more naturally. By creating events that are family oriented, you communicate your values in many ways and predispose prospects to be interested in you.

There are many different types of activities you could plan. We know advisors who have rented out an arcade for the whole family to enjoy. Other advisors have rented out an entire theater for the premiere of a family movie such as Atlantis.

The following case study walks you through an event as an illustration.

## Exhibit 10.5
### Family Steward Case Study

*There is a financial representative named Robert in Southern California that likes to work with Family Stewards who are also small business owners. He prospects for these types of clients by organizing a baseball outing every year where he invites affluent Family Steward clients and prospects and their families.*

*Robert identifies potential guests by networking with his current Family Steward clients. His approach is to invite his current Family Stewards to his annual baseball outing. Then he tells his current clients that he enjoys and specializes in working with small business owners, and asks if they know any other small business owners who might like to bring their family to the baseball outing.*

*Robert's rationale is that any leads he gets this way are likely to be affluent since they're business owners, likely to be Family Stewards since they're referred by another Family Steward and likely to be family oriented if they agree to come to an event of this kind.*

*He sometimes supplements his guest list by obtaining a list of businesses that sponsor the local Little League. These businesses, too, are typically run by Stewards who themselves have a child playing Little League and have sizable assets.*

*Once Robert has his guest list established, he invites the Stewards and their families to his baseball outing. He chooses a Fan Appreciation day so that the Stewards can take their kids to meet the players and get autographs. The kids love the opportunity, and his prospects like it, because it makes them heroes in their children's eyes—something that is invaluable to a Steward.*

*Robert takes the time to make the outing into something special. The opportunity to meet the players and get autographs is a key element, but he does other things to add value to the day:*

➢ *He sets up lunch or dinner immediately prior to the game when everyone is excited and the kids are well-rested. He usually chooses a nearby restaurant with a small private room and arranges a ballpark theme buffet. Everyone is in a controlled environment and he is free to talk business with his core group of Stewards while their families are occupied.*

➢ *Unless all of the guests already know each other, he has tasteful, pre-printed nametags available for everyone*

➢ *He makes a gift bag for each child which includes peanuts, a scorecard, a baseball program, a toy catcher's mitt, and other toys such as bubble-blowing kits, coloring books, and crayons, etc. Each gift bag is appropriate to the child's age, and is personalized with the kids' names in advance.*

➢ *He takes an instant camera along and snaps pictures of the group.*

*He gives most of them away to the families, but keeps some to pin on his office bulletin board. Family Stewards appreciate seeing them when they visit-it reinforces how well he understands their values. (Some advisors now use digital camera to take photos of an event).*

*Robert has been very successful with his baseball outings. Not only are they well-organized events with a built-in element of fun, but they're perfect for him because he himself is a baseball fan and truly enjoys the experience.*

Advisors like Robert who have created ongoing, systematic prospecting events like this have been quite successful. Obviously, these events take time to put together, but they do deliver good results for the effort. The key to success is to keep them fun and family-focused. Your clients will do all your talking for you. All you want is for new, prospective clients, to feel good about you in a family context and to take your call when you want to talk to them about investing.

## Exhibit 10.6
### Sample Invitation Text

*(Representative Name) of (Firm Name) Investments cordially invites you and your family to the "Take Me Out to the Ballgame" Baseball Outing & Lunch (Supper) (Date & Time) (Location). Our party has a block of (xx) seats reserved in the (xx) area of the ballpark. (It's Fan Appreciation Day) or (We're planning to arrive at the ballpark early) so all of the kids will have a chance to meet some of the players and get an autograph or two. We'll have special gifts for the kids, and it should be a nice chance for all of us to relax, socialize, and enjoy the game.*

*(RSVP info)*

There are ways you can use to make the invitation unusual and to build excitement around the even. For example, you could fold your invitation into a small square and insert it into a pack of baseball cards. Send the card pack out in a bright colored envelope with a piece of your notepaper that instructs the recipient to "Rip into this for more info on a full day of family fun at the ol' ballpark!" Or, you could mail the invitation in a small box along with an actual baseball or a baseball hat or even have your invitation copy transferred onto a t-shirt, then mail the shirt. Think about sending a separate invitation to each member of the family. Kids love getting invitations.

Follow-up is the essential step, as you want that personal meeting later. Be sure to send a follow-up note like the one provided.

## Exhibit 10.7
### Sample Thank You/Follow-Up Note

*Dear (Client Name),*

*I hope you and (spouse / kids names) enjoyed yourselves at the game last week. (Try to add a personal anecdote about one of the family here, such as "I wish I had a picture of the look on John's face when he got that Sammy Sosa autograph!"). (Spouse name) and I certainly had a great time. We realized how much we enjoy baseball and how infrequently we get to the ballpark. Hopefully there will be more opportunities for all of us to get together in the future.*

*(Client Name), we had a chance to talk a little bit about (plug in a specific Family Steward investment opportunity here) at the game and I was hoping we could set up a time for me to explain a little more about it. My office is (plug in location) or I would be happy to meet you at your office or at home, whatever is convenient. I'll give you a call in the next couple of days to check your availability.*

*Thanks again for joining us at the baseball game. I look forward to talking to you soon.*

*Sincerely,*
*(Financial Representative Name)*

The event ideas provided here, the invitation and follow-up notes are all provided as examples. You will want to create your own to reflect your own style. They are provided here just to show you how other advisors have implemented prospecting programs.

### Chapter 10 Big Answer:
**You can create a great practice around Family Steward clients. Family Stewards are one of the most attractive segments to target.**

The key to maximizing the results of your investment in developing this segment is consistency and focus. It takes time to create a pipeline of new clients and new asset streams to manage for existing clients. Big good implementation will create a successful practice.

# Chapter 11:
# Investment Phobics

*A man who has a million dollars is as well off as if he were rich.*

— John Jacob Astor

## Chapter 11 Critical Question:
## How can I grow my client base of Investment Phobic clients?

Investment Phobics have very different needs and wants from their financial advisor than Family Steward clients do. This chapter outlines a business model built around Investment Phobic clients. It includes an Investment Phobic-specific personal marketing plan for a sample client. Of course, all the examples included here are just that, examples. Each of your Investment Phobic clients has their own individuality. Think of the Investment Phobic profile here as a starting point and then tailor your actions to the actual clients you serve. Combine the "Financial Motivator" of the Investment Phobic profile with each client's unique personality for optimum success. In this chapter, we will walk you through the general steps of developing a business around this psychographic profile and illustrate each step with a client story.

## PRACTICE BUSINESS PLAN:

### I. Mission/Vision:
*Become the advisor of choice for Investment Phobic clients. Achieve this goal by creating highly satisfied Investment Phobic clients, with the ultimate goal of increasing assets under management and generating more referrals.*

There are several things to note in this mission statement. It focuses most of the advisor's time on satisfying current clients rather than prospecting. This is for several reasons. For almost all affluent clients, the time and money cost of getting new clients is staggering, it is much better to channel your energy towards client retention and satisfaction. More importantly, satisfied clients will become the most important pipeline of new client referrals. Finally, and most important, Investment Phobics are almost impossible to prospect for using traditional prospecting methods (such as direct mail, calling, seminars). Instead, they listen to their friends and go to the people their friends recommend.

## II. Strategy:

*Invest professional time on current clients. Increase client satisfaction using the insights of the financial motivator and positively impact each component of the C.L.A.S. Client Satisfaction Model in action plans tailored to each target Investment Phobic clients.*

The strategy will be to use state-of-the-art thinking on investor satisfaction to meet the goals of the mission statement. The CLAS model has been proven to increase client satisfaction, and so it is adopted as the central strategy to guide the practice plan in this segment.

While investment performance is important to Investment Phobics, they are quite oblivious to day-to-day market dynamics. They do not pay attention to the DJIA, they do not watch the financial channels and they do not read the financial press. They do want to feel safe with respect to their money, and value performance from that point of view.

Investment Phobics are very sensitive to the CLAS model because these are the relationship related factors. In general, the CLAS relationship factors are 4 times more powerful than investment performance; however, among Investment Phobics they are 10 times more important in engendering client satisfaction.

"C" refers to client orientation, to a high level of client focus. "L" refers to advisory leadership, which is to proactively identify important issues and provide solutions to clients. "A" is attending behaviors, and indicates the number of and motivation of client contacts. Finally, "S" refers to shared values and how an advisor shows their trustworthiness and shared value system.

## Exhibit 11.1
### The CLAS Model

| C | Client Orientation | Your level of client focus |
|---|---|---|
| L | Leadership | Proactively identifying important issues and providing solutions |
| A | Attending Behaviors | The number of and motivation for client contacts |
| S | Shared Values | Trustworthiness and sharing of a similar value system |

### III. Target Clients

*Identify high potential clients to target for relationship development. Select clients based on potential for incremental asst. capture and new client referrals.*

There are only so many hours in the day, and so a key component of your approach is how to allocate your time. We advocate a several step approach. The first step is to determine how intensive the contact per client needs to be. Then you can figure out how much time that will take. Once you have a sense of the effort per client, you can determine how many clients you can manage to work with at this level.

Our research has shown that Investor Phobic clients need a high level of interaction. Research shows that around 15 client contacts must be made over the course of six months to increase client satisfaction.

No one has the time or resources to practice high-impact relationship management with all of their clients. For this reason, you need to focus on your best Investment Phobic clients and/or those clients with significant assets that you might be able to capture.

List your top Investment Phobic clients by assets, and then rank them according to satisfaction level—high, average or low. You can enhance or maintain your current approach with the highly satisfied group, and dramatically improve relationships with the average and low groups.

## Exhibit 11.2
### Client Targeting Worksheet

| Client Name | Assets Under Management | Potential AUM | Current Satisfaction | Satisfaction Goal |
|---|---|---|---|---|
| Irene Davis | $800K | $350K | Average | Improve to highly satisfied |
| | | | | |
| | | | | |
| | | | | |
| | | | | |
| | | | | |
| | | | | |
| | | | | |
| | | | | |
| | | | | |

### IV. Individual Client Relationship Development Planning

*Develop an individual client relationship development plan for each client targeted as high potential through the exercise above.*

We provide an example here by continuing with the Irene Davis case. Irene is a classic Investment Phobic. She has little knowledge about or interest in investments. She thinks of it all as a burden that causes her a good deal of anxiety. She tells you she does not want to lose her money or make a mistake. However, whenever you brought up investing specifics, she will change the subject. You realize she is looking for evidence that she can trust you to watch out for her best interests.

You realize that she has to get to know you better so she can feel comfortable in leaving the details to you. Right now, you think she would rate her satisfaction as "good". You think significant improvement is possible.

You know that an average of 15 client contacts over the course of six months is necessary to increase the satisfaction of an Investment Phobic. You create a six month plan listing possible actions you could take. You label each one a (C), (L), (A) or (S) to designate which component of CLAS you are impacting with a specific action item. Some action items will impact more than one component of the CLAS Model. Your goal is to impact each area three to four times over the six month plan.

## Exhibit 11.3
### Individual Client Relationship Development Plan

**Client Name:** Irene Davis
**Background:** Married for 43 years; husband passed away a year ago. She has received a life insurance payout; receives retirement plan benefits. Two daughters, both married.
**Financial Motivator:** Investment Phobic
**Investing IQ:** Low
**Target Contacts:** 15

| Date | Goal | Action |
|------|------|--------|
| July 1 | Show interest in their lives. (S) | It was pretty clear from the first meeting that Irene is a Phobic. You realize that talking about investments at this point would only cause Irene to tune you out. You decide to learn all about Irene since you already know her family through her husband. You need to know her personally in order to put together an appropriate investment plan. You focus on demonstrating to Irene your interest in her life history. |

| Date | Goal | Action |
|------|------|--------|
| July 18 | Provide leadership by informing the client of the high quality performance you have delivered in the past, being careful not to get too deep or detailed. (L) | Send Irene a simple handwritten note thanking her for telling you about herself in your last meeting. Emphasize something you find you have in common, such as pet cats. Mention that since she shared so much with you, you thought she should know more about you. You enclose your track record from last year, averaging an 18% gain for your clients. You mention that your guiding philosophy is "Safety today, with growth for a secure future." Close the note by saying you will call in a few days. |

| Date | Goal | Action |
|------|------|--------|
| July 25 | Learn a lot about the client's outside interests. (C) | Call Irene to confirm she got your note. Mention that you have learned a lot about her past, but that you'd like to learn more about her current interests to help you get a better idea of how that might affect your investment recommendation. You ask about how she spends her days, what trips she has gone on, and if she has any hobbies. She says that she belongs to several groups that have outings to shows, plays bridge and meets her friends for lunch and dinner. She also visits her daughters and grandkids in Chicago and Wisconsin several times a year. She does volunteer work one day a week for a literacy program. You want to make sure you remember all of this, so you take notes. Getting to know all of her interests helps build the personal trust that is foundation of a relationship with an Investment Phobic. |

| Date | Goal | Action |
|------|------|--------|
| August 9 | Demonstrate leadership in handling the technical issues of investing for people who are not interested in the subject but realize its importance. (L) | You call Irene to schedule a meeting. You preface it by saying that you realize many of your clients don't find investing interesting. In fact, they find it a burden. You say you understand and that it's okay. You say that you enjoy and take pride in watching out for the interests of your clients. You see yourself as their "financial guardian." You arrange a meeting with Irene on the 14th to go over the plan you are putting together. |

| Date | Goal | Action |
|------|------|--------|
| August 14 | Meetings focus on Life-style issues (not financial). (A) | You have prepared a thorough investing plan for Irene and her money. However, you have worked with enough Investment Phobics that you call it their "Life Security Plan." You have identified the key goals, issues and activities in Irene's life in your previous conversations. In your presentation to her, you organize the plan around her top five concerns: 1) Her security, 2) Something to pass on to her daughters, 3) Enough money to live life like she's accustomed, 4) Funds for family travel and gifts, 5) Never being a burden to her daughters. You say that from your previous conversations that these are the top five items in her life that are relevant to financial decisions. You clearly, but briefly go over the action you recommend to ensure each goal. You then hand her a document that explicitly states all of the financial details for her records. You mention that if she would like to discuss it, now or in the future, you'd be glad to explain your recommendations. You have essentially organized the meeting around her goals, touched on the details in a succinct, straightforward fashion and provided her with a record to take home. |

| Date | Goal | Action |
|------|------|--------|
| September 3 | Express your belief that investing is necessary, but being an expert is not. (S) | Send Irene a note thanking her for coming in. Tell her you understand that investing can seem like learning a foreign language. Tell her that not everyone needs to be an expert at investing, but they should have an expert taking care of their interests. Finish your note by saying that you are glad she has chosen you as her expert, and that it is a duty you take great pride in. |

| Date | Goal | Action |
|------|------|--------|
| September 8 | Call client to confirm the number of times they would like to meet going forward, typically a low number is desired by Phobics. (A) | You call Irene to mention that everything is going as planned. Say that you understand your profession is something she's not particularly excited about and that you don't want to be a nuisance to her. However, you will touch base regularly and you would like to schedule meeting once a year to review her progress. You suggest a meeting at the end of October, so that she is updated before leaving town to spend time with her daughters over the holidays. She agrees. |

| Date | Goal | Action |
|------|------|--------|
| September 27 | Demonstrate your knowledge of the client's outside interests. (C) | You come across an article on illiteracy in the United States. You write a very brief note saying, "Irene, I came across this article and you came to mind. Thought you might be interested." With this simple action, you communicate that you remember something important to Irene, and reinforce the fact that you care about her and her welfare. |

| Date | Goal | Action |
|------|------|--------|
| October 9 | Frequently inform the client of high quality performance in a very succinct way. (L) | You call Irene and tell her some positive news about the performance of one of her investments. The answering machine picks up, so you leave a brief message telling her that her mutual fund has gained 5% since she got into it (2 months time), and this is more than CDs are paying right now for the whole year. |

| Date | Goal | Action |
|------|------|--------|
| October 11 | Show interest in their lives and/or activities. (S) | You saw a major, new play is coming to town. You cut the ad out of the newspaper and send it to Irene with a short note, saying "Irene, I saw this ad and I remembered your group always see the new plays. If you get the chance, please let me know what you thought. If you like it, my wife and I may go see it." |

| Date | Goal | Action |
|------|------|--------|
| October 18 | Keep your word by doing exactly what you have said to help establish trust. (A), (S) | Call Irene to say that this is the time of year you want to schedule your annual meeting. You say you realize that you just started the account a few months ago and that if she doesn't see any need to meet now, it's okay with you. But you wanted to just check in and offer. Irene declines to meet with you but says she was glad you called and checked in. |

| Date | Goal | Action |
|------|------|--------|
| November 2 | Keep client posted on new developments or information that concerns investments. (C) | The market has recently experienced unusual volatility over the previous couple weeks. In fact, it has been in the news. As an advisor, you know that even hundred point moves in the Dow are small percentages, and perfectly normal. However, you call Irene to reassure her. You tell her that this is normal and that even though the numbers seem high, they are actually small percentage moves. You finish by saying that you are watching the market very closely for her and will contact her if need be. |

| Date | Goal | Action |
|------|------|--------|
| November 26 | Emphasize your technical expertise. (L) | With an Investment Phobic like Irene, you realize you don't want to demonstrate your technical expertise by discussing the efficient frontier. However, you can emphasize your technical expertise in other ways. For example, send Irene an article written about you and your investing approach from the local paper to Irene. She may not understand it all. But, seeing you mentioned in the article will reinforce your own expertise to her. |

| Date | Goal | Action |
|------|------|--------|
| December 8 | Learn a lot about the client's outside interests and tailor them to their financial plan. (C) | You call Irene to tell her that her first check "to help with holiday expenses" has just been sent to her. You say that like you both planned back in August, this is income from one of her investments, designed to give a payout at this time every year to help cover her holiday travel and gifts. You mention it will be larger next year, because it will have a whole year to work for her, and not just four months like this year. |

| Date | Goal | Action |
|------|------|--------|
| December 11 | Send something to the client of a personal nature. (A) | You send Irene a holiday card with a simple note thanking her for the opportunity to be her financial guardian and that you look forward to working on her behalf in the coming year. You close by wishing her happy holidays and to have a nice visit with her daughters. |

## V. Collect Relationship Development Ideas

*Continually upgrade your archive of ideas to use to cement relationships with Investment Phobics.*

To advisors trained in the technical aspects of investing, this relationship model does not come easily. You can help yourself by collecting and referring to ideas you come across. Here is a list of quick and effective ideas that you can use to build relationships with Investment Phobics. Using one or more of these tools on a regular basis will reinforce how much you care about your relationships with your Investment Phobic clients and will demonstrate the high standards of service you provide.

## Exhibit 11.4
### Relationship Development Ideas

*The following is a list of places to start in collecting ideas to deepen your relationship with Phobics. This list is not intended to be exhaustive, it is provided here to get you going.*

➤ Collect and send magazine & newspaper articles about non-financial topics that may be of interest to Investment Phobics. Always be sure to consider each client's individuality when choosing articles. Topics could include:
- Local activities/ clubs for seniors
- Activities to do with grandchildren
- Listing of restaurants/ hotels that have tea socials
- Life changes
- Social Security/ pensions
- Things to do and tips for after retirement
- Travel to client destinations of interest
- Healthcare/ Medicare
- Web sites and organizations specifically for widows/widowers
- How to deal with the loss of family members or friends
- Political issues
- New books due to come out
- Family
- Hobbies—baking, flea markets, crossword puzzles, etc.
- AARP news
- Shows coming to town with performers from their generation

➤ Familiarize yourself with events and activities that your clients individually enjoy and talk about these things with them. You can also talk with them about activities you enjoy. This shows them that you want to build a relationship.

➤ Keep an eye out for events that they can bring their grandchildren to, such as the circus or ice skating shows.

➤ Likewise, keep an eye out for events that your clients might enjoy, such as plays, musicals or movies.

➤ Set up your own seasonal events that your clients can attend, such as holiday socials. You can also set up seasonal events that they can bring their grandchildren to, such as baking Christmas cookies, making Valentines or coloring Easter eggs.

➢ Send out handwritten cards for birthdays and all major holidays.

➢ Send out reassurance letters when there are major turns in the market. This will help to build trust with your clients, and confidence that you are watching out for their interests.

➢ Send out handwritten notes to your clients for no particular reason or call them. This shows them that you care about your relationship with them.

Search out Investment Phobic oriented websites for additional relationship management ideas to brainstorm with your staff. Here are a few examples:

www.grandtimes.com/index.html
A unique weekly Internet magazine for seniors. Controversial, entertaining and informative. Grand Times celebrates life's opportunities and examines life's challenges.

www.aoa.dhhs.gov/default.htm
This is the site for the U.S. Department of Health and Human Services Administration on Aging. It is an excellent source for information on aging and it has a great section on volunteer work for seniors.

www.aarp.com
The AARP site provides links ranging from healthcare, grand parenting and investing money for your grandchildren, travel and leisure, government issues among various other relevant topics.

www.verybestbaking.com
A web site with recipes, baking tips and kitchen talk chat rooms provided by Nestle.

www.justgive.org
Justgive.org is a charitable giving site that lets you search over 850,000 charities and provides ideas for volunteer activities as well.

www.collegeplan529.com/index.htm
A web site devoted to understanding 529 Plans and how to take advantage of them to save for the college education of your family.

www.nationalgeographic.com/traveler
The web site for National Geographic Traveler magazine. This magazine and web site is for the active, curious traveler. One who is more inquisitive than acquisitive. Every department and article is designed to inspire readers to pick up and go—and to provide them with the tools and orientation to do so.

www.grandparents-day.com/index.html
This site is devoted to National Grandparents Day. It provides links to how the day originated, activities to do with grandchildren, contests, projects, etc.

www.grandmasue.com
Gifts, toys, books, artwork and conversation for and about children and grandchildren.

www.aboutseniors.com.au/Hobbies.html
Hobbies, interests, lifestyle, recreation, leisure, cooking, models, card games, board games, trains, collectibles, gardening, genealogy, information for senior citizens.

## VI. Implement Prospecting Program
*Create a reliable pipeline of new, qualified, Phobic clients through a systematic program of referrals from current Phobic clients.*

Investment Phobics' core investing motivation is to feel confident that everything is being taken care of, while avoiding it as much as possible. In fact, people who fit this profile do not like discussing investments at all, and they would never initiate a discussion on investing. The majority of Investment Phobics fall into one of two categories. The first category is widows or widowers who have received the payout from a large life insurance policy. The second category is young adults who have inherited a large sum of money. For our purposes, we will focus on the first group.

When prospecting Investment Phobics, investment representatives should focus on building a personal relationship. The advisor should also concentrate on establishing trust.

In addition to networking through your existing clients you should look for affluent Investment Phobics by networking within your community. To network for Investment Phobic prospects seek:

➤ Community centers with activities like bingo, bridge and dancing
➤ Neighborhood social groups that may have activities like tea socials
➤ Church senior groups
➤ Retirement communities
➤ Activities that their grandchildren may be involved in, such as swimming or piano lessons
➤ Veteran Groups
➤ Elderly singles organizations

## Exhibit 11.5
### Phobic Networking Case Study

*Susan Newman is a Florida based investment advisor who enjoys working with Investment Phobics (most of whom are widows). She prospects these clients by organizing a formal "Sweetest Day" luncheon every year, in which she invites Investment Phobic clients.*

*Ms. Newman identifies potential guests by networking with her current Investment Phobics. Her approach is to invite her current Investment Phobic clients and ask them to invite a friend to her luncheon and tea.*

*Her idea for hosting the event came from the thought that many of these people may be lonely on Valentine's Day. Ms. Newman thought this occasion might be a nice opportunity for them to get together and socialize with others who are in similar situations. It is also a time to build relationships and trust with these clients and prospects, achieving her goal as an investment representative.*

*Once Ms. Newman has her guest list established, she invites the Investment Phobics to the luncheon. She chooses to have a long event to allow time for activities and an additional opportunity for her to get to know the guests in a more intimate setting. Her schedule is built around a luncheon, afternoon games or socializing and ends with tea. During the event, Susan acts as the master of ceremonies. After greeting her guests, she outlines the afternoon's activities. Group introductions start the session, followed by group photos of each table, lunch, a few games & activities, tea and a brief testimonial from a willing attendee about a special need the advisor helped them with, and closes with a raffle with free prizes, like lunch for two. She never discusses investing during the luncheon. To her, the luncheon is about getting to know people, creating relationships and building trust. Only at the end does she offer to meet with them if they need help. That's it.*

The investment representative described in this case study takes the time to make the event something special. Holding the tea in addition to the luncheon, is a key element, but she also does additional things to add to the excitement and pleasure of the day:

➢ She has tasteful, pre-printed nametags that match the original invitations she sent out to the guests.

➢ She makes a welcome gift bag for every guest that includes chocolates, a small silk flower bouquet, a box of assorted herbal teas and a picture frame.

➢ She takes pictures at the luncheon of each table of guests, and she mails the developed pictures to each guest in her follow-up note. The guests can then put their picture of the event in the frame that they were given. She keeps some of the pictures of the event and puts them up in her office, in order to put emphasis on the relationships that she has built with the guests.

This investment representative has been very successful with her luncheon and tea socials. Not only are these events well-planned, creative and exciting, but they are fun for her because she enjoys providing a nice afternoon for her clients and getting to know potential new clients.

## Exhibit 11.6
### Sample Invitation Text:

*(Representative Name) of (Firm Name) Investments cordially invites you to the "Sweetheart" Sweetest Day Luncheon and Tea on (Date) from (Time) to (Time) at (Location). Our party will begin with the luncheon at (Time) in the (Banquet Room Name). After the luncheon, our party will move into the (Other Room Name) for tea and desserts, in order to have an opportunity to mingle and get to know everyone a little more in a relaxed environment. We will have special "sweetheart" gifts for all who attend. This should be a nice opportunity for all of us to socialize and have a nice time with good company. The attire for the event is formal.*

*(RSVP information)*

There are a variety of invitation format ideas you can try. In using any of these, be sure the invitation you send is conservative, straightforward and tasteful:

Use a calligrapher to hand write and address each invitation. Have the name of the event, location and date transferred onto a tea cup and send it in a small box, along with the invitation. Send a formal, elegantly designed invitation, along with a small box of chocolates and a silk flower.

## Exhibit 11.7
### Sample Follow-Up Note:

*Dear (Client Name),*

*I sincerely hope that you enjoyed yourself at the luncheon and tea social last week. (Try to add a personal comment about something that happened at the event or about a conversation that you had with the person). I certainly had a great time, and I realized how infrequently I have the opportunity to meet new people.*

*(Client Name), I am an expert in financial planning. I take pride in watching out for my clients' best interests and taking care of them. If you are interested, I would be more than happy to meet with you at your home or my office (plug in location) to discuss any financial help you may need.*

*I'd like to thank you once again for joining us at the luncheon and tea. I hope you enjoy the enclosed picture of the event! Please feel free to call me if you ever have a question or need any assistance.*

*Sincerely,*
*(Financial Representative Name)*

### Chapter 11 Big Answer:
**It is possible to build a thriving advisory practice around Investment Phobics. You just have to understand their unique needs.**

This chapter lays out a practice business plan you can follow to create a practice around Phobic clients. To do so, you need to think of the Investment Phobic profile described here as a starting point and then tailor your actions to the actual clients you serve. What you need to do is combine the "Financial Motivator" of the Investment Phobic profile with each client's unique personality as you develop your client-centered programs.

This section has walked you through the steps of developing a business around this psychographic profile. Every step has been illustrated with a case study or example. As you can see from all this material, Investment Phobics have very different needs and wants from their financial advisor than Family Steward or any other type of clients do. This chapter outlines a business model built around Investment Phobic clients. It includes an Investment Phobic-specific personal marketing plan for a sample client. Of course, all the examples included here are just that, examples. Each of your Investment Phobic clients has their own individuality.

# Chapter 12
# Independents

> *"He does not possess wealth that allows it to possess him"*
>
> — Benjamin Franklin

## Chapter 12 Critical Question:
## How can I create a practice around Independent-type clients?

Like other clients, Independents have their own unique needs from their financial advisor. If you find that Independent-type clients are a natural focus for your practice, you will want to create a general practice plan around this segment and client-specific marketing plans for your clients who fit the Independent profile. This chapter will help you do both of these things.

## PRACTICE BUSINESS PLAN

### I. Mission/Vision
*Build on current success to become the area advisor of choice for Independent clients. Attain this goals though a focus on relationships, asset capture and client referrals.*

This mission statement communicates an intention to create highly satisfied Independent clients, with the ultimate goal of increasing assets under management and generating more referrals. There is a large body of research that proves the cause and effect relationship that high client satisfaction will lead to more assets and referrals. This is especially the case among Independent clients, who are quick to add assets to advisors they like. They are also responsive to requests to refer friends of theirs to their advisor.

## II. Strategy

*Identify high potential prospects among current clients, focus relationship development efforts on those in order to increase perceived satisfaction. Use the CLAS model to organize these efforts.*

You understand that the more a client is satisfied, the higher the rate of asset capture and the higher the rate of new client referrals. In applying the CLAS model, you will leverage that insight to your advantage. Specifically, you will focus on increasing client satisfaction by using the insights of the financial motivator. By using the proactive planning approach outlined here, you will positively impact each component of the CLAS Client Satisfaction Model for your targeted clients.

Investment performance is important to Independents, but what is even more important to them is their goal of financial and personal independence. As a financial professional, you will do your best to achieve the best in investment performance. But you also recognize that you do not control what the market will do.

On the other hand, you do control what you do. You do control how much time you spend with clients, the kind of attention you give them and what you say to them. This brings us to the relationship factors, or the CLAS model. Independents are very sensitive to the CLAS model, in fact, CLAS relationship factors are 4 times more powerful than investment performance, and they are strong among Independents as well.

"C" refers to client orientation, to a high level of client focus. This means focusing in on what your clients really need and want. "L" refers to advisory leadership, which is to proactively identify important issues and provide solutions to clients. For Independents, this means reinforcing their goal of financial independence. "A" is attending behaviors, and indicates the number of and motivation of client contacts. Independents need periodic contacts to reassure them that you are on top of their account. Finally, "S" refers to shared values and how an advisor shows their trustworthiness and shared value system.

# Exhibit 12.1
## The CLAS Model

| C | Client Orientation | Your level of client focus |
|---|---|---|
| L | Leadership | Proactively identifying important issues and providing solutions |
| A | Attending Behaviors | The number of and motivation for client contacts |
| S | Shared Values | Trustworthiness and sharing of a similar value system |

## III. Target Clients

*Identify target clients for the CLAS strategy based on their overall potential for asset capture and client referral.*

No advisor has the time or resources to practice high-impact relationship management with all of their clients. For this reason, you need to focus on your best clients and/or those clients with significant assets that you might be able to capture. List your top clients who fit the Independent model on a form like the one we have provided below. Then note the current level of assets under management, and what you believe the potential is. Next, rate their satisfaction. This will be your estimate, although you could interview these clients to find out (actually, clients welcome the opportunity to share what is working and what could be improved in your relationship). Next, figure what you could improve their satisfaction level to.

## Exhibit 12.2
### Client Targeting Worksheet

| Client Name | Assets Under Management | Potential AUM | Current Satisfaction | Satisfaction Goal |
|---|---|---|---|---|
| George Young | $50K | Do not know | Good | Improve to very satisfied |
| | | | | |
| | | | | |
| | | | | |
| | | | | |
| | | | | |
| | | | | |
| | | | | |
| | | | | |

Review your chart. Look for patterns. Are there are lot of assets you do not have under management, or do you not know? Do you think your clients are as satisfied as they could possibly be, or (honestly) is there room for improvement? Have you selected the right clients for targeting? If not, revise your list. Once you have the right clients targeted, proceed to the next section to develop a relationship plan for each and every one of these key clients.

## IV. Individual Client Relationship Development Planning

*Create and implement an individual client relationship development plan targeted at each high potential targeted client.*

In this section we will walk you through how to develop such a plan by providing the example of George Young. Keep in mind that this is a general example for an Independent, and real clients will vary somewhat from the model. However, as long as you focus on your clients prime financial type (such as Independent) and take their individuality into account, you will not go wrong.

It is imperative that you understand your client's profile as well as their individuality. Think of the Independent profile as your starting point, and customize your plan to the individual with these directional insights. Combining the "Financial Motivator" of the profiles with each client's unique personality is the essential step necessary for developing successful plans.

To increase satisfaction among Independent clients, an average of 15 contacts must be made over the course of six months. Each contact should be made with a specific goal based on the CLAS model. As you develop your plan, mark each action item with a (C), (L), (A) or (S) to designate which component of CLAS you are impacting. Some action items will impact more than one component of the CLAS Model. The goal is to impact each area three to four times over the six-month plan.

As you think of actions to fill you're your client development plan, keep two other criteria in mind. You want each action to take into account the client's financial motivator (in this case – Independent) and their investment IQ (in this case – average to above average).

## Exhibit 12.3
### Individual Client Relationship Development Plan

**Client name:** George Young

**Background:** George is 41 years old and is a senior executive at a large publishing company. He spends every weekend sailing his boat. He dreams of being able to sail full time by age 50 (you think he could realistically achieve this by age 55). He currently owns an 18-foot boat and he hopes to buy a larger boat that he can use for ocean sailing. George is married and has no children.

**Financial motivator:** Independent

**Investing IQ:** Above average

**Target contacts:** 15

| Date | Goal | Action |
|---|---|---|
| July 1 | Talk about how appealing you think the idea of financial freedom is (S) | It was quite obvious from your recent meeting with George that he was an Independent. You suggest that your next meeting with George should be in a more relaxed environment, instead of in an office setting, so you can get to know each other a little bit better. He insists that you come to his yacht club for lunch. |

| Date | Goal | Action |
|---|---|---|
| July 18 | Express shared values (S) | During lunch at his yacht club, you get George to talk about his sailing adventures. You express to George a little bit about what financial freedom means to you and relate your ideas back to his. You agree that both of you have a dream to be independent. From this meeting you come away with a much clearer idea of what George's dreams are, and you have established that you share those very same values. You both also agree that it is important to put together an appropriate investment plan so he can achieve his goal. |

| Date | Goal | Action |
|---|---|---|
| July 25 | Provide frequent updates on progress toward goal of financial independence (A) | Follow up with George with a phone call thanking him for lunch. Let him know you are beginning to put together an investment plan that you believe will help him reach his dream of personal freedom. You say you would like to schedule a meeting with him to share what you have come up with. He agrees. |

| Date | Goal | Action |
|---|---|---|
| August 9 | Avoid technical discussions irrelevant to the client's goal (C) | You have prepared an investment plan and you present it to George when he comes to your office. You have focused on George's main goal— personal freedom, when you prepared the plan. When you explain the plan to him, you avoid any technical discussions that do not pertain directly to his goal of comfort. |

| Date | Goal | Action |
|---|---|---|
| August 20 | Communicate your understanding of the client's goals (S) | You find an article on sailing in the Caribbean and send it to George with a brief note that says: "Thought of you when I saw this." |

| Date | Goal | Action |
|---|---|---|
| September 3 | Frequent updates on issues related to client's goal (A) | You read an article by recognized authorities that projects the cost of living 30 years in the future. You fax it to your client with a note that says these are some important numbers to be aware of. |

| Date | Goal | Action |
|---|---|---|
| September 8 | Be task driven and focused on the client goal (C) | Select and show an aggressive portfolio of funds, show how the investments can become more conservative as he moves closer to retirement – show the shift in asset allocation parameters. |

| Date | Goal | Action |
|------|------|--------|
| September 27 | Talk about successful experiences in working with similar clients (C) | Call George to tell him you would like to share a success story. Briefly tell him about a client you have who has just retired, and how pleased you are he is now living the life he always wanted, kayaking in the Northwest. Invite George and his wife to a small get-together at your house. |

| Date | Goal | Action |
|------|------|--------|
| October 9 | Show the client you are thinking of them and caring (C) | Have your small get-together. Invite people like George and your recently retired client, as well as people who share the goal of early retirement. Keep bringing the conversation around to retirement issues. |

| Date | Goal | Action |
|------|------|--------|
| October 11 | Call to update the client (A) | Call George to give him a brief update on his account. Point out an area where performance has been strong and connect that performance to George's goal of early retirement. |

| Date | Goal | Action |
|------|------|--------|
| October 18 | Talk about how appealing you think the idea of financial freedom is (S) | Send George an article that you come across about people who retire early and live out their dreams. Attach a handwritten note saying that you read this and think his retirement goal sounds very appealing. |

| Date | Goal | Action |
|------|------|--------|
| November 2 | Open up a discussion on planning needs (A) (L) | Call George to open up a discussion of alternative distribution strategies for his company retirement plans. Explain that there are some alternatives you think he should look at, and the more time he has to evaluate alternatives, the better he will be able to shape his overall plan. You agree on a date a few weeks away. George thanks you for being on top of his situation. |

| Date | Goal | Action |
|------|------|--------|
| November 26 | Show leadership by anticipating client planning and investment needs (L) | Preliminary distribution planning meeting – present scenarios for distribution strategies. You call George to set up a meeting. You tell him he's on track with his goal. However, so that he is financially set through retirement, you tell him that you feel you should meet to discuss retirement distribution planning. You present him with three different distribution strategies. |

| Date | Goal | Action |
|------|------|--------|
| December 8 | Demonstrate your shared value system (S) | You select a card to send to George and clients with similar values and goals. You choose one that features a picture of you and your wife on the golf course. Your handwritten note to George says: "Wishing you your dream for the coming year – this is mine." |

| Date | Goal | Action |
|------|------|--------|
| December 11 | Reinforce your understanding of client goals (C) | You select a special type of gift basket for George – one filled with tropical fruit. Your note says something like, "You'll have this every day, sooner than you think." |

## V. Collect Relationship Development Ideas

*Continually update your portfolio of ideas to use to cement relationships with Independent-type clients.*

Independents seek personal freedom and independence above all else. An investment representative's prospecting strategies should focus on helping the Independent achieve his or her dreams of financial freedom. The advisor should network and become familiar with this profile's activities, hobbies, and goals because these are commonly their motivation for achieving their financial independence.

Stay on the look-out for new ideas to deepen your relationships with your Independent clients. Keep being deliberate about this until it becomes second nature. We know an advisor who keeps a folder of ideas, even classifying them C, L A or S. We have collected a list of quick, effective ideas for you to use to jump-start your thinking.

The key is to stay in contact with your Independent clients. Using these ideas or ones you come up with will reinforce how well you understand the Independents' dreams, and remind your clients of your commitment.

# Exhibit 12.4
## Relationship Development Ideas

Following is a list of suggested ideas for developing relationships with Independent clients. As you become more experienced with this approach, you will develop your own strategies. This list is provided to get you started.

➢ Collect and send newspaper or magazine articles about non-financial topics that may be of interest to Independents. Of course, only send articles to people with that specific interest. Topics could include:

- Suggestions of things to do for those who go into early retirement
- Boating/ sailing
- Biking/ golfing/ skiing
- Travel
- Art shows
- Theater, plays
- Wine tastings

➤ Collect stories of other Independents that describe how they made their dreams come true.

➤ Keep yourself well informed about the activities and interests of your Independent clients so you can talk about them. Perhaps you can invite them to go golfing, biking, etc., with you if you share that interest.

➤ Plan smaller, more intimate events that you can invite your clients to, in smaller groups or one on one. Perhaps invite them to smaller boat outings, out for a cocktail or dinner, etc.

➤ Plan dinners, cocktail parties, etc. for holidays, such as Christmas.

➤ Send them personal notes or make phone calls to them about the status of achieving their individual goals and give them encouragement.

Search out Independent oriented websites for additional relationship management ideas to brainstorm with your staff. Here are a few examples:

www.greatvacationhomes.com
The Great Vacation Homes site is well known for its intelligent search engine. Detailed information is displayed per search assisting renters in quickly finding vacation rentals that meet their vacation needs. You can search the U.S., Europe, South America, Mexico, among many other countries.

### www.retireearlyhomepage.com
This is an online magazine for people who "used to work for a living." This site provides information ranging from safe withdrawal rates, retirement reports, retirement news and has message boards to chat with other early retirees as well.

### www.lgca.com
The leading golf course of America web site guide. This site provides everything from golf course searches, golf news to golf trip packages.

### www.digitalnomad.com
This site logs the travel of an individual's adventures traveling around the world. It includes a journal of where he has been, where he is going next, pictures, among other interesting information.

### www.fishinginternational.com
This site helps you to plan your dream international sport fishing trips, based on what country you want to go to and what kind of fish you want to fish for. It allows you to search the site in English, Spanish and French, and also provides you information for fishing travel consultants.

### www.retirenet.com
An on-line retirement resource, featuring homes, properties, golf course and water front living. Manufactured and site built homes are also available for searching on this site.

### www.ssa.gov/retire2
This Social Security retirement planner site will help you find more information about your Social Security retirement benefits and how they will affect your retirement plans. The site provides interesting information facts you need to know about retiring, as well as retirement calculators and other resources.

### www.bednbreakfastconsult.com
A site to help you plan for opening your own Bed and Breakfast. Helps you with the complete process including the early stages of

Site Selection, Design Planning, and Construction Consulting. It also has sections on Financial Projections (Income and Overhead), Promotion & Advertising, your Marketing Focus, even Room Design and your Inn's Amenities.

http://entrepreneurs.about.com/cs/secondcareer
A site providing information and resources for and about entrepreneurs who are on their second career. These entrepreneurs are usually over the age of 45. The site provides a wide variety of links, including financing, getting started, chat rooms and how to sell a business.

www.travelandleisure.com/travelplanners/index.cfm
A travel and leisure site with the world's best travel destinations. Includes links on weather, currency, maps, safety, etc.

## VI. Implement Prospecting Program

*Proactively cultivate referrals from existing clients. Develop new clients among affinity groups of Independents.*

Your current clients are the best sources of referrals. They know you and your services best. Because of that, they are convincing when they tell others about you. Remember that your current clients will not think about making referrals on their own (they have other things to think about). You need to prompt them, which means ask them. The best time is after you have completed a major piece of work for them, such as a retirement plan or yearly review. You also have to ask for something they can provide. They won't know, off hand, of people they can refer to you. But they will be able to introduce you to people they know who you want to be introduced to. Do your homework. Know their contacts. Know who you want to meet. This will help your clients learn that you do want referrals. That way, if a friend does approach them asking about advisors, they will think of you right away.

Another thing current clients can do is to introduce you to other Independents who share their particular interests. If their dream is boating full time the way George Young's was, they can introduce you to people from their yacht club. If its to follow the sun golfing, they will know other golfers.

You can look for Independents by networking and sponsoring events that connect with their dream of independence. Remember that Independents are working and investing for the day they are free to do anything they want. Accordingly, seek out Independents in seminars or classes where they may be learning the skill or activity they plan to pursue upon retirement. Try looking for prospects at:

➢ Hobbyist groups of almost any kind
➢ Sailing/ yachting clubs and classes
➢ Becoming a chef/ opening a restaurant
➢ Opening a bed and breakfast
➢ Travel groups/ clubs
➢ Ski clubs and groups
➢ Wine tasting/ vineyard cultivation
➢ Bicycling travel groups
➢ Charitable organizations
➢ Golf classes and country clubs

So that you can see these strategies being used, we provide the following case study.

## Exhibit 12.5
### Independent Networking Case Study

*Wayne Bragg is a financial representative in Chicago who is an avid sailor. An Independent type himself, he dreams of the day he can retire to spend more time sailing. He has found he enjoys working with people with similar interests and goals like his own, and for that reason he actively prospects Independent clients*

*Because he has an interest in sailing, he does basic prospecting at a few major boat dealerships. Every year, these boat dealers have cocktail receptions open to customers and current boat owners, displaying the new models for the coming year. To gain access to the event, he offers the dealership a co-payment for the cocktail reception. In return, they agree to allow him to network with attendees, wherein he passes out invitations to an event that he organizes. The event offers attendees the opportunity to have a group lunch with a man who sailed his boat around the world. The lunch is held on a chartered boat, and includes an entertaining presentation on the trip around the world.*

*The man who sailed around the world finishes his presentation by explaining that he became financially independent at the age of 49, allowing him the luxury to pursue his love of sailing full time, fulfilling his dreams. This point is critical because it serves as a convenient segue for the financial representative who sponsored the lunch to offer all attendees the opportunity to develop their own financial plan that may help them achieve their own financial independence.*

*Wayne does not give a presentation on a financial plan during the outing, but merely offers to create a plan for each attendee. At the end of the outing, Wayne gives each guest a tasteful, bound journal. He tells his guests that the purpose of the journal is to write down their personal and financial goals and dreams, as well as to develop a plan toward achieving them. He then tells them that by writing down their goals, they are significantly more likely to achieve them. This gives them encouragement, as well as motivation that they can achieve what they desire.*

By using this prospecting strategy, this investment representative achieves his goal of gaining access to people who have demonstrated a certain amount of financial success. In addition, these people are also likely to be Independents because of their interest in hearing someone speak about living their own dream—achieving financial independence in order to pursue dreams like sailing around the world.

## Exhibit 12.6
### Sample Invitation Text

*You and a guest are cordially invited to a cruise and lunch on (Date & Time) at (Location). Please join me in an afternoon of fun aboard the Resurgent, a 60 foot trawler. The afternoon will start with a cocktail reception and lunch, immediately followed by an entertaining presentation by David Arnman about his trip around the world on his sailboat. We will then have a couple hours of cruising Chicago's shoreline for socializing. I urge you to join us in this rare opportunity to hear firsthand about the fun, excitement and challenge of taking a sailboat around the world.*

*(RSVP info)*

Like the sample, the invitation should be simple, elegant and to the point. You will want to refer to the attraction at the event (man who sailed around the world) to make sure you connect with your Independents along the lines of their particular dream of independence. This way, you are appealing to them with more than just a free lunch and a show. You are sharing a dream of independence with them.

To create added interest, you could try sending the invitation in one of these unusual ways:

➢ Send the invitation in a box along with a small, framed picture of a sailboat on the sea. Attach a note to the picture that says, "Wouldn't you like the freedom to sail around the world one day? Join us to hear from a man that made this dream a reality."

➢ Send the invitation along with a copy of a map of the world with the areas denoted that the man who sailed around the world stopped at during his trip. Enclose with it a note that says, "Where would you stop to visit if you were to sail around the world?" This will enforce the idea in the their minds that it is possible for their dream to come true, too.

## Exhibit 12.7
### Sample Follow-Up Note

Dear (Client Name),

I hope you enjoyed yourself at our yacht outing last week. (Add a personal comment about something that happened during the day). I really enjoyed the opportunity to get out on Lake Michigan and take in the fresh air. We couldn't have asked for better weather! I sincerely hope there will be more opportunities for all of us to get together to take another cruise in the future.

(Client Name), I mentioned during the cruise that I would be happy to create a financial plan to help you achieve your own independence. I would like the opportunity to set up a time to meet with you and discuss a possible plan. My office is (plug in location) or I would be happy to meet with you at your office or home, whatever is most convenient for you. I will call you within the next couple of days to check your availability.

Thanks again for joining us for the yacht cruise. I look forward to speaking with you again soon!

Sincerely,
(Financial Representative)

The sample invitation and follow-up are here as examples. You will tailor them to your own setting, clientele and event. They are here to show you how successful advisors have developed a pipeline of Independent clients for their practices.

## Chapter 12 Big Answer:
*You can create a strong practice around Independent-type clients. It takes discipline and focus to do so, but the rewards are tremendous, especially if you are an Independent yourself.*

This chapter was designed to help you do two things. First, it was written to help you create a general practice plan around this segment and. Second, it shows you how to build client-specific marketing plans for your clients who fit the Independent profile. Like all the other clients, Independents have their own unique needs. If you decide that Independent-type clients are a natural focus for your practice, you will want to use these programs to create a thriving advisor business centered on this segment.

# Chapter 13
# Anonymous

*"The fortune which nobody sees makes a person happy and unenvied."*

— Francis Bacon

### Chapter 13 Critical Question:
### How can I establish and grow a practice built around Anonymous-type clients?

Anonymous clients have their own unique profile. Above all else, they value their privacy and the confidentiality of their information. If you know and respect this, you can become a highly successful advisor to Anonymous clients.

To build a practice around anonymous clients takes care and time, but is well worth it. This chapter outlines a business plan you can use as a take-off point in developing your own practice model. It starts with a mission statement and develops a strategy of relationship enhancement. Most of the chapter is devoted to an example of a six-month client development plan, and to sample prospecting activities. The key, as always, is to start with the financial motivator of the client front and center. In the case of the Anonymous, it is to protect privacy at all times.

## PRACTICE BUSINESS PLAN

### I. Mission/Vision
*Create highly satisfied Anonymous clients in order to increase assets under management and generate client referrals from advisors.*

In addition to providing excellent technical and financial management skills, you will focus on developing your relationships with your Anonymous clients. As you saw from the earlier chapters of this book, research overwhelmingly proves the cause and effect relationship between high satisfaction and more assets under management and client referrals.

There is, however, an important caveat with Anonymous clients. Anonymous clients will rarely refer other clients to you. Recall that they are obsessive about privacy and confidentiality. They simply will not discuss their private financial affairs with others, and so the subject of making a referral will simply never come up.

However, they will confide in their trusted advisors. You can leverage this positive word-of-mouth into other referrals from the same advisor. This is one area where strategic alliances with advisors is critical. There will be more discussion about this later.

## II. Strategy

*Increase Anonymous-type client satisfaction using the insights of their financial motivation. Do so by positively impacting each component of the CLAS Client Satisfaction Model.*

Your strategy will be to structure your practice around delivering against the relationship needs of this segment of clients. Of course, you will continue to do an excellent job of providing investment advisory service. The four components relating to the relationship – the CLAS – actually deliver more value to clients as measured by how much they contribute the probability that the client will add assets to be managed.

For all clients, the CLAS model refers to the way in which you interact with the client to increase their satisfaction with their relationship. In the CLAS model, the "C" refers to client orientation (the amount of focus on the client), the "L" refers to advisory leadership (proactively providing solutions to clients), the "A" refers to attending behaviors (client contact behavior) and the "S" refers to shared values (how an advisor shows their trustworthiness). In general, the "CLAS" portions of the model are 4 times more important than investment performance in producing client satisfaction.

## Exhibit 13.1
### The CLAS Model

| C | Client Orientation | Your level of client focus |
|---|---|---|
| L | Leadership | Proactively identifying important issues and providing solutions |
| A | Attending Behaviors | The number of and motivation for client contacts |
| S | Shared Values | Trustworthiness and sharing of a similar value system |

### III. Target Clients and Advisors

*Identify high-potential Anonymous clients in your current client base for the purpose of asset capture. Review your advisor referral network to determine the advisors you want to build strategic alliances with.*

It isn't possible to boost your client contact time and effort with all your clients. You have to prioritize. You simply do not have the time to practice high-impact relationship management with all of your clients. For this reason, you need to focus on your best clients, which are clients with significant assets that you might be able to capture.

You can easily do this if you list your top clients by assets (remember, they should all by Anonymous-type clients for this purpose). Then fill in your estimate of potential assets available for capture. Next, rank them according to what you think their satisfaction level is — high, average or low. Finally, for each client, decide on what your goal for increasing the satisfaction is, and fill that in.

## Exhibit 13.2
### Client Targeting Worksheet

| Client Name | Assets Under Management | Potential AUM | Current Satisfaction | Satisfaction Goal |
|---|---|---|---|---|
| Dr. Imana | $750K | $750K (estimated) | Not Known | Improve to highly satisfied |
| | | | | |
| | | | | |
| | | | | |
| | | | | |
| | | | | |
| | | | | |
| | | | | |

Once you have completed your listing of Anonymous clients, inspect it. Look for patterns and opportunities. How much do you really know about your client's total assets and the AUM potential that they have for you? Are they really as satisfied as they could be, or do you not know for some of them? This is your time to be as honest as possible.

Revise your notations until they are as accurate as you can make them. Then prioritize your clients in order of their important to you is building up your practice. You will want to focus on your biggest clients, you least satisfied ones and ones with the greatest potential for asset capture.

Most advisors decide to enhance or maintain their current approach with the highly satisfied group, and work on dramatically improving relationships with the average and low groups.

Once you have the right clients targeted, you will want to create a plan for improving their satisfaction with you. In the next section we walk you through the process of creating a client-specific plan.

### IV. Individual Client Relationship Development Planning

What follows in an example of an individual client relationship improvement process. This is a general example for an Anonymous; you will want to adapt the example to your own style and the needs of your individual clients. Always remember that have to understand your client's profile, but also take their individuality into account at all times. Think of the Anonymous profile as your starting point, and customize your plan to the individual with those directional insights. Combining the "Financial Motivator" of the profiles with each client's unique personality is the essential step necessary for success.

In our example, we decided that eight to 10 client contacts over the course of six months would be the target. Anonymous clients like less contact than the other profiles do. The Anonymous require fewer, but more focused, contacts. Each of the following action items will be marked with a (C), (L), (A) or (S) to designate which component of CLAS you are impacting with a specific action item. Some action items will impact more than one component of the CLAS Model. The goal is to impact each area 3 to 4 times over the six-month plan.

### Exhibit 13.3
#### Individual Client Relationship Development Plan

**Client name:** Dr. Carlos Imana

**Background:** He was born in a foreign country and immigrated to the U.S. after graduating from medical school and getting married to a U.S. citizen. Dr. Imana was referred to you by your attorney. He invested $750,000 in treasuries more than a year ago with you. He never discusses himself and does not like being asked questions. He only calls if he absolutely has to (such as when a bond reaches maturity). From time to time, you have suggested that the client invest in some equity funds to help increase his return, but he always declines vehemently.

**Financial Motivator:** Anonymous

**Investment IQ:** Below average

**Target contacts:** 8 to 10

| Date | Goal | Action |
|------|------|--------|
| July 1 | Communicate that you believe privacy is an increasingly important issue (S) | In a meeting with the Doctor, you bring up privacy as an issue in the discussion. You say there is too much personal information readily available through the Internet, and that you should never say something in an e-mail that you wouldn't want to show up in court. Emphasize how disturbing this is to you. Note that because you have expressed how you feel, the client will understand you share the same values. You go on to explain that your firm has many security and privacy features in place to counter this serious issue. |

| Date | Goal | Action |
|------|------|--------|
| July 18 | Discuss your security procedures with the client (L) | Tell the client that anytime he needs to correspond with you that he should always use a certified letter via U.S. mail, not an overnight letter service. The reason is that it is a federal crime to open or tamper with U.S. Mail and that acts as a strong deterrent. You mention that law firms require their clients whom are parties to lawsuits to mail them information the same way. |

| Date | Goal | Action |
|------|------|--------|
| July 25 | Show great attention to client privacy needs (C) | Review some of your security procedures with the Doctor—corporate computer system firewall, your own advanced computer sign-on system, enhanced firewalls in computer systems, use of an ID number system in place of client names on all communications, a secure, locked file cabinet for all client files, etc... |

| Date | Goal | Action |
|------|------|--------|
| August 9 | Tell client about you and your firm's security procedures (L) | You identify an industry or firm-specific article about security measures in the financial services business and set it aside for your Anonymous clients. |

| Date | Goal | Action |
|------|------|--------|
| August 14 | Send investment information in a secure manner (A) | Send the article to the client. Be sure it, and all reports and envelopes are all stamped private and confidential. Have the client's I.D. number on the letter, not their name. |

| Date | Goal | Action |
|------|------|--------|
| September 3 | Mention you like working with clients who understand the importance of information security (S) | You call to be sure the Doctor has the material you sent last week and say how much you enjoy working with clients who share the same values. During the same call, you suggest a meeting and ask the client where he would like to meet. You mention that sometimes your clients like to meet in their own homes or office. You can also meet in your office, which as he knows is very private. The Doctor opts for his office. |

| Date | Goal | Action |
|---|---|---|
| September 8 | Explore client preferences for maintaining privacy (L) | Meet the Doctor in his office to review your plan to increase his return without taking excessive risks. Only after the client enters the room do you remove files from your locked briefcase. The client is never identified in the report, only his I.D. number is used. Every page has a "Confidential" watermark on it. After a thorough discussion, the client agrees to transfer $400,000 into a large cap-value mutual fund. You explain that you see no need to schedule any meetings for the next few months unless a key issue arises. Plus, you mention that when there's no communication, there are no security concerns. He agrees. You tell him you will send confirmation that everything was done properly. |

| Date | Goal | Action |
|---|---|---|
| September 27 | The Anonymous prefer fewer face to face meetings than most clients (A) | Send confirmation of your account transactions by certified mail. Include a note saying that you think you will meet on an "as-need" basis going forward, but that you are immediately available if any issues arise. |

| Date | Goal | Action |
|---|---|---|
| December 27 | Send a holiday card (A) | Be sure the card is simple and discrete. It should feature generic "Holiday Greetings" with your firm name printed on it. You simply want to make the point that you remembered them during the holidays. Handwrite "Personal & Confidential" on the outside of the envelope. |

## V. Collect Relationship Development Ideas

*Constantly increase your knowledge of privacy and security concerns. As appropriate, implement these measures in your practice.*

The following is a list of highly effective ideas that you can use once you have gained Anonymous clients. You can use these to stay connected with them and to convey your priority of confidentiality. Using these tools will reinforce your high standards of service that you practice with your clients.

As you become more practiced and conscious about dealing with Anonymous clients, you will naturally develop your own ideas (and sources for new ideas). The ideas we provide below were culled from advisors who have already implemented practice programs targeted at Anonymous-type clients.

## Exhibit 13.4
### Relationship Development Ideas

You will quickly develop your own ideas for working with you Anonymous clients. Here is a list of ideas to get you started.

- Discuss investments that enable them to preserve their privacy or their assets from taxation. Contact them when there are new opportunities for these investments as well.

- Buy them a document shredder for their home as a "welcome aboard" gift. Make sure it is a cross-cutting shredder and include a note that it is important for them to make sure all of their financial statements and other sensitive documents are disposed of properly to ensure their privacy and protect them from the growing risk of identity theft. A gift of this size (approx. $200) should only be given to appropriate clients.

- Offer to contact their bank, insurance and credit card relationships to ensure that their personal information is not being sold or shared with any other firms for any reason. This is called activating the "opt-out notification". You can inventory their relationships, then have your assistant contact these banks or you can merely suggest they do it themselves to "stay under the radar." For more on this, go to www.privacyrights.org

- When meeting, visit them to ensure confidentiality. Mark all of their folders and documents "confidential." Remember that Anonymous clients will reward their advisors with loyalty who understand them.

- When sending them documents, always use a carrier with instructions that the addressee is the only one permitted to sign for the document. Don't send them faxes or e-mails, they are too accessible to others.

- Keep a locked file cabinet in your office. Unlock and remove your client's file in their presence only. Return it to the cabinet and lock it before they leave.

- Never talk about any personal information about your other clients to an Anonymous. They will worry that you will talk about them to other clients as well.

- When talking to them on the telephone, ask them to hold on for a moment while you shut the door. Also, you should ensure there are no interruptions.

- Ask your client what other practices they would like to see you use to ensure confidentiality. This will impress them that you want to do whatever it takes for them to feel secure.
- Keep an eye out for articles or books that cover secure and confidential investing. Send them a copy of it with a note that says, "I have read this and have gotten some ideas from it. I thought you might like to read it too, and we can discuss it."
- Contact them by phone or note (that will be delivered by carrier) when you have new ideas or updates on their account. Remember that Anonymous clients are willing to concentrate on their portfolio when needed.
- Be careful not to suggest or push investment ideas that are too risky. Remember that Anonymous clients are risk adverse.

The Anonymous are so focused on this one idea you can even develop programs that will interest and appeal to them. We have seen several advisors develop programs on "How To Prevent Identity Theft." Some of the things that affluent people and their advisors need to know to prevent identity theft include:

➢ Shred all credit card, bank and other financial statements.
➢ Always use secure Web sites for Internet purchases.
➢ Do not discuss financial matters on wireless or cellular phones.
➢ Write or call your Motor Vehicles Dept. to have your personal information protected from disclosure.
➢ Do not use your mother's maiden name as a password on your credit cards.
➢ Be wary of anyone calling to "confirm" personal information.
➢ Thoroughly review all bank, credit card and phone statements for unusual activity.
➢ Monitor when new credit cards, checks or ATM cards are being mailed to you and report any that are missing or late.
➢ Close all unused credit and bank accounts, destroy old credit cards and shred unused credit card offers.
➢ Remove your Social Security number from checks, driver's licenses or other identification.
➢ Always ask for the carbon papers of credit purchases.

- ➤ Do not leave outgoing credit card payments in your mailbox.
- ➤ Do not carry your Social Security card in your wallet unless needed.
- ➤ Order your credit report once a year and look for anomalies

Search out Anonymous oriented websites for additional relationship management ideas to brainstorm with your staff. Here are a few examples:

www.anonymizer.com
A free, anonymous web site to keep hackers and advertisers from knowing who you are and what web sites you visit.

www.privacycouncil.com
The Privacy Council is a company devoted to helping businesses of all sizes address the increasingly complex issues surrounding privacy.

www.taxreductioninstitute.com
The Tax Reduction Institute site provides tips on reducing your taxes. Links include articles and tips, tools, a tax IQ test, among various others.

www.epic.org/privacy
The Electronic Privacy Information Center site provides articles and official papers on privacy laws. It includes features on privacy for consumers, travelers, and Internet users.

www.eff.org
This is the site for the Electronic Frontier Foundation, a civil liberties group with a mission to protect privacy, free expression, and public access to information in new media.

www.dol.gov/dol/pwba/public/pubs/protect/guidetoc.htm
Protect your pension is a site put out by the U.S. Department of Labor, Pension and Welfare Benefits Administration. It is a quick reference guide to protecting your pension money.

www.lbl.gov/Education/ELSI/privacy-main.html
With the rapid advances in the computerization of medical data, the question of the protection of medical records privacy has begun to arise. Storing a large amount of sensitive information in a central location (databases) could open the door to "invasion of privacy" issues that were not as common as with the keeping of paper files. This site provides links including who has access to your files, disadvantages of a database, the government's role, etc.

www.ftc.gov/bcp/conline/edcams/kidzprivacy
This site is put out by the U.S. Federal Trade Commission. It is specifically designed to educate kids, parents, and businesses about the privacy rights of children online.

www.aesecurity.com
A&E's Home Security site is a source for do-it-yourself alarm systems, home security systems, and security monitoring.

www.hushmail.com
Looking for the most secure web-based e-mail available? Consider hushmail for the information that is appropriate to e-mail.

www.sia.com/publications/html/online_investing_tips.html
This Securities Industry Association site is designed to assist investors with online trading access. It provides a brief overview of the issues when investing online. Including a Privacy Tool Kit, Professional Conduct Program and Promissory Notes.

## VI. Implement Prospecting Program
*Develop client and advisor relationships to create a stream of new client referrals.*

The core investing motivation for the Anonymous profile is confidentiality about their finances and personal information above all else. Secondarily, they are also quite concerned about the possibility of losing their money.

When investment advisors seek clients from this profile, it is imperative to emphasize that complete client confidentiality is one of the foundations of their business. They also need to convey to the Anonymous client that they truly understand the need for confidentiality when it comes to all financial dealings.

It is important to understand that prospecting the Anonymous profile is very different from prospecting all other profiles. Due to their secretive nature, it would be difficult, if not impossible, for an advisor to prospect in the traditional manner for people in the community who fit the Anonymous profile.

However, there are some approaches that have been successful. Some advisors have placed a discrete ad in the yellow pages emphasizing the confidentiality that their company prides itself on. It is also possible to propose an idea to your local newspaper on a timely topic related to security and confidentiality, such as identity theft. Some newspapers also do profiles on local businesses; it might be possible to develop a piece about your company and the strict security measures that it takes with clients' information. In looking for Anonymous clients, it is crucial to build relationships with other professional advisors (i.e. lawyers, CPAs, insurance agents) because they may refer Anonymous clients that they already work with to you.

In the Exhibit below, we present a case study of an advisor who has targeted Anonymous clients. The case is about Aaron, who is an investment advisor in Arizona. Several years ago he had a computer crisis that changed his thoughts about the importance of security. A computer virus attacked his office's computer system and the result was a shut down of his entire system. Although he was able to recover most of his files, it convinced him that he needed to step up security practices in all aspects of his business. Now, Aaron is very conscious about the need for security and confidentiality in his office. As a result, clients that Aaron would later identify as Anonymous, have become an increasingly important component of his business. He now actively pursues Anonymous clients.

## Exhibit 13.5
### Anonymous Networking Case Study

When Aaron decided to prospect for Anonymous clients, he realized that he wouldn't be able to go directly to the source. He recognized that an Anonymous will never refer another Anonymous client. It is simply not their nature. Instead, his chances for referrals would most likely come from professional advisors who have Anonymous clients of their own.

*With this in mind, Aaron decided to build relationships with other professional advisors, specifically lawyers and accountants. He began by getting introductions to lawyers and CPAs from people he knows. He also looks at local newspaper advertisements, flyers and in the phone book. He then calls the advisors to introduce himself and tells them a little bit about his business. He usually then asks to arrange a time to drop by their office to meet with them in person if the advisor is receptive. During the visit Aaron explains in more detail why he initially called the advisor. He tells them that he enjoys networking with other professionals and that he also likes to refer his clients to advisors he knows when they are in need of other professional service. Aaron does all of these things to work on building relationships with these other advisors with the hope that these other advisors may refer Anonymous clients to him.*

*In order to give these other professional advisors a further reason to refer their clients to him, Aaron also formally invites them to take a tour of his office. During these tours, he points out the important security features of his computer system and office. He also highlights all of the measures he takes with his clients to ensure confidentiality. He offers to work with these other advisors on aspects of their own security systems. After the tour, he arranges to take the professional advisor to lunch in order to build relations and answer any questions they may have about his company and business practices.*

By building relationships and giving these tours to other professional advisors in his community, Aaron has been very successful in getting Anonymous clients via referrals from these advisors. Aaron has also found this prospecting activity to be very rewarding both personally and professionally. The Exhibit below provides an example of an invitation that could be used with an advisor.

## Exhibit 13.6
### Sample Invitation Text

*Dear (Professional advisor name),*

*I know we have had the opportunity to talk a few times regarding my investment approach and philosophy. However, I would like to invite you to take a tour of my office to see how my business works and the security measures that I have in place. Afterwards, I would like to take you to lunch to answer any questions that you may have. I will call you within the next few days to arrange a date that is most convenient for you.*

*Sincerely,*
*(Investment representative name)*

The best way to prepare an invitation for a professional advisor is to have it typed on company letterhead. Consider sending the invitation to the advisor via carrier with instructions that he or she is the only one who can sign for it. This conveys a sense of confidentiality to the advisor. As always, follow up all interactions with a note.

## Exhibit 13.7
### Sample Follow-Up Note

*Dear (Professional advisor name),*

*Thank you for taking the time out of your schedule to review my place of business. I appreciate you letting me talk to you more in depth about my business and the advanced security practices that I follow. You asked me some good questions when we went to lunch, and I am glad I could answer them for you.*

*(Professional advisor name), we are both in services in which the public looks to us for advice and assistance. I want you to know that when my clients look to me for (type of advice he or she specializes in) that I cannot help them with I would feel very comfortable referring them to you. I would also appreciate any referrals that you could guide to me. I hope you left our meeting feeling confident about the service I would provide to any referrals.*

*Please feel free to call me with any questions you may have at any time. Thanks again for joining me last week. I hope to be able to get together again sometime.*

*Sincerely,*
*(Investment Advisor Name)*

The case and samples are provided as illustrations of a client-centered approach. You should adapt them to your personality and situation. However, by looking over a package that is built around one type of client psychology, you can see how much thinking and planning goes into this type of marketing. But it is worth it.

## Chapter 13 Big Answer:
### You can establish and grow a practice built around Anonymous-type clients?

Anonymous clients have their own unique financial motivator and profile. Above all else (above investment return, above other aspects of service), they value the privacy and confidentiality of their information. If you know and respect this, you can become a highly successful advisor to Anonymous clients.

To build a practice around Anonymous clients and their other advisors takes careful planning and execution, but is well worth it. Here we have outlined a business plan, a practice model, a six-month client development plan, and prospecting activities. It is up to you to customize these suggestions to your own practice, and to implement them. Remember to keep the financial motivator of the client front and center — in the case of the Anonymous, it is to protect privacy at all times.

# Chapter 14
# Moguls

*"The only point in making money is*

*you can tell some big shot where to go."*

— Humphrey Bogart

## Chapter 14 Critical Question:
## How can I create a successful practice centered around Mogul clients?

Creating successful practices build around client types with whom you have an especial affinity is the theme of this book. This chapter outlines a practice strategic marketing plan on what to do if you have determined that one of your key client types is Moguls. We start by describing the mission and vision such a practice would have, the client-oriented strategy that you should adopt, and the CLAS model that would orchestrate your actions. We add an approach you could adopt for identifying high potential clients, and a step-by-step approach to creating individual client marketing plans. Sample invitations and follow-up notes are also included to give you concrete examples of this approach.

You, of course, are an individual as are your clients. You will want to customize the approach outlined here, and you should. Each advisor is unique, as are clients. However, never forget that the goal is to address client financial motivators – their real reason for investing. That is why it is vital for you to create a practice business plan built around financial motivators.

# PRACTICE BUSINESS PLAN

## I. Mission/Vision

*Grow the size and production of the practice by becoming the leading advisor to Mogul clients.*

The key to becoming a million-dollar advisor lies in a focus on particular clients that fit your style. In this instance, we are showing how to do this by focusing on Moguls. Paradoxically, you can grow a practice faster by restricting your focus to just a few client types instead of trying to serve all types of clients.

Moguls crave power and acknowledgement of that power by others. One of the elements that make than a useful client type to focus on is that they are quite social and expressive. They know a lot of people. As a result, they are excellent referral sources. Develop a Mogul client well, and you can leverage that client into an ongoing new client pipeline. A great deal of research in the industry has established this cause and effect relationship between highly satisfied clients and growing a practice through referrals.

## II. Strategy

*Increase client satisfaction by applying the CLAS Client Satisfaction Model to individual, high-potential clients.*

Each letter of the CLAS model refers to an aspect of your service that the client values. The four letters all refer to aspect of relationship management. "C" refers to client orientation, to a high level of client focus. This means focusing in on what your clients really need and want. "L" refers to advisory leadership, which is to proactively identify important issues and provide solutions to clients. For Moguls, this means reinforcing their goal of personal power. "A" is attending behaviors, and indicates the number of and motivation of client contacts. Moguls need frequent contacts to reinforce their perception of personal power. Finally, "S" refers to shared values and how an advisor shows their trustworthiness and shared value system.

The value of the CLAS model is that it directs your attention to those aspects of your service that you control. It is hard to have complete control of investment performance because you can't control market volatility. Fortunately, Moguls are especially sensitive to the relationship components of the CLAS model. Overall, the CLAS relationship factors are 4 times more powerful than investment performance, and they are strong among Moguls as well. You control how much time you spend with clients, the kind of attention you give them and what you say to them. Overall, you control what you do in the way of service.

## Exhibit 14.1
### The CLAS Model

| | | |
|---|---|---|
| **C** | **Client Orientation** | Your level of client focus |
| **L** | **Leadership** | Proactively identifying important issues and providing solutions |
| **A** | **Attending Behaviors** | The number of and motivation for client contacts |
| **S** | **Shared Values** | Trustworthiness and sharing of a similar value system |

This is a general example for a Mogul. It is always imperative that you not only understand the client's profile, but also their individuality. Think of the Mogul profile as your starting point, and customize your plan to the individual with those directional insights. You must combine the "Financial Motivator" of the profile with each client's unique personality. This is an essential step necessary for success.

### III. Target Clients
*Focus on your best clients and/or those clients with significant assets that you might be able to capture.*

No advisor has the time or resources to practice high-impact relationship management with all of their clients. Focus is essential. You need to select top clients for targeting with this approach in order for it to pay off. Use the framework below to list your top clients, note the assets that you do manage, and estimate assets you do not manage. Then rate your perception of their current satisfaction level — high, average or low, and think about where you can improve.

## Exhibit 14.2
### Client Targeting Worksheet

| Client Name | Assets Under Management | Potential AUM | Current Satisfaction | Satisfaction Goal |
|---|---|---|---|---|
| James Ascher | $275K | (Short term) assests managed by another advisor, (medium term) 401(k) rollover | Average-Good | Improve to very satisfied |
| | | | | |
| | | | | |
| | | | | |
| | | | | |
| | | | | |
| | | | | |
| | | | | |
| | | | | |
| | | | | |

For most advisors, it is enough to maintain your current approach with the highly satisfied group, and practice high impact relationship management with the average and low groups in order to improve their perceptions of your quality.

To increase (or hold) satisfaction among Moguls, 15 client contacts should be made over the course of six months. Since most advisors make far fewer, you will stand out from the crowd. The important thing is that there be a strategic reason for each contact. In the individual client action plan we lay out below as an example, we have coded each action item with a (C), (L), (A) or (S) to show which component of CLAS is being impacted with a specific action item. Some action items will impact more than one component of the CLAS Model. The goal in the design of this plan is to impact each area 3 to 4 times over the six-month plan.

## IV. Individual Client Relationship Development Planning

*Develop an individual client relationship development plan for each targeted Mogul.*

Developing an individual client development plan is challenging at first. It can even seem a little forced. But if you keep focusing on the twin goals of addressing the client's financial motivator and making a high number of contacts, it will become second nature. To walk you through the process, we have created such a plan for a client example.

The client is a Mogul named James Ascher. Imagine that you met him in his office over a year ago. To get to him, you had to go through three gatekeepers. All of these people referred to him as "Mr. Ascher" (not as "James" or "Jim") and they said it in hushed tones. Upon entering his office, you noticed that he had one picture of his wife and kids on his desk and a wall of photos of himself with various politicians and prominent executives at dinners and golf outings. Another wall held his degrees and various awards.

In the next Exhibit, we outline a relationship development plan built for this Mogul client. It will show how you can think through a sequence of actions that will help clients. Note that the coding of the various actions refers to the CLAS model.

# Exhibit 14.3
## Individual Client Relationship Development Plan

**Client name:** James Ascher

**Background:** Senior Vice President for a large corporation. He's 57 years old, married, three sons, ages 12, 14, 17. You have helped him invest in a mixture of funds, stocks and bonds.

**Financial Motivator:** Mogul

**Investing I.Q.:** Below average

**Target contacts:** 15 contacts over six months

| Date | Goal | Action |
|------|------|--------|
| July 1 | Show that you think their accomplishments are significant (S) | You saw in the newspaper that Mr. Ascher's company reported its 2nd Quarter earnings, and they came out very well. You send him a personal note on your firm's tasteful stationary as an acknowledgement of this fact, and tastefully allude that some credit for these results belongs to him. You close the note by saying that it has been awhile since you have met and that you will call his assistant in a week to schedule an appointment to get his decisions on some of his investments. |

| Date | Goal | Action |
|------|------|--------|
| July 18 | Meetings are organized around decisions they are asked to make (A) | You are able to meet with Mr. Ascher in his office again. You have brought a review of the various investments' performance. All are doing as good or better than their respective benchmarks. You point this out to him and say that it is your recommendation that he build his position in two funds that are poised for growth due to economic conditions. You tell him that you just need his decision on this. He says he wants to think about it and to call him next week. |

| Date | Goal | Action |
|------|------|--------|
| July 25 | Provide immediate follow-up on all requests (A) | You fax Mr. Ascher some favorable performance figures that have developed in your two recommendations during the past week. You mention on your fax the recent uptick in performance, and reiterate your recommendations. You close by saying that you know he is very busy and that you will call in hour to get his decision. When you call his assistant says that Mr. Ascher is too busy to talk but that he received your fax and agrees with your recommendation. He will be sending a check today. You ask his assistant to thank Mr. Ascher and tell him that you think it was a wise decision. |

| Date | Goal | Action |
|------|------|--------|
| August 9 | Make client feel they are working with a top firm in terms of performance & service (L) | You discover a favorable article written about your firm in one of the major business publications. You purchase a copy of the magazine and send it off to your client with a note attached. You write, "I thought you might be interested…This article reviews my firm and our competitors. You'll notice my firm ranks very high on both its service and performance. If there's ever a concern or need you want addressed please don't hesitate to call." |

| Date | Goal | Action |
|------|------|--------|
| August 30 | Demonstrate to the client that they are one of your most important clients (L) | The market has been experiencing some volatility due to an adjusting economic outlook. You call Mr.Ascher to discuss the situation. He's not available so you opt for his voicemail. You say that he may have noticed the recent market volatility. Because he is one of your most important clients you wanted to give him your perspective. You close by saying that it is not urgent, but that you may want to meet to adjust a few things. You offer to put together a list of recommended actions for him to approve. You just need him to give you the word. He calls you back in the evening and leaves you a voicemail saying to put it together and schedule a meeting with his assistant. |

| Date | Goal | Action |
|------|------|--------|
| September 1 | Communicate to the client that the firm's top talent advises on their portfolio (C) | You call Mr. Ascher back to confirm a meeting time for September 9th. You mention that you would normally try to meet sooner. However, you are asking your firm's top equities strategist to meet with you to discuss Mr. Ascher's portfolio and he is in Asia until the end of the week. Mr. Ascher agrees to the 9th in his office after 5:00 PM. |

| Date | Goal | Action |
|------|------|--------|
| September 9 | Create decision points for client to choose among several options (C) | As you discussed with him, due to changing economic conditions, you put together an investment plan that is designed to thrive in this environment. You also provide three fund options for Mr. Ascher to choose from for each of his investment goals. When you meet, you review the various strengths of each fund given the situation. You answer Mr. Ascher's questions along the way, and then ask him for his decision. He says he would like to think it through for a week and to call him then. |

| Date | Goal | Action |
|------|------|--------|
| September 16 | Set up choices for the client, but don't question or second-guess their decisions (S) | You call Mr. Ascher back to discuss your plan. He agrees with two of your recommendations but declines the other, without offering an explanation.You thank him for taking the time to review this material and say you will immediately implement his decisions. |

| Date | Goal | Action |
|------|------|--------|
| October 4 | Respond immediately to client requests and follow-up accordingly (A) | You send Mr. Ascher confirmations of his transactions. You include a note that says, "In our conversation, I received your directions after the close of the market. However, I had our Asian office immediately execute your buy orders to lock in the numbers you approved. Thanks again for your decisions." |

| Date | Goal | Action |
|------|------|--------|
| October 9 | Demonstrate the client's importance to you and your familiarity with them (C) | You send the client a news clipping about a benefit dinner for a local politician. He is one of the politicians Mr. Ascher had his photograph taken with and now hangs in his office. You attach a short note simply saying, "I noticed your photo with (the politician) in your office. I thought you might be interested in this, if you haven't already heard about it." |

| Date | Goal | Action |
|------|------|--------|
| October 30 | Reinforce previous client decisions (A) | Some positive performance news develops from the decisions the client made back in the beginning of October. You send a fax to the client with the increases in percentages and dollars on your company letterhead. The fund he rejected was also up but you purposely make no mention of it so you don't appear to challenge the client's authority. |

| Date | Goal | Action |
|------|------|--------|
| November 2 | Address the client's needs thoroughly (C) | You call the client and mention that your firm is currently in the process of doing an asset protection review for its major clients. Mr. Ascher is one of them. You say that affluent and prominent clients tend to be magnets for lawsuits, and that if he'd like, you can do a complete review of all his assets from his home to his portfolio to determine his level of vulnerability, if any. You can then review this material with your expert (internal or external) to determine any required preventive measures. The client agrees and you arrange for the necessary information to be sent to you. You schedule a review for November 24th. |

| Date | Goal | Action |
|------|------|--------|
| November 24 | Reinforce to the client that they are in control at all times (C) | You present your liability review to the client to show them what assets could be lost in the event of a lawsuit. You review several options with the client including the purchase of a PLUP (Personal Liability Umbrella Policy), which acts as a buffer against lawsuits. The client thanks you for the review and says he wants to get a PLUP. You refer him to a reliable and qualified agent to provide the policy, since this is not part of your product mix. You tell him that the agent will call tomorrow to arrange a policy. You close by saying that even though prominent people may be attractive targets for such problems, they are also in a position to do something about it. |

| Date | Goal | Action |
|------|------|--------|
| December 8 | Show that you think their accomplishments are significant (S) | Send the client a holiday card. It should be a simple, elegant design. Include a note saying that you think they have made some excellent decisions this year and it shows in their portfolio. Close by saying you look forward to working for them in the coming year. |

| Date | Goal | Action |
|------|------|--------|
| December 11 | Demonstrate to the client that they are one of your most important clients (L) | You send a gift to the client that demonstrates they are one of your top clients. You also send Mr. Ascher a package of gourmet foods with two tickets to your firm's skybox seats for the local NBA team. You enclose a note saying, "My firm is offering tickets to its skybox for its top clientele. I'll see you at the game. Happy Holidays." |

## V. Collect Relationship Development Ideas

*Identify and use ideas for developing your relationships with Moguls.*

As you get used to this system, you will be alert to any new ideas you could use in this relationship development system. At the beginning, you should develop a habit of collecting ideas and referring to your file. We know at least one advisor who tears out articles to keep in a file. He writes a C,L,A or S on each so he can find a suitable idea quickly.

## Exhibit 14.4
### Relationship Development Ideas

The following is a list of quick and effective ideas that you can use to maintain and/or improve your relationships with your Mogul clients. Using these tools will act as a reminder of your commitment to serve your clients.

➢ Call or write letters to congratulate your Mogul clients when you know of awards they've received or accomplishments they have made. Remember that Moguls love to be recognized for their accomplishments.

➢ Give your Mogul clients a gift of customized stationery for their personal correspondence. Such a unique and prestigious gift makes an extraordinary impact with status conscious moguls. This can be easily completed by contracting a company that specializes in this type of work. One such company is www.cranes.com and you can find others if you search for "fine stationary".

➢ Send them articles from newspapers or magazines that are about non-financial topics that may be of interest to them. Example topics could include:

- Local politicians
- A listing of local hangouts of politicians, corporate heavyweights, etc.
- Upcoming important benefits, charities, etc.
- Write ups about benefits, political dinners, etc. that were

in town or that they may have attended
- Hot travel destinations of the powerful and elite
- Powerful social figures
- CEOs, CFOs, COOs
- Listings or write ups of exclusive conferences
- Write ups about recognition that people they admire or know have received
- Write ups about any recognition they've received

➢ Set up seasonal, exclusive dinners or cocktail parties, inviting all of your clients who are powerful, social figures, politicians, as well as other powerful and famous people you may know.

➢ Keep an eye out for tickets and invitations to invite your Mogul clients to, such as political dinners, benefits, charities, black-tie events, even openings of shows or art galleries.

➢ Send them articles or books about investing approaches of powerful or wealthy people. Include a note that says, "We may want to consider this. Let me know if you are interested."

➢ Invite them out individually to exclusive restaurants, bars, etc., patronized by powerful people.

➢ Always introduce them or tell them about new powerful clients you or your firm has. Also tell them about or introduce them to powerful people you have met.

➢ Send them personal letters about the latest accomplishments of your company, and remember that presentation is very important to Moguls.

➢ Emphasize the prestigious name and/or clientele of your firm.

Search out Mogul oriented websites for additional relationship management ideas to brainstorm with your staff. Here are a few examples:

www.businessweek.com/bizbooks
*Business Week*'s site for business book reviews. You can search archives, best sellers and even read book chapters.

www.politics.com

Politics.com is a web site devoted solely to political news. It includes links for news, editorial, discussion, polls, rants and gossip.

www.forbes.com

Forbes.com is the "homepage for the world's business leaders." *Forbes* site has links to business conferences, *Forbes* magazine, newsletters, among various other business topics of interest.

www.echaritygolf.com

eCharityGolf.com provides professional service packages for charity golf events. It has listings for tournaments taking place all over the country for various charitable causes. You can participate, sponsor or volunteer.

http://conferences.businessweek.com

*BusinessWeek's* listing of unparalleled executive events –covering the most salient issues and themes in business, technology, and economics today. Exclusive forums feature the sharpest minds in the corporate, government, and academic worlds and deliver the kind of business acuity that attendees can translate into bottom-line success. Includes forums for CEOs, CFOs, and CIOs.

http://tsn.sportingnews.com/features/powerful

A listing of the 100 most powerful people in sports.

www.tlelitetraveler.com

Travel and Leisure Elite Traveler's site boasts the world's best vacation packages, exclusively for T+L Elite Traveler members.

www.summary.com

A site of summaries of the best business books, in print, audio and electronic formats, on management methods, personal skills, sales and marketing, business trends and strategies, customer service, leadership, the Internet, entrepreneurship and more.

www.topperformancecoaching.com
Top Performance and its web site is devoted to coaching CEOs, senior level managers, successful entrepreneurs, professional athletes, and high profile artists, musicians, and writers with demanding time constraints, and uncontested agendas.

www.time.com/time/2001/influentials
TIME and CNN's collaboration of the 20 most influential global executives.

## VI. Implement Prospecting Program
*Direct the future flow of new clients by consistently prospecting through client networks.*

In working with the affluent, mass market or undirected marketing efforts simply are ineffective. The affluent simply do not find their investment advisors by responding to direct mail or advertising. Wealthy people do find advisors through referrals from other clients and advisors. Word-of-mouth recommendations bring people to advisors.

Therefore, the very best prospecting you can do is to make your current clients so satisfied they are delighted to recommend you to their friends and associates.

In addition to unsought recommendations, top advisors are also proactive in asking their clients for referrals. The most effective recommendation s a personal introduction and endorsement. In the relationship development plan above, you will note that quite a few social events were included. Such activities make introduction easy.

It is also possible to prospect this profile through networking more generally. In prospecting this profile, investment advisors should keep in mind that presentation is an important element to Moguls. Advisors need to convey that they understand the importance of influence and power to Moguls. It is a wise idea for investment advisors to drop a few names of political or social power figures when prospecting these profiles.

Look for Moguls by networking within your community in the following areas:

➢ Political fund-raising events
➢ Political debates
➢ Political party groups at local, state and national levels
➢ Local hangouts of politicians, corporate heavyweights, etc.
➢ Exclusive conferences
➢ Large benefit and charity dinners
➢ Directors of community organizations
➢ Award banquets

Prospecting and new account generation is one of the more frustrating parts of the advisory business. Here is a case study of how one advisor created a process that has been very effective for him.

## Exhibit 14.5
### Mogul Networking Case Study

Don is an investment advisor in Texas who has developed a specialized game plan for networking with Moguls. Don particularly likes working with Mogul clients, and is glad to note that one in ten high net worth clients fit the Mogul profile. In developing his strategy, he observed his Mogul clients' needs to connect with "affluential" people. He saw that they seem to regard their wealth as a gateway to community power. He found that one particular Mogul client of his talked at length about local and state issues.

Don decided to call a friend who worked for the political party that this client belonged to, with the intent to learn about upcoming fund-raising events. Don's friend also agreed to arrange an introduction between the client and a prominent candidate at an upcoming fund-raiser. Don purchased three tickets to the fund-raiser and called the Mogul client to invite him and a guest to the event. The client agreed.

Don said he couldn't have been more pleased with the way the fund-raiser worked out. Although his client and the candidate only spoke for five minutes before the event began, the client was clearly pleased to have the opportunity to voice his support and opinions. Don also noticed his client enjoyed the ambiance of the fund-raiser, and was impressed by the connections Don had.

*The introduction seemed to energize his client and stimulated an evening of involved political discussion. It also helped Don figure out other issues that were near and dear to his client's heart — education and downtown development. Don would later make it a habit to discuss issues in the local news with this Mogul client, as well as with other Mogul clients of his.*

The case shows you how this kind of networking can create a referral pipeline. In arranging for this event, Don recognized and appealed to his client's desire to connect to people on issues of power and influence. Don also benefited by getting to know his client better. An unintended additional benefit was that the guest that his client brought along was herself a successful consultant, and subsequently sought out Don's advice on some tax issues. She later became a client.

Since the first time he used this approach, Don has made it a practice to do several each year. He keeps the outings very small (just one client and the guest) because Mogul clients should be treated as important and powerful people, deserving of their advisor's undivided attention.

The Exhibit below provides you with an example of how you might invite a client to an event such as this. Hand writing the invitation on your company letterhead is the best idea for the presentation of any invitation to a Mogul client. The handwritten note shows personal attention and using the company letterhead highlights the prestige of your company.

Send the invitation via messenger to the client or prospect's office. Doing this will demonstrate attention and intimacy to the Mogul. Sending an article that previews the event is also a good idea because it puts emphasis on the importance of the event.

## Exhibit 14.6
### Sample Invitation Text

*Dear (Client or prospect name),*

Enclosed please find an invitation to attend the (Name of fund-raiser) on (Date) with me. I have also enclosed an article from (Name of newspaper) that previews the fund-raiser and the politicians that will be attending. We will be taking a limousine to the event and you will be picked up at your home at (Time).

*I am looking forward to attending, and I hope that you are as well.*

*Sincerely,*
*(Name of Financial Representative Name)*

After the event, there is another natural opportunity to have another contact with the client. You should send a follow-up note. Once again, it is a good idea to do handwritten thank you notes. Doing this shows personal attention. The best idea for presentation again, is to use company letterhead to reiterate the prestige of your company in the Mogul's mind.

## Exhibit 14.7
### Sample Follow-Up Note Text
*Dear (Client Name),*

*I sincerely hope that you enjoyed yourself at the fund-raiser last week.*

*(Add a personal comment about something that happened during the evening). I know that I had a good time and was very interested in hearing (Name of politician)'s views about (Topic that you know the client was interested in too). I hope there will be an opportunity for us to attend a similar event again sometime.*

*(Client name), I would like to offer my assistance to you if there are any investment decisions you are currently making or plan to make in the future. My office is (Location) or I would be happy to meet with you at your office or home.*

*Thanks again for attending the fund-raiser. I look forward to talking to you again soon.*

*Sincerely,*
*(Financial Representative Name)*

All of the material has been provided to you as examples and illustrations. You will want to customize all of these materials to your own practice and clients.

## Chapter 14 Big Answer:
### Moguls are an attractive segment to build a practice around.

Because Moguls account for one in ten affluent investors, they are well networked and they control significant assets. They respond well to advisors who understand and work with their primary financial motivator – power. You can build a highly successful practice around Moguls by leveraging the Mogul relationships you already have and by strategically seeking new Mogul clients through the kind of prospecting we describe here.

# Chapter 15
# VIPs

*"He Who Dies with the Most Toys Wins"*

— Unknown

## *Chapter 15 Critical Question:*
## *How can I establish and grow a practice built around VIP clients?*

The key to establishing and growing a practice built around VIP clients is to start with the financial motivator of the VIP client front and center. In the case of VIPs, it is to support them in increasing their status and prestige.

This chapter outlines a business plan you can use as a take-off point in developing your own practice model for a VIP-centered practice. It starts with a mission statement and develops a strategy of relationship enhancement. An example of a six-month VIP client development plan, and suggested prospecting activities comprise most of the chapter.

To build a practice around VIP clients takes care and time, but this effort pays off. VIP clients have their own unique profile. Above all else, they value status and prestige. If you understand that they amass money and invest it in order to enhance their status and prestige, you can become a highly successful advisor to VIP clients.

## PRACTICE BUSINESS PLAN

### *I. Mission/Vision*
*Build a successful practice by increasing assets under management and generating more referrals by creating highly satisfied VIP clients.*

The theme of this book is that wealth management practices can be grown organically through client satisfaction. The reason is that all the research we have conducted over decades proves that among affluent clients, creating high satisfaction leads to more assets and referrals. Our research also shows that many of the usual forms of promoting a practice simply do not work with affluent clients. Cold calling, direct mail, seminar selling, advertising and the like simply are unproductive in attracting new affluent clients or boosting asset capture rates. The only thing that does work is personal networking. The most efficient and effective form of personal networking is leveraging high client satisfaction.

## II. Strategy

*Increase VIP client satisfaction by focusing on their financial motivation. Do so by systematically and positively impacting each component of the CLAS Client Satisfaction Model.*

Our recommendation is that you should structure your practice around delivering against the relationship needs of VIP clients. Continue to do an excellent job of providing investment advisory services. The four relationship components – the CLAS model – actually deliver more value to clients as measured by how much they increase the probability that clients will refer other people to you and that they will add assets to be managed.

For VIP clients, the CLAS model refers to the way in which you interact with them in order to increase their satisfaction with you and your services. In the CLAS model, the "C" refers to client orientation (the amount of focus on the VIP client), the "L" refers to advisory leadership (proactively providing solutions to VIP clients), the "A" refers to attending behaviors (contacting VIPs) and the "S" refers to shared values (how an advisor shows their trustworthiness to VIPs). In general, the "CLAS" portions of the model are 4 times more important than investment performance in producing client satisfaction.

The implication is that if you focus on satisfaction, clients will stick with you even if the market creates poor investment performance. Again, the research bears this out.

## Exhibit 15.1
### The CLAS Model

| C | Client Orientation | Your level of client focus |
|---|---|---|
| L | Leadership | Proactively identifying important issues and providing solutions |
| A | Attending Behaviors | The number of and motivation for client contacts |
| S | Shared Values | Trustworthiness and sharing of a similar value system |

### III. Target Clients

*Identify high-potential VIP clients in your current client base for the purpose of asset capture and developing referrals.*

As a busy practice manager, you need to manage your time. Creating satisfied clients takes more time per client. You need to create priorities because it is not possible to boost your client contact time and effort with all your clients. You simply do not have the time to practice high-impact relationship management with all of your VIP clients. For this reason, you need to focus on your best clients, which are the clients with significant assets that you might be able to capture.

You can easily do this if you list your VIP clients. Then select just your top VIP clients, the ones with the most potential for asset capture or client referral. You can use the worksheet below for this purpose. Fill in your estimate of potential assets available for capture and rank them according to what you think their current satisfaction level is — high, medium or low. Finally, for each client, decide on what your goal for increasing the satisfaction is, and fill that in.

## Exhibit 15.2
### Client Targeting Worksheet

| Client Name | Assets Under Management | Potential AUM | Current Satisfaction | Satisfaction Goal |
|---|---|---|---|---|
| Trevor Lawrence | $135K | $65K | Low-medium | Improve to highly satisfied |
| | | | | |
| | | | | |
| | | | | |
| | | | | |
| | | | | |
| | | | | |
| | | | | |
| | | | | |

Once you have completed your chart, look it over. Especially, look for patterns. Are there are lot of assets you do not have under management, or do you not know? Do you think your VIP clients are as satisfied as they could possibly be, or might there be room for improvement? Have you selected the right clients for targeting? If not, revise your list. Once you have the right clients targeted, proceed to the next section to develop a relationship plan for each and every one of these key VIP clients.

### IV: Individual Client Relationship Development Planning

*Create and implement an individual VIP client relationship development plan targeted at each high potential targeted client.*

It is easier to understand how to create an individual client relationship by working through an example. In this section we will walk you through how to develop such a plan by using an example of Trevor Lawrence. Remember that that this is a general example for a VIP, and your real clients will have their own unique needs. However, as long as you focus on your clients' prime financial motivator (such as VIP) and take their individuality into account, you will not go wrong.

It is imperative that you understand your VIP client's profile as well as their individuality. Think of the VIP profile as your starting point, and customize your plan to the individual with these directional insights. Combining the "Financial Motivator" of the profiles with each client's unique personality is the essential step necessary for developing successful plans.

To increase satisfaction among VIP clients, an average of 15 contacts must be made over the course of six months. As you plan each contact, think of a specific goal based on the CLAS model. As you continue to develop your plan, mark each action item with a (C), (L), (A) or (S) to remind yourself of which component of CLAS you are impacting. Some action items will impact more than one component of the CLAS Model. Your goal should be to impact each area three to four times over the six-month plan.

As you think of actions to fill out your VIP client development plan, keep two other criteria in mind. You want your every action to address the VIP client's financial motivator and their investment IQ (in this case – average to above average).

Trevor always insists on the best. The priority he places on lifestyle spending and on being associated with celebrities and important people enables you to easily classify Trevor as a VIP.

## Exhibit 15.3
### Individual Client Relationship Development Plan
**Client name:** Trevor Lawrence
**Background:** Trevor is married and has two children, both in private schools. His corner office is expensively decorated. It is clear he is an avid golfer from the items you see around his office. Trevor is expensively dressed and very well-groomed. He has a wall of photos of himself with celebrities.
**Financial motivator:** VIP
**Investing IQ:** Average
**Target contacts:** 15

| Date | Goal | Action |
|------|------|--------|
| July 1 | Provide first class treatment. Talk about highly visible people in the community (C), (S) | Your firm has season tickets to the local minor league baseball team, but you know just a night at the game isn't Trevor's style. As a VIP, he will want something more. You decide on an elegant, but casual dinner before the game and carry in gourmet treats to share during the game. You know someone who knows the team manager, who was a famous player in his day. You are able to set up a meeting between Trevor and the manager after the game, and take a photo. |

| Date | Goal | Action |
|------|------|--------|
| July 18 | Reinforce appreciation of highly visible people in the community (S) | Have the photo blown up to the size of Trevor's other pictures, place it in a nice frame and send it over to his office with a personal note. |

| Date | Goal | Action |
|------|------|--------|
| July 25 | Schedule frequent meetings to address their ego needs (A) | You know Trevor and his family went to Hilton Head for their summer vacation and that he enjoyed the golfing there. You call Trevor and ask him to join you at the new Tuscan restaurant that just opened to tell you about his trip. |

| Date | Goal | Action |
|------|------|--------|
| July 30 | Make them feel as though they are in the same class as celebrity clients. Provide first class treatment (C), (L) | At the restaurant, you get him talking about golfing and the summer, and ask if he ever considered buying a spot in a gated community or resort area. You tell him a few stories of highly visible people you know who have bought vacation homes in wonderful places. VIPs like Trevor like to talk about possessions and real estate with people who share their values. |

| Date | Goal | Action |
|------|------|--------|
| August 9 | Give them the sense that many people are involved on their behalf (C) | Schedule a meeting with Trevor at your country club, and have the chef come out to meet Trevor. VIPs like Trevor like to feel that they are getting special treatment. You bring along some timelines you have worked up, and explain the nature of the data you will need from him. You think he has assets in other financial advisors' firms, but this gives you a great opportunity to find out for sure. |

| Date | Goal | Action |
|------|------|--------|
| September 3 | Stress the sterling image of the firm. Give them the sense that many people are involved on their behalf (C), (L) | Send Trevor a copy of the new brochure from your firm. In your cover note, point out the people and departments who are backing him up technically on his account. |

| Date | Goal | Action |
|------|------|--------|
| September 8 | Schedule frequent meetings to address their ego need (A) | Call Trevor about a meeting you would like him to have with the Regional Vice President of your firm. |

| Date | Goal | Action |
|------|------|--------|
| September 27 | Insure meeting content is not exceedingly challenging. Provide first class treatment (C) | Hold the meeting with the Regional VP in your firm's board room. Position the meeting as an executive briefing on broad financial trends, and avoid getting into detailed technical issues. |

| Date | Goal | Action |
|------|------|--------|
| September 30 | Talk about highly visible people in your firm or community (S) | Call Trevor to follow-up on the meeting with the Regional VP. Mention that the Regional VP wanted you to thank him for coming in to talk with him. |

| Date | Goal | Action |
|------|------|--------|
| October 9 | Provide first class treatment ( C) | Invite Trevor and his wife out for dinner, preferably at a newly opened "hot" spot. |

| Date | Goal | Action |
|------|------|--------|
| October 11 | Schedule frequent meetings. Insure meeting content is not exceedingly challenging. Make them feel as though they are in the same class as celebrity clients (L), (A) | In the elegant and quiet restaurant you have selected, you talk about some of the topics you have already established in common with Trevor; the vacation house, good restaurants, golfing, kids, schools. You talk about some of the celebrity clients of the firm and mention the types of investments you are currently recommending to them. Ask Trevor if he might be interested enough to have you call him. |

| Date | Goal | Action |
|------|------|--------|
| October 12 | Make them feel as though they are in the same class as celebrity clients (L) | Call Trevor to recommend the new fund you were talking about last night. He is interested, and he messengers over a check for $40,000. |

| Date | Goal | Action |
|------|------|--------|
| October 13 | Give the impression that many people are involved on their behalf (C) | Call and say the trade has been made. Mention that the other clients you talked about made the same move. You assure Trevor he is in good company. |

| Date | Goal | Action |
|------|------|--------|
| November 5 | Stress sterling image of the firm (L) | Send a newspaper clipping that mentions the firm. VIPs like Trevor enjoy being associated with a prestigious firm. This reinforces their positive impression of the firm. |

| Date | Goal | Action |
|------|------|--------|
| December 8 | Demonstrate many people working on client behalf (C) | Send out a holiday card to Trevor and your other VIP clients. Consider cards from museums or have a card custom printed. Be sure it is expensive and of high quality. Sign it with a fountain pen, "Wishing you the very best in life for the New Year." Have a few other people from the firm who you have introduced to Trevor, like the Regional Vice President, sign the card as well. |

| Date | Goal | Action |
|------|------|--------|
| December 11 | Send the client your annual holiday gift (A) | Send the client a holiday gift. This gift can be the same as you send to others but customize it to your VIPs. For example, if you send a fruit basket, make sure it is elegantly wrapped and presented, and tuck in a pair of grape scissors. Your note can say something like "Let's celebrate the best things in life this year." Such sentiments reinforce to a VIP client that you, too, enjoy the good life. |

### V. Collect Relationship Development Ideas

Continually update your portfolio of ideas to use to cement relationships with VIP clients.

VIPs want status, prestige and the good life. They like "toys" and the ability to buy them. Your strategy at all times is to mirror this vale set with your VIP clients. We have suggested many ideas in the sample six-month client development plan, but you should seek out new ideas to deepen your relationships with your VIP clients. Keep being deliberate about this until it becomes second nature. We know an advisor who keeps a folder of ideas, even classifying them C, L A or S.

## Exhibit 15.4

### Relationship Development Ideas

The following is a list of quick and effective ideas that you can use to stay connected with your VIP clients. Using one or more of these ideas on a regular basis will reinforce how well you understand your VIP clients' desire for prestige and will also act as a reminder of your commitment to service.

➢ Collect and send magazine or newspaper articles about non-financial topics that may be of interest to your VIP clients. Topics could include:

- Large benefit events in town
- Exclusive shows/plays coming to town
- Fine dining restaurant/exclusive bar and cigar bar openings
- Listings of the most exclusive, local fine dining restaurants
- Hobbies, antiques or collectibles
- Antique shows coming to town
- Celebrities coming to town
- Write-ups of celebrities they admire
- Exclusive vacationing destinations
- Exclusive homes and vacation homes
- The latest, most expensive cars
- Car or boat shows coming to town
- Latest technology, gadgets, watches

➤ Keep an eye out for tickets and invitations to openings of high-profile shows, plays, musicals, etc., as well as wine tastings and fine dining restaurant openings that your clients may enjoy attending.

➤ Find out what your VIPs' hobbies are and what collections interest them. Invite them to go to collectible shows with you. Show them your own collections.

➤ Try to arrange an introduction with them and any celebrity clients you have. Share with them what investments the celebrity clients have.

➤ Call them or write them a personal letter when new, exclusive investments or private equities come out.

➤ Call or write them a letter to discuss ideas that may appeal to them, like creating a private foundation in their name or sponsoring a large benefit and having their name in print inside of the program.

Search out VIP oriented websites for additional relationship management ideas to brainstorm with your staff. Here are a few examples:

www.worldartantiques.com
An international listing of art and antiques dealers, museums and auction houses. The World of Art & Antiques is an online gallery

featuring works by artists and artisans, along with antiques and collectibles of world wide age and origin.

www.usachefs.com
A guide to fine dining with menus, recipes, and food photography from top chefs in major cities from New York to San Francisco.

www.primetickets.com
A site that specializes in obtaining premium, hard-to-get, sold-out tickets for Broadway shows and events.

www.slh.com
A guide to small luxury hotels of the world, including resort hotels, historic châteaux, and country houses throughout the world.

www.kruseinternational.com
Kruse International's site, one of the world's leading auction firms and the largest collector car auction company, allows you to browse available cars and view upcoming auctions.

www.sharperimage.com
Sharper Image's site offers an assortment of products in the electronics, recreation and fitness, personal care, houseware, travel, toy, gift, and other categories.

www.thecelebritycafé.com
A celebrity insight web site featuring interviews with bands, authors, actors, super-models, musicians, and other celebrities.

www.world-world.com
A site that lists exclusive apartments, condos, homes, and villas for rent directly from the owners in Europe, Australia, and the Americas.

www.finertimes.com
Finer Times Vintage Wrist Watches sells and purchases vintage and fine American and European watches.

<u>www.clubsites.com</u>
A site listing golf, country, yacht, city, tennis, and social clubs throughout America.

## VI: Implement Prospecting Program

Proactively cultivate referrals from existing VIP clients. Develop new clients among affinity groups of VIPs.

The core investing motivations for VIPs are to receive social recognition and prestige. To this group, investing is a means of keeping score with other affluent people.

Your current VIP clients are the best sources of referrals to other VIPs. Current VIP clients know you and your services well, and so they are very convincing when they tell others about you. Of course, your current clients will not think about making referrals on their own (they have other things to think about). You need to ask them for referrals. Wait until after you have completed a major piece of work for them, or had a success. You also have to ask for something they can provide. They won't know, off hand, of people they can refer to you. But they will be able to introduce you to people they know who you want to be introduced to. Do your homework. Know their contacts. Know who you want to meet. This will help your clients learn that you do want referrals. That way, if a friend does approach them asking about advisors, they will think of you right away.

Keep in mind that VIP clients can introduce you to other VIPs who share their values and interests. VIPs are generally gregarious and well networked. Look for VIPs by leveraging your VIP client's networks. Since VIPs like to acquire and display tangible symbols of success, you know they will concentrate at events like antique auctions, boat shows and wine tastings.

When prospecting this profile, advisors should focus on communicating the prestige of their firm. Advisors might also mention various famous clients that you or your firm have accounts with. Relay to them that you understand that money is the means to their ends, like a yacht or a vacation home. Try prospecting for VIPs at the events you are attending with your clients, events such as gallery openings, charity benefits, country clubs and the like.

We can show you how this technique of VIP focused networking works by providing an example or case study.

## *Exhibit 15.5*
### *VIP Networking Case Study*

*Craig is an investment representative in New York that enjoys working with VIPs and is a VIP himself. He prospects for VIP clients through his current clients. He has connections in the theater industry and makes use of them by reserving a block of tickets to a new (and hot) play or musical or to an opening night. He invites current VIP clients to the show, and asks them if they know of any friends who might enjoy the show as well. He had found that VIP clients tend to know VIPs. Once Craig has put his guest list together, he invites his clients and prospects to a formal dinner at an exclusive restaurant near the theatre.*

Craig takes the time to make the event very special. Taking the guests to an exclusive restaurant where celebrities are likely to be seen is key, but he also does other things to add to the prestige of the evening:

➢ *He arranges for a local celebrity (a radio personality) that is a client of his to stop by the table during dinner to converse with his guests and to give Craig a plug.*

➢ *While the celebrity is conversing with the guests, Craig snaps a few photos. He sends a copy of the photo to each guest in the thank you note he sends out after the event. Remember that most VIPs like to hang pictures around their office of themselves with celebrities. Craig also hangs a copy of the photo up in his office, along with all of the other photos he has of himself and his clients with celebrities. This always gets the attention of VIP clients and prospects in his office.*

➤ *He also has programs for the show in advance to give to the guests at the dinner. This helps build the excitement and anticipation.*

Craig's program has been very successful. Some of his VIP clients look forward to being invited every year. They appreciate the opportunity to see a show everyone is talking about, and to meeting others like themselves. They understand that the reason Joe is doing this is to meet others, but they know it will be done in such a low-key way no one will ever be offended. Craig, who is a VIP himself, likes prospecting this way because he personally enjoys going to exclusive restaurants and the premieres of shows.

## Exhibit 15.6
### Sample Invitation Text

*(Representative Name) of (Firm Name) cordially invites you to dinner at (Name of Restaurant) and the exclusive opening night of (Name of Show) on (Date). We will meet in the bar at (Name of Restaurant) at (Time) for cocktails and will sit for dinner at (Time). After dinner, we will go to the theatre where we have a block of seats reserved for our party. The night will be a wonderful time for all of us to get to know each other a little better, and to take in the premiere of (Name of Show).*

*(RSVP information)*

Invitations sent to VIPs should be simple and direct, yet classy. Try using dark, rich-looking colors for the design of the invitation along with a metallic color, for example burgundy or forest green with gold. You can be creative if you want to, but be sure to keep it tasteful. For those advisors who want to do something extra special, send the invitation in a small box along with a bottle of champagne.

## Exhibit 15.7
### Sample Thank You/ Follow-Up Note

*Dear (Client or Prospect Name),*

*I sincerely hope that you enjoyed yourself at the dinner and show last week. Enclosed please find a copy of the picture that I snapped at dinner. (Try to add a personal comment about the evening). I truly had a wonderful time and hope that there will be more opportunities for all of us to get together in the near future!*

*(Client Name), we had an opportunity to talk a little bit about (plug specific investment opportunity here) during the evening and I was hoping that we could set up a time for me to explain a little more about it. My office is in (location) or I would be happy to meet with you at your home or office, whichever is most convenient for you. I will give you a call within the next couple of days to check your availability.*

*Thank you once again for joining us for dinner and the show. I look forward to talking to you soon.*

*Sincerely,*
*(Financial Representative Name)*

The sample invitation and follow-up are provided here as examples. Of course, you will tailor them to your own setting, clientele and event. They are here to show you how successful advisors have developed a dependable stream of VIP clients for their practices.

### Chapter 15 Big Answer:
### You can create a thriving practice around VIP clients. It takes discipline and focus to do so, but the rewards are tremendous, especially if you are a VIP yourself.

*The key is in understanding and empathizing with their financial motivations. You know they desire social recognition, status and prestige. To create highly satisfied VIP clients, you have to reinforce these needs. In this chapter we have provided a step-by-step outline you can use to identify your VIP clients with greatest potential, create high levels of satisfaction y using the I-CLAS model and prospect for new clients.*

# Chapter 16
# Accumulators

> *"I want to be Rich, lots and lots of money"*
> — Bobby McFarland

## Chapter 16 Critical Question:
## How can I create a successful investment advisory and wealth management practice around Accumulator clients?

Accumulators are the stereotypical affluent client. The financial motivator of Accumulators is to amass assets. They want more for the sake of having more. Like other clients, Accumulators are distinctive, with their own financial needs. They want help from their financial advisor in accumulating more assets. If you decide that Accumulator-type clients are a natural focus for your practice, your next step will be to create a business plan. This will have two parts; one is a general practice plan built around this segment and the other is how to do client-specific marketing plan for each Accumulator client. This chapter will help you do both of these things.

## PRACTICE BUSINESS PLAN

### I. Mission/Vision
*Create a successful practice by focusing on increasing the satisfaction of Accumulator clients. Increase assets under management and generate more referrals from and through Accumulators.*

This mission statement emphasizes satisfaction. In fact, it focuses on satisfying current Accumulator clients rather than prospecting. The reason satisfaction is so important is that it is very costly (in terms of time) to get new clients. It is much better to use that time to increase satisfaction and therefore improve client retention rates. More importantly, satisfied clients will become the most important pipeline of new client referrals. Among Accumulators, many research studies prove a cause and effect relationship in that highly satisfied clients lead to more assets and referrals.

## II. Strategy

*Increase client satisfaction using the insights of the financial motivator to positively impacting each component of the CLAS Client Satisfaction Model.*

In order to achieve the goals of building a large and sustainable practice, the strategy will be to implement state-of-the-art thinking on investor satisfaction. The CLAS model incorporates that thinking and so it should be used to guide action.

Investment performance is especially important to Accumulators as their financial motivator is to increase their assets. They are very sensitive to day-to-day market dynamics, they watch the financial channels and read the financial press. They expect their advisor to be as focused on performance as they are.

However, Accumulators are also responsive to the CLAS model, but less so than the other profiles. In general, the CLAS relationship factors are 4 times more powerful than investment performance; however, among Accumulators, they are just 2 times more important in engendering client satisfaction.

"C" refers to client orientation, to a high level of client focus. "L" refers to advisory leadership, which is to proactively identify important issues and provide solutions to Accumulator clients. "A" is attending behaviors, and indicates the number of and motivation of client contacts. Finally, "S" refers to shared values with the Accumulator client and how an advisor shows their trustworthiness and shared value system.

## *Exhibit 16.1*
### *The CLAS Model*

| C | Client Orientation | Your level of client focus |
|---|---|---|
| L | Leadership | Proactively identifying important issues and providing solutions |
| A | Attending Behaviors | The number of and motivation for client contacts |
| S | Shared Values | Trustworthiness and sharing of a similar value system |

### *III. Target Clients*

*Identify the most high potential Accumulator clients in the current client base for special focus with the goal of asset capture and client referral.*

You are already busy and have many clients. Your issue is whether you are spending your time with the right clients. This section helps you address that issue.

This is a several step approach. The first step is to determine how intensive the contact per targeted client needs to be. Then you can figure out how much of your time it will take. Once you have a sense of the effort per client, you can determine how many clients you can manage to work with at this level.

Our research has shown that Accumulator clients need a relatively high level of interaction. Research shows that around 15 client contacts should be made over the course of six months to increase Accumulator client satisfaction.

You probably do not have the time to practice high-impact relationship management with all your clients. Instead, you should focus on your best Accumulator clients and those clients with significant assets that you might be able to capture.

The recommended approach is for you to list your top Accumulator clients by assets, and then rank them according to satisfaction level—high, average or low. Then set a satisfaction goal for each client. You can enhance or maintain your current approach with the highly satisfied group, and decide to significantly improve relationships with the average and low groups. We have filled in the top line as an example.

## Exhibit 16.2
### Client Targeting Worksheet

| Client Name | Assets Under Management | Potential AUM | Current Satisfaction | Satisfaction Goal |
|---|---|---|---|---|
| *Joan Harrison* | *$2M* | *unknown* | *Medium* | *Improve to high* |
| | | | | |
| | | | | |
| | | | | |
| | | | | |
| | | | | |
| | | | | |
| | | | | |
| | | | | |

Once you have completed your chart, look it over for patterns. Are your clients as satisfied as they could be or is improvement possible? Are there sizable assets you could be targeting (or do you not know)? What does the data suggest your plan should be?

### IV. Individual Client relationship Development Planning
*Develop an individual client relationship development plan for each client targeted as high potential through the exercise above.*

It is very hard to increase the overall satisfaction level of your clients without working on them one at a time. That is why the core of this system is working on one client at a time with an *Individual Client relationship Development Plan*.

We provide an example here by continuing with the Joan Harrison case. Joan is an Accumulator. She owns a market research firm in the city with six employees. She travels extensively in her business and always seems stressed. She is divorced and has no children. She is a marathon and long distance runner (at the Masters level), and has a vacation home, as well as her place in the city. Whenever you talk with her, she emphasizes race times ("a new personal best!"), recent company billings and gains in her stock portfolio ($2 million in investable assets; she wants $10 million). She is very performance oriented.

You do not think she is as satisfied as she could be, and decide to set a target of increasing her satisfaction with you and your services. You know that an average of 15 client contacts over the course of six months is usually necessary to increase the satisfaction of an Accumulator. You create a six month plan listing possible actions you could take. You label each one a (C), (L), (A) or (S) to designate which component of CLAS you are impacting with a specific action item. Some action items will impact more than one component of the CLAS Model. Your goal is to impact each area three to four times over the six month plan.

This individual client plan is, of course, a general example for an Accumulator. It is imperative that always take your client's individuality into account. Think of the Accumulator profile as your starting point, and customize your plan to the individual with these directional insights. Combining the "Financial Motivator" of the profiles as with each client's unique personality is the essential step necessary for success.

## Exhibit 16.3
### Individual Client Relationship Development Satisfaction Plan:
**Client name:** Joan Harrison
**Background:** Owns a market research firm. Has $2 million stock portfolio. Single, no children.
**Financial Motivator:** Accumulator
**Investment IQ:** Above average
**Target contacts:** 15

| Date | Goal | Action |
|------|------|--------|
| July 1 | Report frequently on superior performance compared to selected benchmarks (L) | Watch Joan's portfolio this week for a performance gain worth commenting on. As soon as you identify one, you call Joan with the news, but leave a voice mail because she is not in the office. |

| Date | Goal | Action |
|------|------|--------|
| July 18 | Communicate a sense of urgency around financial performance (C) | Since Joan is an Accumulator, she will want to be reassured that she is on track with whatever the current growth trends are and in on what gains there are to be made. Knowing today is the time to communicate with Joan, you think for a minute about what is really hot right now. Let's say it is value or recovery in emerging markets. With these ideas in mind, you check her portfolio and look for a match. You find one. You have her in an emerging market fund that has bottomed out and is showing some gains. You call Joan with the following message. "Today's numbers out of Asia confirm the recovery is beginning. Your position in our fund sets you up for participating in those gains. Let's keep an eye on this." Notice you don't ask for a new investment (although you could have). The point to relationship building is just that – to reinforce that you are looking out for their interests, not just trying to sell them at every chance you get. |

| Date | Goal | Action |
|------|------|--------|
| July 25 | Communicate a sense of urgency (C) | You call Joan and mention that the value story is now turning around and that timing is critical. You tell her you think she should decide as soon as she can to insure the best returns over the long haul. Joan acts on your advice and wires you $48,000 to invest in the fund you recommend. You set up a time for a breakfast meeting to go over this decision and the rest of her portfolio, in light of current market conditions. |

| Date | Goal | Action |
|------|------|--------|
| August 9 | Conduct frequent meetings, reinforce investment expertise (A)(L) | At the breakfast meeting with Joan, you review her portfolio and show the placement of the value investment decision in the context of the overall asset allocation plan. You reinforce her perceptions of your investment expertise as you walk her through the portfolio analysis process. You quickly map out a sequence of planning exercises you will have to jointly do to get to her goal of $10 million. |

| Date | Goal | Action |
|------|------|--------|
| August 20 | Reinforce value of accumulating wealth (S) | You see an article about the growth of wealth in the country among women entrepreneurs. Some of these self-made women have gotten together to started a venture capital fund to fund businesses of other women entrepreneurs. |

| Date | Goal | Action |
|---|---|---|
| September 3 | Involve their other professional advisors (C) | You call Joan to suggest that it is time to coordinate a plan with her other advisors and to consult with her on how best to involve them in her financial planning process. You say you think that trusts may be involved (which calls for her attorney) and that the overlap with the business is an issue (which calls for sitting down with her accountant).You ask her for their phone numbers and say you will set up the meeting. |

| Date | Goal | Action |
|---|---|---|
| September 8 | Organize the meeting (C) (S) (L) | You call Joan and give her a few days everyone else can meet and say you will fax over the agenda everyone has agreed to. You wrote the agenda around Joan's goal of achieving $10 million, including such issues as asset protection planning (the attorney) and deferred comp through the business (the accountant). The agenda clearly positions you as the facilitator of the process. |

| Date | Goal | Action |
|---|---|---|
| September 27 | Personal meeting with her and her advisor team (L), (C), (A) | You and Joan meet an hour earlier than the official meeting to review the agenda, your goals and the direction of the overall process. When the two advisors arrive to join you, you focus the meeting on her goal and the importance of having an expert in each of the three areas present to help her do so –legal, accounting and investments. You have organized the meeting around several decision points, which she is able to make on the spot because she has been so well prepared. |

| Date | Goal | Action |
|---|---|---|
| October 9 | Show the belief that private wealth is what made this country great (S) | Send her a copy of Warren Buffet's autobiography. You just finished reading it and found it fascinating. You attach a short note that points out that in your view, she has the same values that led to his own wealth. |

| Date | Goal | Action |
|---|---|---|
| October 16 | Focus on results (A) | Give Joan a call to report on the value investment you worked on earlier. Point out that she got in at the right time – buying a dollar's worth for 50 cents. |

| Date | Goal | Action |
|---|---|---|
| November 2 | Demonstrate your own value of accumulating assets (S) | Statements were sent out at the end of the month. You pull up Joan's records and note where good gains were made. Call Joan to bring one of these to her attention. Add that you appreciate working with a client who looks for the same things you do. This will reinforce to Joan that you are watching out for her interests, and underscore that you share the same values towards investing. |

| Date | Goal | Action |
|------|------|--------|
| November 26 | Conduct frequent meetings (A) | Call Joan and suggest that is it time to meet to review performance over the last three quarters, make any adjustments necessary before the end of the year and plan for next year. You know she is on the road most weekdays, so you ask about getting together on the weekend. Suggest a few specific dates and times (Accumulators don't like ambiguity). |

| Date | Goal | Action |
|------|------|--------|
| December 8 | Communicate a sense of urgency around financial performance (C) | Meet with Joan about her portfolio. Communicate your urgency about keeping her fully invested, and highlight her progress towards her goal of accumulating a $10 million nest egg. As usual, you don't waste her time during the meeting with social talk. Come in with charts, records and highly organized, specific programs. Lay out her alternatives crisply and clearly, emphasizing your investment expertise, and follow her pace. |

| Date | Goal | Action |
|------|------|--------|
| December 11 | Show you know enough about the client to do a thoughtful thing (A) | Send over a gift basket from a health food store (filled with organic food) with a note that says you hope this will help Joan's winter training program. |

## V. Collect Relationship Development Idea:
*Constantly collect and implement new ideas for improving relationships with Accumulator clients.*

Accumulators value you for your investment skills. They also need your relationship skills. To advisors trained in the technical aspects of investing, this emphasis on relationships does not come easily. You can help yourself by collecting and referring to ideas you come across. Here is a list of some ideas that you can use to build relationships with Accumulators. Feel free to using one or more of these tools in order to show how much you care about your relationships with your Accumulator clients.

## Exhibit 16.4
### Relationship Development Ideas
*The following is a list of places to start in collecting ideas to deepen your relationship with Accumulators. This list is not intended to be exhaustive, it is provided here to get you going.*

➤ Complete a financial plan for the client. Find out their goal ($5MM by age 60). Recalibrate the goal if it is unrealistic given their current age and asset base. Once goal is set, provide the client annual net worth and cash flow statements.

➤ Conduct a financial efficiency audit for them. Inventory their bills and financial practices and offer ideas on how to save more money. Reduce the number of credit cards they hold, ensure insurance coverage for all policies is pooled at one provider for maximum discounts, avoid use of credit for large ticket purchases, etc…

➤ Send them articles, books or even provide a seminar on the benefits of tax efficiency over the long term. Be certain, of course, not to direct them to a seminar out of your control.

➤ Include money saving tips as a P.S. on all of your handwritten notes to them. Use a book or website (just type in "money saving ideas" at a search engine) for ideas on this subject. Also ask your clients to send in their own money saving ideas, and share them with your other clients.

➤ Share news of other clients that have hit their goals by sticking to their long term plans (without names or personal specifics of course)

➤ Send them articles and books of individuals that became wealthy by adhering to a long term investment philosophy and plan, such as Warren Buffett. Include a note about the long term benefits of adhering to a financial plan

Search out Accumulator oriented websites for additional relationship management ideas to brainstorm with your staff. Here are a few examples:

www.compareinterestrates.com
A loan calculator site to determine loan amounts and mortgage

payments. Also allows you to search for current mortgage interest rates from lenders and brokers nationwide.

www.angelfire.com/co/simplewealth/buffettips.html
A listing of commonly referred sayings of Warren Buffett.

www.kiplinger.com/calc/calchome.html
This is the site of Kiplinger's financial calculators. It provides a collection of calculation forms ranging from how much your savings will be worth and what will it take to pay off credit balances.

www.winnerstrategies.com/Wealth.htm
A web site listing books and tapes on secrets of how to accumulate wealth from experts like Dale Carnegie and Stephen R. Covey.

www.isgplanning.com
The ISG™ site highlights its sophisticated software that includes features like a Wealth Accumulation Schedule, allowing a user to creating a meaningful accumulation plan.

www.calccentral.com
Online calculator center with links to calculators for business, finance, investment, mortgages, retirement, and more.

www.buffetwatch.com
BuffettWatch was developed to provide detailed information on the investment decisions of Warren Buffett.

www.quicken.com
Quicken.com provides a vast amount of information from investment news to allowing you to monitor your portfolio and receive alerts on investments you want to track.

www.taxreductioninstitute.com
The Tax Reduction Institute site provides information on tax planning, including how to reduce your taxes, tax law changes, etc.

www.sensible-investor.com
Sensible Investor provides ratings and analysis of finance websites, magazines, and television, with a focus on long-term investing.

## VI. Implement Prospecting Program
*Create a reliable pipeline of new Accumulator clients through a systematic program of referrals from current Accumulator clients.*

Accumulators desire solid investment returns and good service. Satisfied Accumulator clients will refer you to other people that share their same values. That is the reason you have been concentrating on increasing their satisfaction.

You need to ask clients for referrals. Because your current Accumulator clients know you well they can be very convincing when they tell others about you. Of course, your current clients will not think about making referrals on their own (they have other things to think about). Wait until after you have completed a major piece of work for them, or had a success. In general, they won't know, off hand, of people they can refer to you. But they will be able to introduce you to people they know who you want to be introduced to. Do your homework. Know their contacts. Know who you want to meet. This will help your clients learn that you do want referrals. That way, if a friend does approach them asking about advisors, they will think of you right away.

When prospecting this profile, advisors should focus on their success in managing investment portfolios. You should communicate knowledge of the leading indices in each sector and your performance against them. Accumulators are always looking for a new edge or method for boosting their investment return, and are responsive to seminar selling. You can also use the technical investing resources of your firm to good effect with Accumulators. This group likes meeting portfolio managers and analysts.

## Chapter 16 Big Answer:
### *It is possible to build a successful and profitable advisory practice around Accumulators.*

This chapter lays out a practice business plan you can follow to create a practice around Accumulators. Use the Accumulator profile provided here as a jumping off point and then tailor your actions to the actual clients you serve. Combine the "Financial Motivator" of the Accumulator profile with each client's unique personality as you develop your client-centered programs.

Now that you have finished this chapter, you have an understanding of how to develop a business around this psychographic profile. Now you should develop your own plan. Start with your vision or mission, address satisfaction and strategy. Then identify the clients you will target and develop a personal marketing plan each Accumulator client you decide to target. You are well on your way to building a successful, focused, practice.

# Chapter 17
# Gamblers

> *"Past Performance Is No Guarantee of Future Results.*
> *And If It Was, What Fun Would That Be."*
>
> — Josh Billings

## *Chapter 17 Critical Question:*
## *How can I build a successful practice focused on Gambler-type clients?*

Gamblers have a distinctive financial motivator, and it is the excitement and thrill of the investing process itself. In this way, they are very different from the other types of affluent investors. Here, this chapter, we provide a framework for a business model built around Gambler-types clients. We include an example of a Gambler-specific marketing plan for a sample client. Keep in mind that all the examples included here are just that, examples. Each of your Gambler-type clients has their own individuality. Think of the Gambler financial motivator as a starting point and then tailor your actions to the actual clients you serve. Combine the "Financial Motivator" of the Gambler with each client's unique personality for optimum success. In this chapter, we will walk you through the general steps of developing a business around the Gambler profile and we will illustrate each step with a client story.

## PRACTICE BUSINESS PLAN:

### *I. Mission/Vision:*
*Increase assets under management and generate more referrals by being the advisor of choice of Gambler clients; achieve this goal by creating highly satisfied clients.*

Every mission statement deserves to be read closely and this one is no exception. There are several things of note in this mission statement. It focuses most of the advisor's time on satisfying current clients rather than prospecting. The reason is that the time and money costs of getting new clients is huge, and it is much more efficient to direct those energies towards client retention and satisfaction. More importantly, satisfied clients will become an important pipeline of new client referrals.

## II. Strategy:

*Invest professional time on current Gambler-type clients. Increase client satisfaction using the insights of the financial motivator and positively impact each component of the C.L.A.S. Client Satisfaction Model in action plans tailored to each target client.*

The core strategy will be to use world-class thinking on investor satisfaction to meet the goals of the mission statement. In the financial services industry, the CLAS model has been proven to increase client satisfaction. We strongly recommend that advisors adopt this model as their central strategy.

Among Gamblers, investment performance is of obvious importance. They are quite attuned to day-to-day market dynamics, and to the performance of their own securities. They pay close attention to the Dow and the other indices. They watch the financial channels on TV and read the financial press. Investing is their hobby and passion.

However, Gamblers are also very sensitive to the CLAS model. In general, the CLAS relationship factors are 4 times more powerful than investment performance.

"C" refers to client orientation, to a high level of client focus. For Gambler clients, this means being as excited and enthusiastic about investing as they are. "L" refers to advisory leadership, which is to proactively identify important issues and provide solutions to clients. For Gamblers, this means More ways of being involved in investing and financial markets. "A" is attending behaviors, and indicates the number of and motivation of client contacts. Gamblers are very needy clients; they want a lot of contacts. Finally, "S" refers to shared values and how an advisor shows their trustworthiness and shared value system which in this case is a zest for the investing process.

Quite a few Gamblers became day-traders, and some people speculate that they are not good target clients for advisors. Our research shows that quite a few Gamblers do like working with advisors, but that they do not want to delegate investment decisions. Instead, they want a "playmate", someone else to swap stories and news with.

## Exhibit 17.1
### The CLAS Model

| C | Client Orientation | Your level of client focus |
|---|---|---|
| L | Leadership | Proactively identifying important issues and providing solutions |
| A | Attending Behaviors | The number of and motivation for client contacts |
| S | Shared Values | Trustworthiness and sharing of a similar value system |

### III. Target Clients
*Identify high potential Gambler-type clients to target for relationship development. Select clients based on potential for incremental asset capture and new client referrals.*

As a business person, you know that you have to manage your own time carefully. Your time is a scarce resource. A key element of building a successful practice is how to allocate your time.

We advocate a several step approach. The first step is to determine how intensive the contact per client needs to be. Then you can figure out how much time that will take. Once you have a sense of the effort per client, you can determine how many clients you can manage to work with at this level.

Our research has shown that Gambler clients need a very high level of interaction. Research shows that around 20 client contacts must be made over the course of six months to increase satisfaction among this group.

This is a very demanding rate of contact. For this reason, you need to focus on your most high-potential Gambler clients — clients with significant assets that you might be able to capture.

List your top Gambler clients by assets, and then rank them according to satisfaction level—high, average or low. You can enhance or maintain your current approach with the highly satisfied group, and dramatically improve relationships with the average and low groups.

## Exhibit 17.2
### Client Targeting Worksheet

| Client Name | Assets Under Management | Potential AUM | Current Satisfaction | Satisfaction Goal |
|---|---|---|---|---|
| John Pelligrino | $800K | $350K | Average | Improve to highly satisfied |
| | | | | |
| | | | | |
| | | | | |
| | | | | |
| | | | | |
| | | | | |
| | | | | |
| | | | | |

### IV. Individual Client relationship Development Planning
Develop an individual client relationship development plan for each Gambler client targeted as high potential through the exercise above.

The key to increasing client satisfaction is focusing on each client one at a time. In this section, we provide you with a sample client plan. It is geared around the example of a client we call John.

John is a new client who calls you frequently. He is always interested in what's going on, and wants the inside story every time there is significant market activity. John is focused on the quick gain, and the lure of finding the undiscovered gem among low-priced stocks. John seems obsessed with getting rich quick, and his portfolio is a hodge-podge of stocks he bought on tips. You are able to tab John as a Gambler without too much trouble.

If a client is a Gambler, 20 or more client contacts must be made over the course of six months. Each of the following action items will be marked with a (C), (L), (A) or (S) to designate which component of CLAS you are impacting with a specific action item. Some action items will impact more than one component of the CLAS Model. The goal is to impact each area about 5 or 6 times over the six-month plan, with an emphasis on Attending Behaviors.

## Exhibit 17.4
### Individual Client relationship Development Plan

**Client Name:** John Pelligrino
**Background:** John is 35. He is divorced and sees his two kids regularly.
**Financial Motivator:** Gambler
**Investment IQ:** High
**Target Contacts:** 20

| Date | Goal | Action |
|------|------|--------|
| July 1 | Mirror emotional intensity (S) | Call John to share excitement about today's market volatility, and the top-level resignation at the Federal Reserve. Mention that small-cap growth funds are a great opportunity now. |

| Date | Goal | Action |
|------|------|--------|
| July 3 | Quickly respond to client calls (A) | John called you this morning, and you get right back to him. You show your excitement in your voice about the market. John shares in your excitement, and tells you to take $60,000 from his money market account and invest it in the small-cap fund you recommended the last time you talked. |

| Date | Goal | Action |
|------|------|--------|
| July 6 | Highest possible interaction (C) | Send him a report from one of the analysts at your firm talking about the opportunity in small cap growth. |

| Date | Goal | Action |
|------|------|--------|
| July 18 | Emphasize expertise in taking advantage of market movements and volatility (L) | Today the markets are moving a lot and the small-cap fund had an up-tick. You call John to share the news. |

| Date | Goal | Action |
|------|------|--------|
| July 25 | Show you have an appreciation for quickness, risk-taking and action (S) | You come across an article from a technical journal saying that astute trading strategies have beat buy-and-hold strategies. This is right up John's alley. You send it to him with a short note saying: "Looks like we are on the right track." |

| Date | Goal | Action |
|------|------|--------|
| August 9 | Initiate many contacts between meetings (A) | You know that Gamblers like it when you pitch new ideas to them. You happen to like emerging markets right now and decide to give John a call. It turns out he is lukewarm, but says he appreciates your call. |

| Date | Goal | Action |
|------|------|--------|
| August 15 | Communicate trading vs. buy-and-hold orientation (L) | You notice that emerging markets didn't make a quick move, and you call John to let him know you noticed this. You say that you are learning that he likes things to move quickly, and you will keep that in mind as you look for opportunities for him. You talk about small cap some more because you know he is pleased with the performance in that sector, and you discuss benchmarks for getting out of that position. You also explore how he stands on other investment alternatives and in particular sector funds. It turns out he does follow them, especially the high-tech ones. |

| Date | Goal | Action |
|------|------|--------|
| August 21 | Initiate many phone calls between meetings (A) | You follow some of the high-tech sector stocks after your last call, and see some opportunity. You call John to talk about some options. He appreciates your research and asks you to move funds from his money market account to buy the fund. |

| Date | Goal | Action |
|------|------|--------|
| September 8 | Emphasize receiving the highest possible interaction with a portfolio manager (C) | Call John to say the small-cap fund manager is coming in, and you would like to have him meet John. |

| Date | Goal | Action |
|---|---|---|
| September 11 | Initiate many phone calls between meetings (A) | Confirm the meeting with the portfolio manager. |

| Date | Goal | Action |
|---|---|---|
| September 27 | Highest possible interaction with portfolio manager, communicate trading vs. buy-and-hold orientation (C), (L) | You introduce John to the small-cap fund manager. They get along well, John is excited about the fund. They spend a lot of time talking about specific stocks in the fund, about the potential of these stocks to take off and about the trading philosophy of the portfolio manager. |

| Date | Goal | Action |
|---|---|---|
| September 28 | Initiate many phone calls between meetings (A) | Call John to share excitement about the meeting. John says he will wire over an additional $250,000 to invest in the fund. |

| Date | Goal | Action |
|---|---|---|
| October 1 | Initiate many phone contacts between meetings (A) | You call John to say you have received the wire transfer and that the trade has been executed. In that conversation you talk about two of the companies in the fund that are really starting to make a move. These two companies were the ones John and the portfolio manager talked about a lot in their meeting together. |

| Date | Goal | Action |
|---|---|---|
| October 8 | Initiate many phone contacts between meetings (A) | You call John to give him updates on the two funds you have him in. He is pleased. |

| Date | Goal | Action |
|---|---|---|
| October 18 | Highest possible interaction with portfolio manager. (C) | You have the portfolio manager drop John a note with a comment on how he thinks things are going. |

| Date | Goal | Action |
|---|---|---|
| November 2 | Communicate excitement and enthusiasm for investing, communicate trading orientation (C), (L) | Call John to schedule a comprehensive portfolio review. You also include a few comments about individual stocks or funds Tony has in order to show you are on top of the market and his position at all times. |

| Date | Goal | Action |
|------|------|--------|
| November 4 | Initiate many phone contacts between meetings. (A) | You call Tony on some of the agenda items you are planning for the meeting and to update him on the two funds you have him in. |

| Date | Goal | Action |
|------|------|--------|
| November 22 | Initiate many phone contacts between meetings (A) | You call John to confirm the meeting and share some exciting performance reports. |

| Date | Goal | Action |
|------|------|--------|
| November 26 | Mirror emotional intensity. (C), (A) | You and John meet for a couple of hours to go over his portfolio and positions. You place emphasis throughout the meeting on the proactive actions you and John have taken throughout the year – especially the major move into the small-cap growth fund and the individual equities you have purchased for him. You mention he has been a fun client to have. |

| Date | Goal | Action |
|------|------|--------|
| December 8 | Show you share an appreciation for quickness, risk-taking and action (S) | Send out a holiday card to John and your other Gambler clients. Find a way to show you share these values; perhaps a snapshot of you skiing, or a note to the effect that you enjoyed the wild year with him and look forward to more excitement next year. |

| Date | Goal | Action |
|------|------|--------|
| December 11 | Communicate excitement and enthusiasm for investing (C) | Send John your annual holiday gift, the one selected especially for Gamblers. Select something with a connection to the market such as bear and bull cuff links. |

## V. Collect Relationship Development Ideas

*Continually upgrade your archive of ideas to use to cement relationships with Gamblers.*

To advisors trained in the technical aspects of investing and who have a personal zest for investing, working with the Gambler type comes easily. Even so, you can help yourself by collecting and referring to ideas you come across. Here is a list of quick and effective ideas that you can use to build relationships with Gamblers. Using one or more of these tools on a regular basis will reinforce how much you care about your relationships with your Gambler clients and will demonstrate the high standards of service you provide.

**Exhibit 17.4**
**Relationship Development Ideas**
Here is a set of ideas you can use as a jumping-off point for your relationship development activities with your Gambler-type clients.

➤ Collect and send magazine and newspaper articles about new financial topics that may be of interest to Gamblers. Gamblers are technically savvy, so sending things via e-mail is an alternative. Always be sure to consider each client's individuality when choosing articles. Topics could include:

- New stock issues
- New investment styles
- Articles about companies they are invested in
- Bios of successful investors
- Investment trends
- Research reports on industries
- Investment opportunities

➤ Find out about firm events on investment topics that you could invite your Gambler to. Be certain that the presenter and the topic are appropriate for the Gambler financial motivator.
➤ Familiarize yourself with events and activities that your clients individually enjoy and talk about these things with them. Sharing other interests gives you even more opportunities to bring up topics related to investing.
➤ Many Gamblers are also puzzle fans. See if your Gamblers are; that will give you other themes to use in communications with them.
➤ You can also talk with them about activities you enjoy. This shows them that you want to build a relationship.
➤ Set up your own seasonal events that your clients can attend, such as a casino trip or a benefit casino night.
➤ Send out handwritten cards for birthdays and all major holidays. Be sure all communications reflect your shared intensity.

➢ Call whenever there are market events. Always have a suggestion or two that will capitalize on current opportunity.

➢ Send e-mails to your clients often. This shows them that you care about your relationship with them, and respect their preference for speed.

Search out Gambler oriented websites for additional relationship management ideas to brainstorm with your staff. Here are a few examples:

www.stock-commodity-day-trading-education.com
This site offers stock and commodity day trading education. It offers information about trading methods.

www.mesquite-nv.com/hotel.htm
A complete guide to Las Vegas casinos and hotels.

www.stock-reports.net
The Independent Analyst's Report provides stock selections, analyses and commentaries. Each issue of the report contains background information on each company, an earnings projection and a target stock price.

www.tradescape.com
This site is a provider of trading software that gives the individual investor online access to the stock market, avoiding all middlemen.

www.casino.org
Internet casinos, a web-based gambling site.

www.derivativesweek.com
*Derivatives Week* is dedicated to breaking news on the over-the-counter derivatives market worldwide. Every week, its reporters dig up must-read intelligence on swaps and options on equities, interest rates, currencies and commodities. They reveal who's using derivatives, who's planning to do so and why. Coverage

includes development of new derivative instruments, regulatory changes, firm reorganizations, technology, market trends and risk management.

www.vital-info.com
This site is a publisher of investment newsletters recommending small-cap growth stocks and growth and sector mutual funds.

www.casinolinkslist.com
A listing of both real and online casinos. This site also provides links to downloadable games, tips, and suppliers.

www.HFAlert.com
Every week, Hedge Fund Alert delivers the early intelligence you need to keep up with the latest risks and opportunities facing fund-management firms, their service providers and investors.

www.1daytradingstockadviceandpicks.com
This site offers stock and swing option picks, alerts, and technical chart pattern analysis for full and part time traders.

## VI. Implement Prospecting Program
*Design and implement a consistent prospecting program for new Gambler-type clients.*

The Gambler's core investing motivation is to feel excitement in the investing process. Gamblers like discussing investments, trading, and markets. They initiate discussions on investing at every opportunity.

When prospecting for Gamblers, investment representatives should focus on communicating that they share the same values.

A good way to identify Gambler prospects is to network through your current clients. They may know other Gambler-type investors though work, investment clubs, family connections or non-profits.

Gamblers are a group that responds to seminar selling, if the topic is well chosen. As you might expect, they do not respond well to long-term strategies, buy-and-hold approaches or risk-reduction tactics. They want the new, new thing that active investors are talking about.

It is harder to meet Gamblers in the usual social settings because they are harder to spot. In general, however, you can be on the look-out for anyone who talks about investing or stocks and does so with enthusiasm. Gamblers are known to brag about a recent success in the market.

Below is a sample prospect activity that we provide to show you how a prospecting program for Gambler-type clients can be done. You will customize this approach to your own practice, of course.

## Exhibit 17.5
### Gambler Networking Case Study

*Colin Notting is an advisor who enjoys working with Gamblers. He puts on seminars several times a year and invites current clients and their guests. He also publicizes these seminars. In all communications, he is careful to emphasize his personal excitement and zest for the field, and how much enjoys the sheer pleasure of the investment process.*

*Colin Notting arranges these events carefully. He insures that the speakers are particularly dynamic. He surprises his guests with interesting beverages and a gift of a bag of puzzles. He creates opportunities for people to talk to him and to hear the enthusiasm in his voice.*

This investment representative has been very successful with his seminars. Not only are these events well-planned, creative and exciting, but they are fun for him because he enjoys talking about investing as much as his clients do. The enthusiasm he has for his work is very attractive to Gambler-type clients.

## Exhibit 17.6
### Sample Invitation Text

*(on firm letterhead)*

*In these exciting times, we can't sit still. New issues, new investment tools, new concepts. It is why I got into this field, and why I would like to invite you to join me for an evening seminar. I have arranged for (expert name) of (firm name) to give us an exclusive briefing on their groundbreaking report (title). He has guaranteed that our take-away will be a good sense of the state-of-the-art in (investment topic appealing to Gamblers).*

*Join me on (Date) from (Time) to (Time) at (Location).*

In sending invitations to your seminars in such as way that they appeal to Gamblers, consider these other ideas. For example, speed and excitement are important. You may want to use an overnight delivery service (e.g. FedEx), or use a Treasure Hunt theme.

However you choose to do the invitations, keep the same theme going in the follow-up communications you send. Here is an example.

## Exhibit 17.7
### Sample Follow-Up Note:

*Dear (Client Name),*

*I am glad you were able to join us for the discussion (of topic). I enjoyed our discussion of (insert something investment-related that you talked about), and here is a new article on (topic) that I though you would find exciting.*

*(Client Name), we share an interest in investing and a belief in active management. I look forward to talking to you further about some opportunities.*

*I am an investment advisor, and I work best with clients who are knowledgeable and enthusiastic about investing. If you are interested, I would be more than happy to meet with you at your home or my office (plug in location) to discuss investment topics.*

*Sincerely,*
*(Financial Representative Name)*

### Chapter 17 Big Answer:
### If you are willing to give Gambler clients the extensive personal attention they seek, Gamblers can be a rewarding type to build a practice around.

Gamblers are a challenging group to select as clients to target. They have a distinctive financial motivator — the excitement and thrill of the investing process itself. They need an unusually high number of contacts to be extremely satisfied with their advisors. However, if you understand their needs, and are wiling to invest this much time in each client, Gamblers can be very rewarding clients.

You can use this chapter to create your own practice model built around Gambler clients. Begin with mission and strategy, then select target clients. Finally, create a Gambler-specific marketing plan for each clients according to the sample provided here.

As always, remember that each of your Gambler-type clients has their own individuality. Even though they share the same, Gambler, financial motivation, they remain unique personalities. You can apply these steps to develop a business around the Gambler profile, with this illustrated step by step guide.

# Chapter 18
# Innovators

*"Wealth is in applications of mind to nature."*

— *Ralph Waldo Emerson*

## Chapter 18 Big Question:
### How can a profitable and successful practice be built around Innovator clients?

Innovators are one of the smaller groups of affluent investors, one of the most challenging and also one of the most rewarding. Like the others, Innovator clients have their own unique financial (and life) motivator. Innovators like the new, the state-of-the-art, and the cutting edge. In investing and money management, they like the technical, the new theoretical approach, the strategy that no one else is using. Innovators also like to invest in new technologies. They are smart and well read in investing.

For this reason, they are very challenging to advisors who do not share their passion for betas, formulas and the technical and arcane elements of investing. If this is not your natural type, you may want to consider not pursuing this segment as they will not be happy with you and you will not feel as though you are satisfying their needs either.

As with the other profiles, building a practice around Innovator clients takes care and time, but is well worth it. This chapter outlines a business plan you can adapt to your own clients and practice. As a practice model, it includes a mission statement, a strategy for relationship enhancement, a client development plan, and sample prospecting activities. The key, as always, is to start with the financial motivator of the Innovator client front and center.

# PRACTICE BUSINESS PLAN

## I. Mission/Vision:

*Build a successful and profitable practice by developing high rates of satisfaction among Innovator clients in order to generate high rates of asset capture and client referral.*

The key to building a successful with any practice is satisfied clients. The key to creating satisfied clients is managing to their unique financial motivator. In the case of Innovators, their financial motivator is to be at the state-of-the-art. As you saw from the earlier chapters of this book, research overwhelmingly proves the cause and effect relationship between high satisfaction and more assets under management and client referrals regardless of the type of client. However, the key to what makes a client satisfied is different depending on the type you are taking about.

In the case of Innovators, the key is understanding and addressing their need to be at the state-of-the-art in the technical aspects of investing and financial management.

## II. Strategy

*Increase Innovator client satisfaction using the insights of their financial motivation. Do so by positively impacting each component of the CLAS Client Satisfaction Model.*

We recommend that your strategy will be to structure your practice around delivering against the relationship needs of the Innovator segment of clients. Of course, you will continue to do an excellent job of providing investment advisory service. The four components of the CLAS model actually deliver more value to clients as measured by how much they contribute the probability that the client will refer other clients to you and add assets to be managed.

For all clients, the CLAS model refers to the way in which you interact with the client to increase their satisfaction with their relationship. In the CLAS model, the "C" refers to client orientation (the amount of focus on the Innovator client), the "L" refers to advisory leadership (proactively providing solutions to Innovator clients), the "A" refers to attending behaviors (client contact behavior) and the "S" refers to shared values (how an advisor shows their trustworthiness to Innovators). In general, the "CLAS" portions of the model are 4 times more important than the "I" portion in producing client satisfaction.

## Exhibit 18.1
### The CLAS Model

| C | Client Orientation | Your level of client focus |
|---|---|---|
| L | Leadership | Proactively identifying important issues and providing solutions |
| A | Attending Behaviors | The number of and motivation for client contacts |
| S | Shared Values | Trustworthiness and sharing of a similar value system |

### III. Target Clients and Advisors
*Identify high-potential Innovator clients in your current client base for the purpose of asset capture and new client referrals. Also develop advisor networks for referrals of Innovator clients.*

With only so many hours in the day, you do not have unlimited time for client contacts. You have to ration your time, and spend it on the clients with the greatest potential to help you develop your practice. You have to prioritize in order to practice high-impact relationship management with your Innovator clients.

In order to focus on your best clients (those with significant assets that you might be able to capture) you need to work through a client targeting process. First, list your top clients by assets (remember, they should all be Innovator clients for this purpose). Next, fill in your estimate of potential assets available for capture. Then note what you think their satisfaction level is — high, average or low. Finally, for each client, decide on what your goal for increasing the satisfaction is, and fill that in.

## Exhibit 18.2
### Client Targeting Worksheet

| Client Name | Assets Under Management | Potential AUM | Current Satisfaction | Satisfaction Goal |
|---|---|---|---|---|
| Steve Chung | $150K | $1 M (estimated) | Not known | Improve to highly satisfied |
| | | | | |
| | | | | |
| | | | | |
| | | | | |
| | | | | |
| | | | | |
| | | | | |
| | | | | |

For most advisors, it is enough to maintain your current approach with the highly satisfied group, and practice high impact relationship management with the average and low groups in order to improve their perceptions of your quality.

To increase (or hold) satisfaction among Innovators, 15 client contacts should be made over the course of six months. Since most advisors make far fewer contacts than this, you will stand out from the crowd. The important thing is that there be a strategic reason for each contact. In the individual client action plan we lay out below as an example, we have coded each action item with a (C), (L), (A) or (S) to show which component of CLAS is being impacted with a specific action item. Some action items will impact more than one component of the CLAS Model. The goal in the design of this plan is to impact each area 3 to 4 times over the six-month plan.

In the case below, we show you how an individual client plan can be set up. In this example, we create one for a client we call Steve Chung. In this example, imaging that you met Steve when you joined the board of a local venture center. You both ended up on the finance committee, and shared frustration about the backward ways the non-profit was managing its money. As you talked with Steve, it became clear that he set a priority on implementing well-tuned financial practices, and you initiated discussions about investing. You learned Steve runs some of his own money, but uses several managers for most of his $1 million portfolio. He widely reads financial literature, is fascinated by financial engineering, but isn't excited by risk. He begins to work with you, and you determine that Steve is an Innovator.

## Exhibit 18.3
### Individual Client relationship Development Plan

**Client name:** Steve Chung

**Background:** Steve is a computer engineer who owns his own consulting company. He is married with two school-age children.

**Financial Motivator:** Innovator

**Investment IQ:** very high

**Target contacts:** 18

| Date | Goal | Action |
|------|------|--------|
| July 1 | Position yourself as an educational resource (C) | Steve doesn't like what is hot in investing, he likes what is scientific. You contact your research group to see if they can recommend a recent, good article about this topic. The research group suggests one that reviews the role physicists and scientists have been playing on Wall Street and covers some of the technical aspects. You get a copy of the article, read it, talk again to the analyst who recommended it and send it off to Steve. You clip on a handwritten note: "I came across this and thought of you immediately." |

| Date | Goal | Action |
|------|------|--------|
| July 16 | Have frequent interactions. Share the belief that innovative, cutting edge investing is the way to go (A) (S) | Call Steve to talk about the article and see the kind of thing he would like you to keep your eye out for. Mention to him that this is the kind of material you like to read, too. |

| Date | Goal | Action |
|------|------|--------|
| July 25 | Provide access to technical expertise (C) | Call Steve to set up a meeting. The derivatives specialist and a portfolio strategist are available to talk with him about hedging his portfolio. |

| Date | Goal | Action |
|------|------|--------|
| August 9 | Bringing leading edge investment opportunities (L) | Steve and you meet with the firm specialists. The specialists talk about technical initiatives that they are developing. The discussion turns to Steve's situation, and the specialists make several broad suggestions for Steve to consider. |

| Date | Goal | Action |
|------|------|--------|
| August 10 | Have frequent interactions with the client (A) | Call Steve to collect a little bit more data to use in developing an analysis of these options and ask for dates for the next meeting. |

| Date | Goal | Action |
|------|------|--------|
| August 20 | Have frequent interactions with the client. Reflect their technical turn of mind (S), (A) | Call Steve to confirm a date for the meeting. Mention that you appreciate working with someone who is so interested in sophisticated planning. |

| Date | Goal | Action |
|------|------|--------|
| September 8 | Communicate the importance of staying on top of financial innovations. Talk the technical jargon (L) | You and the portfolio strategist prepare to meet with Steve. You have a series of proposals, each in a separate binder. For each financial issue, you have prepared several alternative ways he could consider. After considerable discussion, Steve agrees to consider your proposals and get back to you. |

| Date | Goal | Action |
|------|------|--------|
| September 16 | Have frequent interactions (A) | You haven't heard from Steve, so you call. Steve says he likes several of the suggestions but is worried about their tax implications, He wants to get his accountant (who is a tax specialist) involved. You offer to set up a conference call. |

| Date | Goal | Action |
|------|------|--------|
| September 21 | Bring leading edge investment opportunities. Reflect their technical turn of mind (L), (S) | You set up a conference call between you, Steve, the portfolio strategist and his accountant. You all talk about Steve's concerns. Steve decides on several issues. On a few others, the accountant needs more information. You say you will follow up with the accountant. |

| Date | Goal | Action |
|------|------|--------|
| October 1 | Position yourself as an educational resource. Share the belief that innovative, cutting edge investing is the way to go (C), (S) | Call Steve back to confirm that you have sent all the material to the accountant and that you will be following up to help Steve complete his analysis. You suggest to Steve that the way is clear to use listed options to create a hedge for a part of his portfolio. Steve agrees, and you work out the details. |

| Date | Goal | Action |
|------|------|--------|
| October 5 | Talk technical jargon (L) | Call Steve to confirm the listed options purchase and say you will be sending a documentation of the process and implications for his whole portfolio. |

| Date | Goal | Action |
|------|------|--------|
| October 15 | Focus on industry news and new products (A) | Send Steve an article about listed options. Attach a handwritten note that says: "It's nice to be ahead of the curve, again." |

| Date | Goal | Action |
|------|------|--------|
| November 2 | Have frequent interactions (A) | Call Steve to say you have been watching the market with his option position in mind and you are even more convinced he made a wise move. You ask how the accountant is coming. Steve says he is ready to move on the other decisions. Specifically, he wants to look at his fund portfolio and make investment decisions based on tax efficiency. You say you will consult with the accountant and revise the proposal. |

| Date | Goal | Action |
|------|------|--------|
| November 26 | Position yourself as an educational resource ( C) | ou set up a conference call between you, Steve, the portfolio strategist and the accountant to review the tax efficient investing proposal. With a few changes, everyone agrees with your plan. You say that you will begin to implement the plan. |

| Date | Goal | Action |
|------|------|--------|
| December 1 | Have frequent interactions (A) | Send out the holiday cards you selected for your Innovator clients. Knowing they like things that are unusual or different, you find a unique card for this group. |

| Date | Goal | Action |
|------|------|--------|
| December 8 | Have frequent interactions (A) | You call Steve to say you are implementing the plan and you review one or two components of it with him. |

| Date | Goal | Action |
|------|------|--------|
| December 10 | Have frequent interactions (A) | YSend Steve confirmation of the tax efficient fund implementation and a documentation of the process and implications for his whole portfolio. |

| Date | Goal | Action |
|------|------|--------|
| December 11 | Have frequent interactions (A) | Send the client a holiday gift that is appropriate for an Innovator. You can use the same gift you use for all your other clients, if you customize it a bit. For example, you could send a fruit basket. But, think about how to customize it to Innovators. Consider several options – an article on genetic engineering of foods, a fancy new kitchen tool, or an organic fruit. You opt for the kitchen tool, and in the note mentions that you hope him and his family enjoy the "gizmo" you sent. |

## V. Collect Relationship Development Ideas

*Identify and use ideas for developing your relationships with Innovators.*

As you get used to using client-by-client relationship development planning and implementation, collect ideas you could use. Create some system for looking for and saving ideas. One advisor we know tears out articles to keep in a file. He codes them C,L,A or S on each so he can find a suitable idea quickly.

## Exhibit 18.4
### Relationship Development Ideas

The following is a list of quick and effective ideas that you can use to increase satisfaction of your Innovator clients. Using these tools will reinforce your positioning with these clients as committed advisor.

➢ Use e-mail to communicate with your Innovator clients. Be sure you always have state-of-the art PDA and communications equipment, and let these clients have your cell and beeper numbers. Innovators notice what technology you use.

➢ Stay on top of awards, patents you clients have received and congratulate them. Innovators work long hours to reach these heights and want people to respect them for their commitment.

➢ Send them articles from newspapers or magazines that are about innovations in the investment field.

➢ Set up seasonal sessions that will interest your clients. These should be technology and innovation focused.

➢ Find a role for yourself in local inventor's societies, university venture groups and in venture funding organizations. These kinds of organizations have events that may interest your Innovator clients.

➢ E-mail clips about financial news about well-known or celebrity Innovators such as Jim Clark (Netscape) or Paul Allen (Microsoft).

➢ Invest in your own web site, make sure it is technologically oriented. Maintain links to interesting sites that cover innovations on other fields. Be sure your site is updated regularly to keep it fresh and interesting.

➤ Your office decor should have the informal and contemporary look of a hi-tech company rather than the traditional and formal look of a law firm or bank.

➤ Create a regular e-mail to your clients with excerpts from the reports of your firm's analysts on small cap stocks, new issues and IPOs, emphasizing technology companies of all kinds.

Search out Innovator oriented websites for additional relationship management ideas to brainstorm with your staff. Here are a few examples:

www.asee.org
This is the site for The American Society for Engineering Education. ASEE is a nonprofit member association, founded in 1893, dedicated to promoting and improving engineering and technology education.

www.innovativetraders.com
Innovative Trading is a leading provider of multi-level educational products and services for the active trading community. They specialize in a variety of market-related topics, such as Technical Analysis, Market Scanning, and advanced Trade Management Techniques.

www.fenews.com
*Financial Engineering News* examines the use of financial instruments to solve problems and exploit opportunities, and explores the use of quantitative methods and computer technology in finance.

www.appliederivatives.com
This site focuses on topical issues within derivatives and related markets with the objective of describing, promoting and explaining the forces of the capital market revolution.

www.efficientfrontier.com
An on-line journal of asset allocation and portfolio theory.

www.thehfa.org
The Hedge Fund Association is an international not-for-profit association of hedge fund managers, service providers, and investors formed to unite the hedge fund industry and add to the increasing awareness of the advantages and opportunities in hedge funds.

www.techcentralstation.com
Tech Central Station is a site to help provide the right answers to many of those questions with the news, analysis, research, and commentary you need to understand how technology is changing and shaping our world, and how you can make sense of it all.

www.stockadvanced.com
Advanced Stock Information is dedicated to helping investors and analysts by offering access to high quality investment research information.

www.nsf.gov/sbe/srs/stats.htm
This the site for The Division of Science Resources Statistics (SRS), which fulfills the legislative mandate of the National Science Foundation Act to provide a central clearinghouse for the collection, interpretation, and analysis of data on scientific and engineering resources, and to provide a source of information for policy formulation by other agencies of the Federal Government.

www.ioniainvesting.com
Ionia Biotechnology Investment Research researches leading biotechnology companies and produces in depth stock reports designed to aid individual investors with their biotech investing decisions.

## VI. Implement Prospecting Program

*Consciously and systematically implement an on-going prospecting program for this unique client profile.*

In working with the affluent, and particularly with Innovators, mass market or undirected marketing efforts simply are ineffective. The affluent simply do not find their investment advisors by responding to direct mail or advertising. Wealthy people do find advisors through referrals from other clients and advisors. Word-of-mouth recommendations bring people to advisors.

Therefore, the very best prospecting you can do is to make your current clients so satisfied they are delighted to recommend you to their friends and associates. In addition to unsought recommendations, top advisors are also proactive in asking their clients for referrals. The most effective recommendation is a personal introduction and endorsement from one Innovator client to another.

Earlier, we listed a number of ways to build your relationship with Innovators through sharing events. All these are excellent places and ways to network as well. Prospecting and new account generation can be a tough part of the advisory business. Here is a case study of how one advisor who targeted Innovators created a process that has been very effective for him.

## Exhibit 18.5
### Innovator Networking Case Study

*David, like his clients, likes being on the cutting edge of technology and investments, He has put the two together in his periodic "Investing in Innovations Evening" series. He sends his clients, advisor-partners and prospects an invitation to this event. He asks his clients to bring a friend who might be interested in this approach to investing.*

David picks a topic that is a technology field in which there are interesting current investment opportunities. Past events have focused on genetically modified food products and optics. He networks with local universities to find speakers. Because technology researchers are often better in a Q&A session than in a talk, he asks them to keep their introductory remarks to about 15 minutes and leave the rest of the session open for discussion. He keeps his groups small to allow everyone a chance to get in on the discussion. He reserves some time at the end to describe two or three investment opportunities.

These evenings have proven popular with his clients, so David does one a quarter. He has found that his expertise has grown substantially with these sessions. They also increase the satisfaction of his current clients as mush as they are effective at bringing in new ones.

The Exhibit below provides you with an example of how you might invite a client to an event such as this. E-mail the invitation (or use company letterhead). Attach (or enclose) an article on the subject matter as background reading for everybody.

## Exhibit 18.6
### Sample E-Mail Invitation Text

(Client name), we share a belief about investing in leading-edge technologies. I have brought (expert) to meet with a small group of us to talk about the competitive and investment implications of genetically modified food technologies driving the 21st century economy.

We can meet (date and time) at (place). We'll have some light refreshments for you as well as some interesting exhibits.

(Name of Financial Representative Name)

After the event, there is another natural opportunity to have another contact with the client. You should send a follow-up e-mail with an attachment or link to information of interest.

## *Exhibit 18.7*
### *Sample Follow-Up E-Mail Text*

*(Client Name), thank you for coming. It seemed like you were as interested as I in (technology). Here is a link to more information about (technology). I have also looked further into some investment plays we might consider and I will call you about those*

### **Chapter 18 Big Answer:**
### **Innovators are an attractive segment to build a practice around, but you may have to also focus on another type.**

While Innovators are very interesting, they are the smallest group. You may find you have to target a second group of investors. Innovators are always interested in new things, and they keep their advisors on their toes. But with market plans such as the one described here, you can learn along with your innovator clients.